Humanistic
Education

Lucy Paine Kezar

Humanistic Education

C. H. Patterson

University of Illinois

Prentice-Hall, Inc., *Englewood Cliffs, New Jersey*

Library of Congress Cataloging in Publication Data

PATTERSON, CECIL HOLDEN.
  Humanistic education.

  Includes bibliographical references.
  1. Education, Humanistic.   I. Title.
  LC1011.P33   370.11′2   72-8374
  ISBN 0-13-447748-0
  ISBN 0-13-447730-8 (pbk.)

© 1973 by Prentice-Hall, Inc., *Englewood Cliffs, New Jersey*

Printed in the United States of America

10   9   8   7   6   5   4   3   2   1

Prentice-Hall International, Inc., *London*
Prentice-Hall of Australia, Pty. Ltd., *Sydney*
Prentice-Hall of Canada, Ltd., *Toronto*
Prentice-Hall of India Private Limited, *New Delhi*
Prentice-Hall of Japan, Inc., *Tokyo*

To Frances Spano Patterson,
1915—1966,
whose humanism facilitated the development
of myself and our seven children.

Education today is faced with incredible challenges, different from, more serious than, it has ever met in its long history. To my mind, the question of whether it can meet these challenges will be one of the major factors in whether mankind moves forward, or whether man destroys himself on this planet, leaving this earth to those few things which can withstand atomic destruction and radioactivity. . . .

Can the educational system as a whole, the most traditional, conservative, rigid, bureaucratic institution of our time (and I use these words descriptively rather than cynically), come to grips with the real problems of modern life? Or will it continue to be shackled by the tremendous social pressures for conformity and retrogression, added to its own traditionalism?

—Carl R. Rogers, FREEDOM TO LEARN, pp. vi, vii.

The secret of education lies in respecting the pupil.

—Ralph Waldo Emerson

Contents

Preface

There has been a flood of books critical of the schools. A considerable literature of a popular nature with this focus has developed. Much of it is of an exposé type, with few if any positive suggestions for correcting or improving the situation. This literature does of course serve a purpose. It informs the public of the conditions which exist, and hopefully arouses a desire, and a climate, for change. It should not be expected that writers who are not professional educators or psychologists would provide remedies for the problems they point out. This extensive literature makes it unnecessary to document in detail the deficiencies and failures of the schools, although Chapter 1 includes some reference to the problems.

Education has of course been the subject of criticism for some time now, but the nature of the criticism has changed. While there are still those who are concerned about the failures of the schools to foster desired levels of academic achievement in children, the brunt of the recent criticism can be summed up in the accusation that the schools are inhuman, that they are unfit environments for children to live in.

The calls to reform the schools have been met, so far, by reforms of the existing curriculum, and by attempts to develop a technology of teaching. But these approaches do not reach to the root of the problem—the schools are not promoting the development of students as persons. As Silberman points out, "The approach to instructional technology that most researchers are following is likely to compound what is wrong with American education —its failure to develop sensitive, autonomous, thinking, humane individuals." [1]

[1] Charles E. Silberman, *Crisis in the Classroom* (New York: Random House, 1970), p. 196.

The call is for a humanistic education, but none of those who have criticized education for being inhumane have come forward with a proposal for a humanistic approach. To be sure, there is considerable writing about humanistic education, but it does not include a systematic, theoretically based foundation. Paradoxically, some writers are suggesting that humanistic education can be implemented by a technological approach, consisting of groups of techniques, exercises or games, to be used with students in the classroom.

The time is ripe, then, for an attempt to present a positive, systematic approach and this book is such an attempt. As a beginning, it certainly will not be the last word. As an introduction, it cannot cover all aspects of humanistic education, nor cover those aspects included in great detail. An effort has been made to be comprehensive, however, and the student or reader who is interested in more detail, or in extending his view, will find relevant material in the references cited. Some of these sources will give the student the feeling of the actual classroom situation to a greater extent than could be done here.

There are two aspects of humanistic education. The first is that of teaching subject matter in a more human way, that is, facilitating subject matter learning by students. The second is that of educating the nonintellectual or affective aspects of the student, that is, developing persons who understand themselves, who understand others, and who can relate to others. Both aspects are considered here.

The book is essentially a textbook for teacher education, urging teachers to be "more human." There is little else in the way of helping them to do this, and their education surely does not now help them. This book should help teacher education students, as well as practicing teachers, in becoming more humanistic in their teaching.

Before teachers can really humanize the classroom, they must have the understanding support of administrators. This book will be useful to administrators in helping to provide them with the understanding which can allow them to let teachers be human in the classroom.

Administrators may not hesitate to support humanistic teachers as much from lack of sympathy with humanistic education as out of fear that the results might disturb school board members and parents. School boards, parents, and the public, then, must also understand the nature of humanistic education and recognize it as the solution to the educational problems which are so well and so often publicized. Thus this book should be useful to all people concerned about education. Humanistic education is not a highly abstruse or technical approach—this book, written in simple, understandable language, should be helpful to parents and others who wish to see the schools become more humanistic in their orientation and practices.

John Holt has written: "There must be a way to educate children so that the great human qualities that we know are in them may be developed." [2] There is a way—the way of humanistic education. It is hoped that this book will help to put education on the humanistic path, and to the development of fully functioning or self-actualizing persons, who are so desperately needed for the future of our society.

The writer wishes to acknowledge the assistance of Betty Burton who performed most of the typing for this book, with some help from Anna Jane Bretzlaff and Pat Rowland.

C. H. Patterson
Urbana, Illinois
September 15, 1971

[2] John Holt, *How Children Fail* (New York: Pitman Publishing Corporation, 1964), p. 141.

Humanistic
Education

1 The Crisis In Education

*At present opinion is divided about the subjects of
education. People do not all take the same position
about what should be learned by the young, either
with a view to excellence or with a view to the best
life; nor is it clear whether their studies should be
mainly directed to the intellect or to moral character.
If we look at actual practice, the picture is also
confusing; and it is not clear whether the proper
studies to be pursued are those that are useful in life,
those that make for excellence, or those that are
non-essential. Each kind of study gets some support.
Even about those that make for excellence there is
no agreement, for men do not all honor the same
excellence, and so naturally they differ about the
proper training for it.*

—Aristotle, POLITICS

THE ATTACK ON EDUCATION

Education has been under severe and constant attack since the Russians launched the first space vehicle in 1957. The self-concept of America as the leader in science and technology was threatened, and the public

1

education system became the scapegoat. Criticism has continued from many sources since then.

The first wave of the attack focused on deficiencies in the academic curriculum. Demands were made for a more rigorous and a more scientifically oriented curriculum, and "soft subjects" and educational "frills" were ridiculed. The criticisms were not, of course, new. The same charges had been made only a few years earlier by Bestor and Hutchins.[1] The critics were representative of the so-called "essentialist" philosophy of education, which would limit the function of the school to the development of the intellect, and leave the personal and social development of the individual to the family and the church. The school is concerned at first with the mastery of the skills of reading, writing and arithmetic—the three R's—and then the transmission of the accumulated knowledge of the human race. Though subject matter is important, there is also emphasis on disciplined intellectual training through the study of classical languages and on developing the power to reason and to think.

Recently, the criticisms of the school, while still insisting that the schools are not fostering the intellectual development or academic achievement of children, have also focused on the psychological atmosphere of the school and the classroom.[2] These critics have questioned the appropriateness or relevance of the goals and objectives of various aspects of the curriculum, as well as methods of instruction. They have placed the blame for lack of achievement of students on the teachers, as well as on poor physical facilities and equipment. Teacher attitudes toward disadvantaged students have been blamed for their lack of success. Teachers, it has been claimed, have expected little and have therefore gotten little. In blaming the teacher for all lack of achievement and academic progress in their students, many of these criticisms are unfair. The attacks on the schools have often been less than constructive.

We shall return to discuss with more detail this second kind of criticism, since it is basic to the thesis of this book. First, however, let us consider a movement in education which appears to be directed toward remedying the conditions attacked by the first group of critics, the ineffectiveness of the schools in teaching basic skills and subject matter.

---

[1] Arthur E. Bestor, *Education Wastelands* (Urbana, Ill.: University of Illinois Press, 1953); Robert M. Hutchins, *The Conflict In Education In A Democratic Society* (New York: Harper & Row, 1953).

[2] See, e. g., William Glasser, *Schools Without Failure* (New York: Harper & Row, 1969); Paul Goodman, *Compulsory Mis-Education and the Community of Scholars* (New York: Vintage Books, 1964); John Holt, *How Children Fail* (New York, New American Library, 1967); Jonathan Kozol, *Death at an Early Age* (Boston, Houghton Mifflin, 1967), (New York, Bantam Books, 1968); George B. Leonard, *Education and Ecstasy* (New York, Dell, 1968); Charles E. Silberman, *Crisis in the Classroom* (New York, Random House, 1970).

THE DEVELOPMENT OF A TECHNOLOGY
OF EDUCATION [3]

Education has been experiencing the beginnings of a technological revolution, the essence of which is the application to educational procedures of techniques developed from research in learning. Skinner has detailed this application in his book *The Technology of Teaching.* "Education," says Skinner, "must become more efficient,"[4] and the systematic application of knowledge about learning, particularly through programmed learning by use of teaching machines, can do this. Machines are necessary, says Skinner, because the teacher cannot effectively control the reinforcement contingencies, that is, provide immediate reward for correct behavior, for a class of children. "The simple fact is that, as a mere reinforcing mechanism, the teacher is out of date. . . . The contingencies of reinforcement which are most efficient in controlling the organism cannot be arranged through the personal mediation of the [teacher]. . . . Mechanical and electrical devices must be used. Personal arrangement and personal observation of the results are unthinkable."[5]

Advantages of Computer-Assisted Instruction

Programmed learning through the use of teaching machines tied into computers (computer assisted instruction, or CAI) is seen by many as the needed revolution in teaching. Its advantages have been widely proclaimed. They include the following:

1. The programming of subject matter leads to a concentration on the careful analysis of the essentials of the subjects which are to be taught, and the reduction of the subject matter to its basic terms, facts, concepts, laws, principles, etc. Then these must be arranged and presented in a logical, systematic, developmental order, with earlier steps leading to later stages, and later material depending on earlier steps. The building of a program is not an easy matter, and the analysis of subject matter which is required is in itself a valuable process which could lead to improvement in education.

[3] The following is based upon C. H. Patterson, "Pupil Personnel Services in the Automated School." *Personnel and Guidance Journal,* 1969, 48, 101–110, and Chapter 21 in C. H. Patterson, *An Introduction to Counseling in the School* (New York: Harper & Row, 1971).

[4] B. F. Skinner, *The Technology of Teaching* (New York: Appleton Century Crofts, 1968), p. 29.

[5] *Ibid.,* pp. 21–22.

2. Programmed instruction provides *individualized* instruction, with each student being able to proceed at his own pace. "A program which is designed for the slowest student in the school system will probably not seriously delay the fast student, who will be free to progress at his own speed." [6] This individualizing of instruction, it is claimed, "will facilitate learning at a speed and depth that now seems impossible to achieve." [7] The use of computers, it is said, will make the teaching machine responsive to the individual learning problems of students, on the basis of data obtained and stored from use of the machines with many different students.

3. A major contribution of the principles of programmed instruction, according to Skinner, is the change of the whole atmosphere of the classroom. At present, according to Skinner, teaching is based upon the use of aversive controls. [8] Students are *punished* for *failure* to learn—no longer with corporal punishment, it is true—but verbally, with ridicule, scolding, sarcasm, criticism, detention, extra assignments, ostracism, etc. Even when rewards are used, the reward is the excusing of students from assignments. Learning is unpleasant, and is avoided by the student. The student escapes by truancy, dropping out of school, inattention and daydreaming, or forgetting. Then again, resentment toward the teacher and the school leads to defiant behavior by the student, which then leads to counterattack by the teachers, escalating into an open, continual conflict. A vicious circle develops in which both teachers and students suffer psychologically.

In contrast to the methods of aversive control of behavior, programmed instruction uses positive reinforcement. Behavior which is desired is rewarded immediately following its occurrence. Programming begins with easy material, giving the student the experience of success as he makes the correct response, and continues by small gradations which continue the success experience.

4. The new technology of teaching frees the classroom teacher from classroom routine. As printing freed the teacher from reading to students from manuscripts, so computer-assisted instruction will free the teacher from the routine of drill. The new technology is most useful in providing the drill and repeated practice necessary in such things as arithmetic skills. The teacher could then devote time to preparing special lectures to be taped or filmed for repeated use, to small group discussions, to individual attention or trouble-shooting with students having difficulty, or even, it is suggested by some, to counseling, though

[6] *Ibid.*, p. 56.
[7] Patrick Suppes, "Plug-in Instruction," *Saturday Review*, July 23, 1966, 25–30. Copyright 1966 Saturday Review Inc.
[8] *Op. cit.*, pp. 95–103.

this term is not actually used in a professional sense. "The teacher," says Skinner, "may begin to function, not in lieu of a cheap machine, but through intellectual, cultural, and emotional contacts of that distinctive sort which testify to her status as a human being." [9]

The promise of the technology of education is appealing. The schools have been severely criticized for not doing a good job of teaching, for not developing the potentials of all students, for not stimulating or retaining their interest in learning, for not keeping them in school by providing an appropriate program or curriculum. Now that we are told that technology can solve all these problems, is it any wonder that there is optimism about its promises? Students will be able to learn faster, and to learn more, so much so that we should be careful about accepting any limits in the capacity of the human being to learn. Subject matter considered to be at the college level, it is suggested, can be learned by elementary school children. [10] We even will be able to teach subjects such as Russian, by means of computers, in schools where there is no one trained in Russian or who can speak it.

Some Flaws in the Technology

The development of educational technology—or the substitution of computers for the little red school house, in the words of a feature writer —would appear to be highly desirable. There are, however, some flaws in the picture which need to be recognized: [11]

1. While computer-assisted instruction is individualized, this is true only for the student's rate of progress. It is limited to a few standard programs. Programs must be laboriously constructed, and the computer does not adapt to individual problems. This is why teachers are needed. However, it is conceivable that not only will the number of programs increase greatly to adapt to individual needs, but that the

---

[9] *Ibid.,* p. 27.

[10] Patrick Suppes, "The Computer and Excellence," *Saturday Review,* January 14, 1967, pp. 46–50.

[11] See the following for a more extensive review of some limitations and problems:

R. S. Barrett, "The Computer Mentality," *Phi Delta Kappan,* 1968, 49, 430–434.

R. F. Bundy, "Computer Assisted Instruction—Where Are We?" *Phi Delta Kappan,* 1968, 49, 424–429.

D. D. Bushnell and D. W. Allen, eds., *The Computer in American Education* (New York: Wiley, 1967).

Philip W. Jackson, *The Teacher and the Machine* (Pittsburgh: University of Pittsburgh Press, 1968).

A. G. Oettinger, "The Myths of Educational Technology," *Saturday Review,* May, 18, 1968, pp. 76–77, 91.

computer can to some extent adapt to the student. Bushnell talks of the development of automated teaching systems modeled after the experienced teacher under student control.[12] But the extent to which instruction can be individualized by machines is still limited.[13] Further, writers confuse individualization of instruction with personalization, and state or imply that machine instruction is personalized, a clear misuse of the term. Instruction can be personalized only by a person.

2. As has been noted, computers are most useful in providing drill-and-practice systems. This is a serious limitation, since education is more than the development of computational, reading, or writing skills. In fact, it may be argued that this is not education at all, but only the preparation for education, the acquisition of the tools with which one attains an education. Their importance is, of course, very great, and any increase in efficiency with which they can be acquired is welcome. But while "training to minimal competence in well defined skills is very important in a variety of military, industrial, and school settings it is not, however, the whole of what the education process should be." [14]

While computers are thus, it appears, currently limited to tool subjects, attention is being given to developing them beyond this level. Suppes projects two additional systems, a tutorial and a dialogue system. In the tutorial system "it is possible . . . to approximate the relationship a tutor would have with a student." [15] This would approach individual instruction, but would still be limited to skill subjects, and would require a very large number of programs. Teachers would be needed as trouble-shooters. The dialogue system would make possible a real interaction between the student and the computer in terms of response to individual questions. The responses must be programmed, however, and so the questions must be anticipated, and the computer must be programmed to recognize questions on the basis of cues or key words.

3. It is claimed that by computer-assisted instruction the student can learn more in less time with less effort.[16] This has not been adequately demonstrated, however. One must be careful about accepting the reports of subjects, and even the objective results of experiments with computers. This is a novel situation for students, and it is subject

---

[12] D. D. Bushnell, "For Each Student a Teacher," *Saturday Review,* July 23, 1966, 30.
[13] Philip W. Jackson, *op. cit.,* pp. 39–43.
[14] A. G. Oettinger, "The Myths of Educational Technology," *Saturday Review,* 5/18/68. Copyright 1968 Saturday Review Inc.
[15] Patrick Suppes, "Plug-in Instruction." *Op. cit.*
[16] B. F. Skinner, *op. cit.,* p. 54.

to the well-known Hawthorne effect. Named from studies conducted at the Hawthorne plant of the Western Electric Company, the Hawthorne effect refers to the influence of interest and attention bestowed upon subjects of an experiment rather than the influence of the specific method or treatment being tested. This has not been taken into account by researchers, perhaps because they themselves have been influenced by it.[17] It may well be that for skill subjects computer-assisted instruction is more efficient, but for subjects where drill is not necessary, fast learners may be slowed, unless different programs are developed. Compared to books, even the simplest program is long for the material covered, but the program may be more efficient for imparting terms, definitions, concepts, etc. For advanced material, for literature, for theory, and for presenting the results of research, books may not only be more efficient, but necessary. Computers are not likely to replace books, even though some publishing companies seem to be afraid of this, as evidenced by their merging with electronics firms.

4. The current appeal of computers on the basis of their novelty points to another caution in the acceptance of computer-assisted instruction as the panacea for what is wrong with schools and education. The basis for the operation of programmed instruction or computer-assisted instruction is, as has been noted earlier, the use of reinforcement as it functions in operant conditioning (the conditioning or modification of behavior through its consequences, usually rewards, which are said to "operate" upon the behavior). So far the problem of effective reinforcers has not arisen, but it certainly will. Skinner states that "the mere manipulation of the device will probably be reinforcing enough to keep the average pupil at work for a suitable period each day." [18] This apparently has been the case so far in the experimental use of computer-assisted instruction for short periods of time.

But as the novelty of the machines wears off, it may be anticipated that other, external, reinforcers will be needed. And as the length of time at the computer increases, the difficulty of getting the student to the computer and to stay at it will increase. Skinner goes on to say that "if the material itself proves not to be sufficiently reinforcing, other reinforcers in the possession of the teacher or school may be made contingent upon the operation of the device or upon progress through a series of problems." [19] What these reinforcers will be in long-term experimental use of computer instruction has not been adequately

[17] R. F. Bundy, *op. cit.*
[18] *Op. cit.,* p. 24.
[19] *Ibid.,* pp. 24–25.

considered. In experimental studies in operant conditioning in schools jelly beans and M&M's have been widely used. Aside from the expense involved in the widespread use of these reinforcers, there will be problems regarding their effects on students, with parental complaints about the school spoiling the appetites, not to mention teeth, of the fast students. There may also be problems regarding the ineffectiveness of such reinforcers when fast students have accumulated a surplus and then take it easy. Satiation is likely to occur, or perhaps the accumulation will be sold or bartered to the slow students, who will then stop working. Perhaps we will see a revival of the use of gold stars and other similar contrived reinforcers.

The problem of reinforcement on a long-term basis has not been solved. Intermittent reinforcement on a high ratio is a powerful method, as evidenced by the gambling machines at Las Vegas, but this method has not been used yet in computer-assisted instruction, and it presents some difficulties. If it comes into use, it may provide a dangerous temptation to overwork the student, since "when properly programmed" the student will not stop working until he is stopped.[20]

The problems, incidentally, do not arise in research with animals. The point is, though, that the problem of motivation, which seems to have been so easily solved by computers, will return to plague us. The student who now creeps "like a snail unwillingly to school," will be creeping unwillingly to the computer. In order for the student to benefit from computer-assisted instruction he must initiate contact with the computer—he must *do* something, and thus *want* to do something—or be made to do something. "A student, like any organism, must act before he can be reinforced. In a sense he must take the initiative." [21] In addition, there is the problem of replacing contrived reinforcers by natural or self-reinforcers, a problem glossed over by Skinner and other enthusiasts for programmed instruction.

Skinner, in his recognition of the need for the use of contrived contingencies for reinforcement, seems to be aware of this problem. And, although he continues to talk about positive reinforcement and the willing attention and participation of the student, he implies, perhaps inadvertently, the need at times or perhaps eventually to resort to aversive control when he says, for example, in referring to the use of a teaching machine: "A child can be *made* to 'look at the sample' by *requiring* him to press the sample window at the top." [22] Presumably when the child is *forced* to interact with the machine, the rewards of success in responding by giving correct answers will keep

[20] *Ibid.*, p. 167.
[21] *Ibid.*, p. 143.
[22] *Ibid.*, p. 73; emphases added.

him at it. But this assumes that such success is rewarding, and this may be true only if the student is curious, intrinsically interested in the subject matter, or has a desire to learn. Of course all children may, as has been suggested, be like this before aversive treatment has killed these characteristics.

5. A final characteristic of computerized instruction is that it is impersonal. It has been pointed out as an asset that no student can complain that the teacher does not like him. It is objective and fair. But the computer is not a teacher, and not a person, and the interaction with the computer is not an interaction with a human. Now it may be true that it is not necessary for the student to be in contact with a person in order to learn, at least in order to learn what can be learned by means of computerized instruction. The point is that the amount of contact the student has with a human environment is reduced by that amount of time which he spends with a computer. It is possible that the computer can be programmed to simulate a human relationship, or to be somewhat human, in that it reflects the humanness of the programmer. Thus computers can, when the student gives his number and first name, respond with his last name—or vice versa—and by means of printed tape, and perhaps eventually by a recorded human voice, give the illusion of being a person. At any rate, it appears that by such programming the student can be led to regard the machine, anthropomorphically, as being almost human. Whether this will be a substitute for relationships with human beings is questionable, however, though it may not be out of place to note that while a computer cannot replace a good teaching relationship, the computer may be better for the student than a bad teacher-student relationship.

These are only a few of the many questions about computer-assisted instruction. Many of these problems are simply technical in nature, and they will soon be remedied or overcome. There is no doubt, as a result of the tremendous amount of money and research being poured into the field, that machines and programs will be perfected. There seems to be no question but that we can look forward, in 20 or 30 years, to computer-assisted instruction as a commonplace in our schools. However, proponents of the technology perhaps underestimate the difficulties of a nontechnological nature as a result of the "breakthrough complex." High costs and implementation problems may slow the pace of adoption. It may be, as Jackson contends, that changes resulting from educational technology will not be as dramatic or occur as rapidly as the headline-makers would have us believe.[23] But there can be no doubt that, as in every other

[23] *Op. cit.,* p. 1.

sphere of our life, technology will eventually prevail. Americans, it has been contended, may not be highly creative in original discovery in science or in philosophy, but they have no peers in technology—except perhaps now the Russians. Though education and educators are, it is claimed, conservative and highly resistant to change, the pressure is on, and the appeal of technology cannot be resisted. Acceptance may occur faster than we think—the adoption of technology will be slowed only by financial considerations. Though at present, in experimental studies, students spend from 15 to 20 minutes a day at a computer, Suppes estimates that in 20 or 30 years the child will be spending 30 to 40 percent of his time in school at a computer.[24] I believe this estimate is conservative, particularly at the elementary school level. Even at higher levels the tremendous amount of information being created by the so-called information explosion will result in increasing pressures on the schools to cram more and more facts into children, and this is the forte of computerized instruction, along with films, slides, recordings, and tapes, all of them being impersonal methods of instruction.

The Classroom as a Factory

With the increasing use of technology in the schools has come an expression of interest by big business in education. The production of the hardware has made education a potential big customer. Many of the giant electronics firms, such as IBM, Xerox, RCA, Raytheon, and General Electric are involved in education. Patrick Suppes, head of the Institute for Mathematical Studies in the Social Sciences at Stanford, is consultant to RCA's Instructional Systems Division, and is only one of many such consultants. Now the goal of business is profits, not education. The appeal of business to education is that of efficiency. "Mass education," it is said, "requires mass production methods." [25]

Picture, then, the classroom of the future, with each student at a computer keyboard. What does the picture remind you of? A factory—a modern, clean, well-lighted factory, but a factory. The teacher is a foreman or supervisor, a trouble-shooter. We read a lot about technology freeing the teacher for other things—to humanize education, to develop personal relationships with students—but nowhere have I seen anything about when and how this is to be done. The technology of education leads to increasing attention to and concentration on the academic progress and development of the student. Wilbur H. Ferry, Vice President of the Fund for the Republic and on the Staff of its Center for the Study of

[24] Patrick Suppes, "Computer Technology and the Future of Education," *Phi Delta Kappan,* 1968, 49, 420–423.
[25] *Ibid.*

Democratic Institutions, warns of the dangers of the invasion of our schools by technology, or technication as he calls it. One of these is that an educational system can be thought of in terms like those of a factory. "Factories," he says, "are fine for producing things, but their record with people is terrible. . . . Technication, as Robert M. Hutchins observes, will 'dehumanize a process the aim of which is humanization.' " [26] Student rebellion is in part a reaction at being treated as a number, an IBM card, rather than as a person.

It may be questioned whether the picture presented here is inevitable, or whether it will actually occur. With our present attitude toward technology, and with the combined acceptance and support by educators and big business executives, automation will, I believe, be widely accepted and carried to extremes. This has been the history of technology in Western civilization. Skinner admits that it may be unwisely used, and may need to be contained or controlled. [27]

THE DEHUMANIZATION OF EDUCATION

The conditions which are suggested above as likely concomitants of the developing technology of education are the very conditions at which humanistic critics of education direct their attention.

The indictment of the schools is detailed in a number of books, several of which were listed earlier in this chapter. One of the earliest writers was Paul Goodman, whose study of the educational system led him to conclude that "the compulsory system has become a universal trap," and that "very many of the youth, both poor and middle class, might be better off if the system did not exist, even if they then had no formal schooling at all." [28] Attending school is, he suggests, not the best use of their time, even though Goodman recognizes that the homes and the streets in which many children live are worse than the schools. He does recommend, of course, that if school attendance is not compulsory, efforts should be made to give something to those whose environment does not offer the opportunity for natural learning. But he suggests an experiment in which children from "tolerable, though not necessarily cultured, homes," in a neighborhood community, would have no school, to see if they would learn anyway. "This experiment cannot do the children any academic harm, since there is good evidence that normal children will make up the first seven years school-work with four to seven months of good teaching." [29]

[26] W. H. Ferry, "Must We Rewrite the Constitution to Control Technology?" *Saturday Review,* March 2, 1968, pp. 50–54. Copyright 1968 Saturday Review, Inc.

[27] *Op. cit.,* pp. 91, 260.

[28] Reprinted from p. 31 of *Compulsory Mis-education and the Community of Scholars* by Paul Goodman, copyright 1964, by permission of the publisher Horizon Press, New York.

[29] *Ibid.,* p. 32.

Education then, retards rather than facilitates the learning of children. The fear of failure, the importance of being right, inhibits learning. Holt describes the classroom behavior of students who are not learning but engaging in strategies to make the teacher think they know the answers and are learning. Though most of the others are not interested, are not attending, and are looking out the window or daydreaming, doodling, passing notes, whispering, those few, who know what is going on, are trying to impress the teacher, to get the "right answers." Both groups' motivation is to get through the daily routine as easily as possible. Underneath it all is constant fear, anxiety and tension. Most children are not only learning, but are becoming neurotic. The uninterested ones give an appearance of stupidity and incompetence to avoid trying and being wrong, to avoid or escape from pressure. As a result they function at a low level, beneath their actual capacity, and after a time they become fixed at this level, and actually are unable to do better. There is nothing in education, in the way they are taught, to catch or command and hold their attention or interest.[30]

The classroom becomes a competitive jungle for those who want to conform—the others, often the majority, function as described. But in such competition there is only one "winner," and many "losers." Henry describes a typical incident:

> Boris had trouble reducing "12/16" to the lowest terms, and could only get as far as "6/8." The teacher asked him quietly if that was as far as he could reduce it. She suggested he "think." Much heaving up and down and waving of hands by the other children, all frantic to correct him. Boris pretty unhappy, probably mentally paralyzed. The teacher, quiet, patient, ignores the others and concentrates with look and voice on Boris. She says, "Is there a bigger number than two you can divide into the two parts of the fraction?" After a minute or two, she becomes more urgent, but there is no response from Boris. She then turns to the class and says, "Well, who can tell Boris what the number is?" A forest of hands appears, and the teacher calls Peggy. Peggy says that four may be divided into the numerator and the denominator. Thus Boris' failure has made it possible for Peggy to succeed; his depression is the price of her exhilaration; his misery the occasion for her rejoicing. This is the standard condition of the American elementary school.[31]

Holt also writes of the effects of failure, when a child makes a mistake, which is recognized by other children who wave their hands, giggle or otherwise call the attention of the teacher to their superiority to the child who has failed. The child, says Holt, not only knows that he goofed, but that others know it, and feels great shame and embarrassment, which

[30] John Holt, *op. cit.*
[31] Jules Henry, "In Suburban Classrooms," in Beatrice & Ronald Gross, eds. *Radical School Reform*, pp. 83–84, © 1969 by Simon & Schuster, Inc. Reprinted by permission of Simon & Schuster. Condensed from Jules Henry, *Culture Against Man* (New York: Random House, 1963). Copyright © 1963 by Random House, Inc. Reprinted by permission of the publisher. British Commonwealth rights by permission of Tavistock Publications Ltd.

paralyzes his thinking so that he cannot correct himself.[32] No wonder, Holt says, that children—and adults—have nightmares about school failures.

Leonard charges that education suffocates the child's potential rather than releases it. He reports on his observations of elementary school classrooms, comparing children in kindergarten to those in fourth grade classes. "It is," he says, "almost as if you are viewing specimens of two different species." The kindergarten children are natural, spontaneous, responding to stories with the emotions they communicate—with suspense, fear, laughter, their faces lighting up and glowing. But in the fourth grade this is all absent in most children. They are quiet, inhibited, painfully self-aware and controlled.[33] Education, he says, seems hellbent on creating joyless drudges out of children.[34]

Leonard, as does Goodman, proposes the elimination of compulsory school attendance, and of school buildings and the teacher-student situation as now practiced. "Practically everything that is *presently* being accomplished in the schools can be accomplished more effectively and with less pain in the average child's home and neighborhood playground." [35]

Charles Silberman, in an evaluation of education following a 3½ year study supported by the Carnegie Corporation, which included visits to more than a hundred schools, contends that even our best schools are so concerned about order and discipline that real education is lacking. In the poorer schools, the picture is depressing. "It is not possible," says Silberman, "to spend any prolonged period visting public school classrooms without being appalled by the mutilation visible everywhere—mutilation of spontaneity, of joy in learning, of sense of self. . . . Because adults take the schools so much for granted they fail to appreciate what grim, joyless places most American schools are . . . what contempt they unconsciously display for children." [36]

In short, the critics are saying that the schools—or at least most schools—are not fit places for human beings. "Many are not even decent places for our children to be. They damage, they thwart, they stifle children's natural capacity to learn and grow healthily." [37] Their hidden function is all too often "the destruction of the human spirit." [38] They destroy the minds and hearts of our children.[39] The schools are inhumane, they do not treat children as persons.

[32] John Holt, *How Children Learn* (New York: Pitman, 1967), p. 100.

[33] George B. Leonard, *op. cit.,* pp. 110–111.

[34] *Ibid.,* p. 15.

[35] *Ibid.,* p. 102.

[36] Charles E. Silberman, *op. cit.,* p. 10.

[37] In Beatrice and Ronald Gross, *Radical School Reform,* p. 13, © 1969 by Simon & Schuster, Inc. Reprinted by permission of Simon & Schuster.

[38] George B. Leonard, *op. cit.,* p. 110.

[39] Jonathan Kozol, *op. cit.,* from the subtitle: *The Destruction of the Hearts and Minds of Negro Children in the Boston Public Schools.*

THE HUMANIZATION OF EDUCATION

These critics of education, and others who will be considered throughout this book, propose a new approach to education. Their voices are just beginning to be heard above those of the technologists. Whereas the technologists may be seen as the successors of the essentialists in education, the new critics are the successors of the life adjustment educators, whose approach resisted the restriction of public education to the development of the intellect. It went beyond the early extension of education to preparation for *making* a living, through the development of vocational technical curricula, to a concern with preparation *for* living. Interest in the individual's physical and mental condition as it influenced academic performance was replaced by interest in the social and emotional development of the student as a person. The focus or emphasis, however, tended to be upon preparing the student for responsible citizenship, rather than the student's development as an individual or a person.

The current successors are more concerned about the development of the student as a person, his growth and development as a free individual. Their approach emphasizes respect for the student as a person, with the rights of a person. Jackson points out that "our most pressing educational problem involves learning how to create and maintain a humane environment in our schools." [40]

There is no clear designation for this approach, but it is characterized as a humanistic approach to education. It is concerned with the psychological or emotional atmosphere of the classroom. It conceives of teaching as essentially a good human relationship, but it goes beyond this in not restricting its concern to cognitive learnings as a goal of education. It includes as goals the development of good attitudes and feelings—it is the education of the emotions, the fostering of adequate emotional development as a legitimate and desirable goal of education. It has been called by some affective education, meaning the education of affect, involving more than the concern with affective techniques in education.

The child, like the pigeon, may be led at first to work continuously "for long periods of time without coercion or threat, showing few signs of fatigue, nervousness, or other forms of escape." [41] The results of this over a period of time can be decidedly harmful if not destructive, however. The conclusion is obvious—to counteract the dehumanizing effects of the machine, we are going to have to be concerned about humanizing the education process. The child will need respite from the machine, and

[40] *Op. cit.,* p. 90.
[41] B. F. Skinner, *op. cit.,* p. 81.

will need human contacts. The restriction of interaction of students with each other by machine instruction will make the need for interaction in groups even more important than it is now. The need for informal interaction will be greater also, so that more attention and time will have to be given to play and recreation.

It has been reiterated again and again, almost defensively, that the machine will not replace the teacher, but will *free* the teacher for other activities, though it is never clear what these activities are, or when they are to be performed. As a matter of fact, some of the talk of business technicians makes no reference to a teacher, who appears to be superfluous to the learning process. But it would appear that the teacher could easily become a technician rather than a professional, a tender of machines and a mediator between the machine and the student to see that they continue to interact productively. The teacher is not going to have much time to do anything else. For if, as is suggested, there are not as many machines as students, mainly because of the cost, so that children have to take turns, the teacher will not be available for those who are not at the machine. It would be interesting to speculate on the implications of this for teaching and for teachers and the teaching profession, but that is beyond our purpose. Jackson notes that "some authorities think that the teacher might become more, rather than less, burdened by clerical work." [42]

In spite of disclaimers that machines will replace teachers, it appears that every effort is being made to have them do so. If this occurs, and all courses are canned (programmed) then the current complaints about standardization, limiting of inquiry and questioning, and originality in teaching will seem trivial. Now the student can question the text or the teacher, can find flaws, can know more about something than the book or the teacher. But will the possibility of this exist in relation to a program carefully created by experts and presented by a machine?

The Reaction Against Technology

Such a situation will not persist—it cannot persist. Even now we find some voices raised against the trend toward the spread of technology. We will recognize that education is more than skill training, more than the three R's, as basic as these are. Teaching machines can never provide an education—they can only foster the skills and provide the materials out of which an education may develop. The realization of this will, no doubt, prevent higher education from becoming highly mechanized. But the picture painted earlier is likely to materialize in elementary, and to a great

[42] This and following quotations reprinted from *The Teacher and the Machine* by Phillip W. Jackson by permission of the University of Pittsburgh Press. © 1968 by the University of Pittsburgh Press.

extent in secondary, education, where the inculcation of skills and the imparting of information are important.

There are those now who are concerned with the fundamental question of "the extent to which a mechanistic ideology should be allowed to permeate our view of the educational process." [43] Such voices are, however, weak and are not likely to be listened to until we experience some of the mixed blessings of technology. To raise such questions now almost amounts to heresy and lack of faith in American ingenuity; such objectors will be, and are, accused of blocking progress. The picture of the classroom as a factory, though, may be overdone. There certainly will be periods for art and music, and for some teacher-student and student-student interaction, although even now there is too often very little of this. But the danger of technology in education is a real one, and its real danger lies in the fact that while it may produce technically skilled individuals it cannot produce free, reasoning, responsible individuals. Education, it has been said, is too important to be left to educators. Actually, it has never been left to educators, who have been controlled by the local school boards. "The use of the computer in education is too serious a business to be left to the computer mentality." [44]

The Fourth R—Human Relations

An important aspect of personal development or self-actualization is interpersonal relationships. One cannot be self-actualizing in a vacuum. Therefore, education must, as must all of society, become concerned with the development of men not just as citizens, but as persons, as members of a community, and as members of the human race. "Where the actions of one can drastically affect the lives of others far distant, it will be crucially important that each person master the skill of feeling what others feel. This skill, more than new laws or new politics, will soon become crucial to the survival of the race." [45]

The emphasis of education of the future, then, will be upon human relations. As Ashley Montagu has said: "Our educational institutions should be training us in the ability to love, not the three R's, or, at the college level, remedial reading, remedial writing, and remedial arithmetic." [46] Rather than having the concern about human relations assigned only to student personnel workers, human relations will be the focus of the curriculum. Machines and computers will have their place, and as-

---

[43] Jackson, op. cit., p. 1.
[44] R. S. Barrett, op. cit.
[45] G. B. Leonard, op. cit., p. 127.
[46] Ashley Montagu, from a speech given at the conference of the International Institute for Euthenics, October 5, 1968, Allerton House, Monticello, Illinois.

sistants, aides, or technicians will be employed to supervise the interaction of students with them. Teachers will then be concerned with the human relations aspects of the curriculum, which cannot be taught or learned by machines. The teacher will be "a specialist in human behavior, whose assignment is to bring about extraordinarily complex changes in extraordinarily complex material. . . . In exposition, discussion, and argumentation (written or spoken), in productive interchanges in the exploration of new areas, in ethical behavior, in the common enjoyment of literature, music, and art—here the teacher is important, and he is important as a human being." [47] This is true, to some extent, at the present time, as Skinner notes, but in the coming age of educational technology, computerized instruction will crowd out or displace much of such teacher activity. When the excesses of such technology are recognized, then the importance of the teacher as a person will be recognized.

Then teachers will no longer be concerned with much of what we now call subject matter; they will not need to be trained to teach the three R's. Subject matter will also be presented by films, slides, recordings, audio and video tapes, and so forth. The teacher, no longer needing to be an expert in subject matter, will, with mechanical aids, be able to teach more than he knows. To the criticism that the teacher will feel inadequate in comparison to the experts presenting subject matter on tapes and films, it may be answered that since the teacher will have other meaningful and satisfying functions, this will not be a problem. Teachers in special subject-matter areas, such as art and music at the elementary level and the liberal arts and sciences at the upper levels will teach through group discussion methods, and will, of course, have to be prepared in the subject matter, but the major preparation of teachers at the elementary level will be in human relationships. The major subject matter of the curriculum will be the fourth R—relationships.

THE REAL REVOLUTION IN EDUCATION

There is much talk about a revolution in education, referring to the rapid increase in technology which we have outlined. But this is not really a revolution, but simply the mechanization of current processes, the application of technology to achieve, more effectively or efficiently, it is claimed, the same objects—the mastery of skills and subject matter.

A real revolution in education would consist of a change in goals and in content. It is such a revolution that I believe will come when we are satiated by the machine technology, when we realize not only its inadequacies even for our present limited purpose, but also the horror of what

[47] B. F. Skinner, *op. cit.,* pp. 254, 255.

might be considered its side effect—the dehumanization of man. In industry this effect has also occurred—it was pictured long ago in the Charlie Chaplin movie, "Modern Times"—and for a long time nothing could be done directly about it. Attempts have been made to counteract it by shortening working hours, and providing personnel services in industry, including recreational facilities, restaurants and cafeterias, and other fringe activities. Now it seems possible that automation may even free man from the machine as far as production of goods is concerned. But by the nature of the learning situation where the individual must be involved, this solution does not appear to be possible in education. We must change the whole focus and goal of the educational process.

It is probably true that we will always have to teach basic skills—the three R's. And it may be that the most efficient way to do this is to use computers. But it will become recognized that this is only a small part of education—actually only preparation for education. The need of society for technicians and scientists will be reduced, and the greater need for people skilled in human relationships will be recognized. Education will be directed toward meeting this need.

"The teacher or the professor will have largely disappeared. His place will be taken by a facilitator of learning, chosen for his facilitative attitudes as much as for his knowledge. . . . Among the most important learnings will be the personal and interpersonal," that is human relationships.[48] Programmed instruction and other techniques such as audiovisual aids, will be used as tools, but will not dominate education, crowding out interpersonal activities.

Rogers describes education of the future as follows:

"Education will not be a *preparation* for living. It will be, in itself, an *experience* in living. Feelings of inadequacy, hatred, a desire for power, feelings of love and awe and respect, feelings of fear and dread, unhappiness with parents or with other children—all these will be an open part of his curriculum, as worthy of exploration as history or mathematics. In fact this openness to feelings will enable him to learn content materials more readily. His will be an education in becoming a whole human being, and the learnings will involve him deeply, openly, exploringly, in an awareness of his relationships to the world of others, as well as an awareness of the world of abstract knowledge." [49]

The succeeding chapters in this book attempt to indicate the nature of education which is concerned with the child or student as a person, whose personal development is facilitated through a humanistic education. We

[48] Carl R. Rogers, "Interpersonal Relationships: U.S.A. 2000," *Journal of Applied Behavioral Science,* 1968, *4,* 265–280.
[49] Rogers, *Ibid.*

shall first examine the nature of the goal of humanistic education. Then we shall consider some earlier and current approaches to education which were and are in nature essentially humanistic. Next, we shall attempt to provide a systematic statement of the nature of humanistic education, including its theoretical base and principles. Finally, we shall suggest some approaches to the implementation and application of this approach in the classroom, in terms of the function of the teacher, the nature of the learner, and the process of learning.

SUMMARY

The schools are under attack. They have been for more than a decade. There have been two major focuses of this attack. The first criticizes the schools for lack of success in fostering high levels of academic achievement. The second, more recent, says the schools are inhuman in their treatment of children, so they are in many cases not fit places for children to be.

Attempts to meet the first type of criticism focus upon the technology of teaching, with emphasis upon programmed instruction. Some consider this development to portend a revolution in education. Other remedies are also being proposed, such as team teaching, new curriculums, audio-video equipment, and other so-called "innovations." Remedies for the dehumanization of education have not been so widely sought or proposed.

What we do about the charges of the critics, which group we listen to and attempt to satisfy, depends upon what we accept as the goal of education. We therefore turn, in the next chapter, to a consideration of the goal of education.

2

The Goal
Of
Education

*In the world which is already upon us, the aim of
education must be to develop individuals who are
open to change.*

—Carl R. Rogers, FREEDOM TO LEARN *

As we have seen, the so-called technological revolution does not involve a change in the goals of education. It accepts the current goals,
mastery of skills and subject matter—and the current education system.
It does not address itself to the problem so well delineated by humanistic
critics—the dehumanizing characteristics of the teacher-directed classroom. Programmed, or computer-assisted, instruction, "innovations" like
the new curricula—new math and new science, as well as many other
developments, do not question the goal toward which they are directed,
nor are they directed to the real or basic reasons that children are not
learning under the present methods. There is no questioning, or even
consideration, of the purposes of all these efforts.

The traditional goal of education is the transmission of the culture, the
preservation of the past and the present, and the development of the intellect. We need, of course, to know about the past, the heritage of the
human race. An understanding of history can help us avoid repeating

* (Columbus, Ohio: Merrill, 1969), p. 304.

the same mistakes. Santayana, the philosopher, has said that those who do not know history are condemned to repeat its mistakes.

But this is not enough. Conditions change, and the knowledge of the past becomes obsolete, irrelevant. Harold Benjamin, in his delightful satire on education, illustrates this problem.[1] We are now in a period of rapid social change. Education must not only provide a knowledge and understanding of the past, and of the present, but prepare people for the future —a future in large part unknown, except that it will involve continuing change. Some talk about *teaching* people how to learn. It is true that our present educational system is not doing this, but it is questionable that this is sufficient, or even possible. Learning is a natural state of the normal organism. Children who can't learn are abnormal—they are often if not usually made abnormal by the nature of the educational process in our schools. It is more important, then, that we provide the conditions which preserve the natural process of learning in individuals. Or, put another way, that we develop people who continue to learn, who are open to change.

THE GOAL OF HUMANISTIC EDUCATION

The humanistic revolution in education involves a change in the goal of education. The problems of individuals, of the nation, of society, of civilization will not be solved by development of intellect alone. Of the many problems facing man today, four major ones are, I feel, poverty, pollution, population and personal (or interpersonal) relations. The first three are essentially technical problems; but the fourth clearly requires more than intelligence and technical know-how.

We need not only men who can think, but men who can feel, and who can act, not only on the basis of intellect but of feeling as well. We need men who can understand other men, who accept and respect others, as well as themselves, and who are responsible.

Silberman, in questioning the developing technology of education, suggests that this approach "is likely to compound what is most wrong with American education—the failure to develop sensitive, autonomous, thinking, humane individuals." He continues, "Our most pressing educational problem . . . is not how to increase the efficiency of the schools; it is how to create and maintain a humane society." [2]

---

[1] J. A. Pediwell, (Foreword by Harold Benjamin), *The Saber-Tooth Curriculum* (New York: McGraw-Hill, 1939).

[2] From pp. 196, 203, of *Crisis in the Classroom,* by Charles E. Silberman. Copyright © 1970 by Charles E. Silberman. This and subsequent excerpts reprinted by permission of Random House, Inc., and William Morris Agency, Inc.

The goal of education, then, is to produce human, or humane, beings, whole beings, not automatons, or intellects, but thinking, feeling, living— or acting—persons, persons who can love, feel deeply, expand their inner selves, create,[3] and who continue the process of self-education.[4]

Another way to put it is to say that the goal of education is to foster the development of persons who can live together as fully functioning human beings. It is not sufficient simply that society be preserved under conditions which prevent the personal development of individuals. If society is to change it can only be through changing individuals. This is the function of education.

What kind of persons, specifically, are necessary to form such a society? What is the nature of a fully functioning person? Writers in the field of counseling or psychotherapy have studied these questions because of their concern about a desirable outcome or goal of counseling or psychotherapy. The work of psychologists and psychotherapists seems to be converging on a definition or description of the fully functioning person, a term introduced by Rogers.[5] Other terms have been used to refer to the same concept: self-enhancement, self-realization, self-actualization. Perhaps the most commonly used term is the last, self-actualization. Self-actualization, therefore, becomes the goal of education or, more accurately, since few if any persons can be said to be fully self-actualized, *the purpose of education is to develop self-actualizing persons.*

In adopting this goal, education is not at odds with other institutions in society. The production of self-actualizing persons is—or should be—the goal of all our social institutions—the family, the church, political institutions, the economic system and other social institutions and organizations.

Moreover, such a goal is not a goal which is external to the individual, and which is forced upon him. It is not inconsistent with the individual's nature and needs. Indeed, this goal is inherent in the human organism, and in this respect it is not only a goal of society, but the goal of the individual, the purpose of life. It is the single, basic, common motivation of the individual. Goldstein said that "an organism is governed by a tendency to actualize, as much as possible, its individual capacities, its 'nature in the world'."[6] Rogers says "The organism has one basic tendency and striving—to actualize, maintain, and enhance the experiencing organism."[7] Combs and Snygg refer to maintenance and enhancement of the

---

[3] George B. Leonard, *Education and Ecstasy* (New York: Dell, 1968), p. 18.

[4] Charles E. Silberman, *op. cit.,* p. 114.

[5] Carl R. Rogers, *On Becoming a Person* (Boston: Houghton Mifflin, 1961).

[6] Kurt Goldstein, *The Organism* (New York: Harcourt, Brace & Jovanovich, 1939).

[7] Carl R. Rogers, *Client-Centered Therapy* (Boston: Houghton Mifflin, 1951), p. 487.

self, which they equate with self-actualization, as the "all inclusive human need which motivates all behavior at all times in all places." [8]

An objection has been made to the concept of self-actualization on the grounds that it leads to selfish and self-centered behavior. This is a misunderstanding of its nature. Every individual lives in a society composed of other individuals. He can only actualize himself in interaction with others. Selfish and self-centered behavior would not lead to experiences which would be self-actualizing in nature. As Rogers states it, the self-actualizing person "will live with others in the maximum possible harmony, because of the rewarding character of reciprocal positive regard." [9] "We do not need to ask who will socialize him, for one of his own deepest needs is for affiliation and communication with others. As he becomes more fully himself, he will become more realistically socialized." [10] He is more mature, more socialized in terms of "the goal of social evolution," though he may not be conventional or socially adjusted in a conforming sense.

THE SELF-ACTUALIZING PERSON

A major criticism of a broad, general goal such as self-actualization is that it is too general and vague to be useful. The behaviorists ask for a specific, objective or operational definition. It is necessary then, to give some consideration to defining or describing self-actualization so that, as an objective of education, criteria can be developed by which we can judge whether the objective is being achieved. While it is not possible at present to provide simple objective criteria, and accurate measures of them, the measurement of self-actualization is in principle possible, and some progress has already been made. A review of some of the discussions of self-actualization will help us to understand its nature and to arrive at a definition, or a description, of self-actualizing persons.

In the first edition of their book in 1949 Snygg and Combs put forth the concept that human beings are motivated by one basic striving, the maintenance and enhancement of the self. Man seeks to develop an *adequate* self.[11] The adequate person perceives himself in positive ways: he has a positive self-concept, he accepts himself. The adequate person also accepts

[8] Arthur W. Combs & Donald Snygg, *Individual Behavior* (New York: Harper & Row, 1959), p. 38.

[9] Carl R. Rogers, "A Theory of Therapy, Personality, and Interpersonal Relationships," in S. Koch, Ed., *Psychology: A Study of Science. Study I. Conceptual and Systematic. Vol. 3. Formulations of the Person and the Social Context* (New York: McGraw-Hill, 1959), pp. 234–236.

[10] Carl R. Rogers, "A Therapist's View of the Good Life: The Fully Functioning Person," in Carl R. Rogers, *On Becoming A Person*, p. 194.

[11] Arthur W. Combs & Donald Snygg, *op. cit.*, p. 45.

others: "we are so entirely dependent upon the good will and cooperation of others in our society that it would be impossible to achieve feelings of adequacy without some effective relationship with them. The adequate personality must be capable of living effectively and efficiently with his fellows." [12] In addition, the adequate person is able to accept into awareness all his perceptions, without distortion, or rejection. From a behavioral point of view, the adequate person is characterized by more efficient behavior, since he is not handicapped by defensiveness and is more open to experience. He is also spontaneous and creative since, being secure, he can take chances, experiment, and explore. Since the adequate person is secure and accepting of himself he is capable of functioning independently, that is, he finds that his own feelings, beliefs and attitudes are adequate guides to behavior. Finally, the adequate person, according to Combs and Snygg, is compassionate. Being less defensive, he can relate closely with others with concern rather than hostility or fear.

Carl Rogers proposes that the organism has "one basic tendency and striving—to actualize, maintain, and enhance the experiencing organism." [13] This tendency leads to or is manifested by growth and maturation, differentiation, independence and autonomy, and self-responsibility. His extensive experience in psychotherapy led him to the conviction that each individual, even though seriously disturbed, manifests this forward-moving tendency.

Rogers later developed the concept of the fully functioning person to describe the results of this striving in the optimal person, whether emerging from completely successful education or psychotherapy. He describes three major characteristics of such a fully functioning person: (1) Such a person is open to his experience, to all the external and internal stimuli; he has no need for defensiveness or distortion. He is keenly aware of himself and his environment; he experiences both positive and negative feelings. (2) The fully functioning person lives existentially. Each moment is new. Life is fluid, not rigid. The person is changing, in process, flexible and adaptable. (3) "This person would find his organism a trustworthy means of arriving at the most satisfying behavior in each existential situation." [14] His behavior is determined from within; the locus of control is internal. Being open to his experience, he would have available all relevant data on which to base his behavior. Behavior would not

---

[12] Combs and Snygg, p. 246. See also Arthur W. Combs, "A Perceptual View of the Adequate Personality," in Arthur W. Combs, ed. *Perceiving, Behaving, Becoming* (Washington, D.C.: National Education Association, 1962), pp. 50–64.

[13] Carl R. Rogers, *Client-Centered Therapy, op. cit.,* p. 487.

[14] Carl R. Rogers, *Freedom to Learn* (Columbus, Ohio: C. E. Merrill, 1969), p. 286. See also C. R. Rogers, "Toward Becoming a Fully Functioning Person," in Arthur W. Combs, ed., *Perceiving, Behaving, Becoming,* pp. 21–33.

always be perfect, since some relevant data may be missing, but the resulting unsatisfying behavior would be corrected on the basis of feedback. Such a person would be a creative and self-actualizing person. As indicated above, such a person is realistically socialized. "We do not need to ask who will control his aggressive impulses, for when he is open to all of his impulses, his need to be liked by others and his tendency to give affection are as strong as his impulses to strike out or to seize for himself. He will be aggressive in situations in which aggression is realistically appropriate, but there will be no runaway need for aggression." [15]

Earl Kelley describes the fully functioning person in terms similar to those of Combs and Rogers. Such a person thinks well of himself, feeling able or competent, though being aware of his limitations. He also thinks well of others, and sees their importance to him as opportunities for self-development. He sees himself as changing and developing. The fully functioning person develops and holds human values; he lives by these values rather than by external demands. Kelley also sees the fully functioning person as creative. In addition to these characteristics which are similar to those included by Combs and Rogers, Kelley says that the fully functioning person recognizes the value of mistakes, since in the process of changing and growing he cannot be right all the time. He sees mistakes as a source of learning and profits from them.[16]

Abraham Maslow has perhaps studied the nature of self-actualization to a greater extent than any one else. His description of the self-actualizing person draws together the characteristics considered above, with others resulting from his work, into a comprehensive picture of the highly self-actualizing person.

Maslow adopted an accepted and sound method in his attempt to study the nature of self-actualization. He selected a criterion group of persons (living and dead) on the basis of a professional judgment that they were outstanding as self-actualizing persons, using as a general definition "the full use and exploitation of talents, capacities, potentialities, etc. Such people seem to be fulfilling themselves and to be doing the best that they are capable of doing. They are people who have developed or are developing the full stature of which they are capable." [17]

These subjects were studied intensively, to determine both what characteristics they had in common, and which differentiated them from ordinary or average people. Fourteen characteristics emerged:

[15] *Ibid.,* p. 291.
[16] Earl C. Kelley, "The Fully Functioning Self," in Combs, ed., *Perceiving, Behaving, Becoming,* pp. 9–20.
[17] Abraham H. Maslow, "Self-Actualizing People: A Study of Psychological Health," in Clark E. Moustakas, ed., *The Self: Explorations in Personal Growth* (New York: Harper & Row, 1956), pp. 161–162.

MORE EFFICIENT PERCEPTION OF REALITY AND MORE COMFORTABLE RELATIONS WITH IT. This includes the detection of the phoney and dishonest person, and the accurate perception of what exists rather than the distortion of perception by one's needs. *Self-actualizing people are more aware of their environment,* both human and nonhuman. They are not afraid of the unknown, and can tolerate the doubt, uncertainty, and tentativeness accompanying the perception of the new and unfamiliar.

ACCEPTANCE OF SELF, OTHERS AND NATURE. Self-actualizing persons are not ashamed or guilty about their human nature, with its shortcomings, imperfections, frailties and weaknesses. Nor are they critical of these characteristics in others. *They respect and esteem themselves and others.* Moreover, *they are open, genuine, without pose or facade.* They are not, however, self-satisfied, but are concerned about discrepancies between what is and what might or should be in themselves, others, and society.

SPONTANEITY. Self-actualizing persons are not hampered by convention, but they do not flout it. *They are not conformists,* but neither are they anti-conformist for the sake of being so. They are not externally motivated, or even goal directed—rather their motivation is the internal one of growth and development, the actualization of their selves and potentialities.

PROBLEM-CENTERING. Self-actualizing persons are not ego-centered, but focus on problems outside themselves. They are *mission oriented,* often on the basis of a *sense of responsibility, duty, or obligation* rather than of personal choice.

THE QUALITY OF DETACHMENT; THE NEED FOR PRIVACY. *The self-actualizing person enjoys solitude and privacy.* It is possible for him to remain unruffled and undisturbed by much which upsets others. He may even appear to others to be asocial.

AUTONOMY, INDEPENDENCE OF CULTURE AND ENVIRONMENT. Self-actualizing persons, though dependent on others for the satisfaction of the basic needs of love, safety, respect, and belongingness, "are not dependent for their main satisfactions on the real world, or other people or culture or means-to-ends, or in general, on extrinsic satisfactions. *Rather they are dependent for their own development and continued growth upon their own potentialities and latent resources.*" [18]

[18] *Ibid.,* p. 176.

CONTINUED FRESHNESS OF APPRECIATION. *Self-actualizing persons repeatedly* (though not continuously) *experience awe, pleasure, and wonder in their everyday world.*

THE "MYSTIC EXPERIENCE," THE "OCEANIC FEELING." In varying degrees and with varying frequencies, *self-actualizing persons have experiences of ecstasy, awe, and wonder,* with feelings of limitless horizons opening up, followed by the conviction that the experience was important and valuable and had a carry over into daily life.

GEMEINSCHAFTSGEFÜHL. *Self-actualizing persons have a deep feeling of empathy, sympathy or compassion for human beings in general.* This feeling is in a sense unconditional, in that it exists along with the recognition of the existence of negative qualities in others which provoke occasional anger, impatience and disgust.

INTERPERSONAL RELATIONS. *Self-actualizing people have deep interpersonal relations with others.* They are selective, however, and the circle of friends is small, usually consisting mainly of other self-actualizing persons. They attract others to them as admirers or disciples.

THE DEMOCRATIC CHARACTER STRUCTURE. *The self-actualizing person does not discriminate* on the basis of class, education, race or color. He is humble in his recognition of what he knows in comparison with what could be known, and is ready to learn from anyone. *He respects everyone* as potential contributors to his knowledge, but also just because they are human beings.

MEANS AND ENDS. Self-actualizing persons are highly ethical. *They clearly distinguish between means and ends, and subordinate means to ends.*

PHILOSOPHICAL, UNHOSTILE SENSE OF HUMOR. Although all the self-actualizing subjects studied by Maslow had a sense of humor, it was not of the ordinary type. Their sense of humor was the spontaneous, thoughtful type, intrinsic to the situation. Their humor did not involve hostility, superiority, or sarcasm.

CREATIVENESS. All Maslow's subjects were judged to be creative, each in his own way. The creativity involved here is not the special-talent creativeness. It is a creativeness potentially inherent in everyone, but usually suffocated by acculturation. *It is a fresh, naive, direct way of looking at things.*

These characteristics give a description of the kind of person who would not only be desirable in our society, but who would be functioning at a high level, using his potentials and experiencing personal satisfaction. In fact, it could be said that unless there are enough individuals possessing a minimal degree of the characteristics of the self-actualizing person society cannot survive. Historically, such men have been contributors to the development of civilization, and where societies have not included some such persons, they have disintegrated and disappeared.

From the standpoint of the individual, perhaps a question could be raised as to whether individuals who are open and honest, and accepting and trusting of others, could exist in a society such as ours. Henry suggests that "in a society where competition for the basic cultural goods is a pivot of action, people cannot be taught to love one another, for those who do cannot compete with one another, except in play." [19] It is questionable, though, that such persons would be at so great a disadvantage. But more important is the question as to how our situation, our society, can be changed. Since society is composed of individuals and consists of interpersonal relations, to change society, one must change both. This is the only place we can start. The outlook is not necessarily grim. One can reason that, since these characteristics are necessary for the survival of society, and societies have survived as long as they have, there must have been, and be, a sufficient number of persons with these characteristics in contemporary society. Moreover, it could be argued that such characteristics being of survival value, persons with these characteristics have to some extent been selected in the evolutionary process. Anthropologists (e.g. Ashley Montagu) have pointed out that cooperation, rather than competition, among men has been the basis for the survival of groups and societies. Thus there is perhaps potential in human beings for the development of these characteristics in greater measure. There is evidence, from the education and training of counselors and psychotherapists, that these characteristics, at least some of them, can be increased by education and training. Finally, there is evidence that the qualities or characteristics of self-actualizing persons are stimulated or brought out in others with whom the possessors have contact, by what is known as the principle of reciprocal affect. We shall consider this in more detail in a later chapter.

MEDIATE GOALS OR SUBGOALS
OF EDUCATION

The self-actualizing person is one who utilizes his capabilities and potentialities to the highest extent. Self-actualization may be considered the

[19] Jules Henry, "In Suburban Classrooms," in Beatrice & Ronald Gross, eds. *Radical School Reform* (New York: Simon & Schuster, 1969), p. 83.

ultimate goal of education, toward which other goals, which may be termed mediate goals, contribute.

It may be argued that, in our society, a person cannot function at his highest level if he is illiterate. Thus, it is necessary that he be able to read and write, and to handle simple mathematics. Certain basic skills are necessary to function at almost any level in our society. Goodman suggests that literacy may be overvalued in our present society, where it is the road to influencing people through the mass media rather than a means for access to the humanities and sciences. "Perhaps in the present dispensation," he says, "we should be as well off if it were socially acceptable for large numbers of people not to read. It would be harder to regiment people if they were not so well 'informed.' " [20] This, however, is hardly desirable for the personal development of individuals.

The humanistic critics of education do not reject the acquisition of such basic skills as a goal of education. They do question the manner in which they are taught, a manner which interferes with or is inconsistent with the development of the characteristics of a self-actualizing person.

In our current society, it appears to be necessary, for most people, at least, to be employed in order to be self-actualizing persons, since having many jobs is normally conducive to self-respect. However, some jobs do not provide a source for feelings of competence or ability. Goodman writes that there isn't enough "man's work" in our society, that is, work that is worth doing, necessary, or useful, a real contribution to society. Much of our production, he says, is useless.[21] There is an argument that work is an aspect of the so-called Protestant ethic which we could well do without. This point of view fails to recognize that there is a basic need, an aspect of the self-actualization process, which requires that man exercise and use his capabilities in some way, and in a way which contributes to others or to society. This need to do something constructive, to make a contribution, to exercise one's abilities and talents, finds an outlet in meaningful work in our society. If and when the time comes when there isn't enough work for all those who can work in our society, a problem will clearly arise. Nevertheless, it may not be necessary, even now, that this always be done through a job. Thus, it may be argued, a job is not a necessary contribution to the process of self-actualization, if the individual has other ways in which to develop and use his talents and potentialities.

This leads to a consideration of some aspects of the relationship of mediate or subgoals to the ultimate goal of self-actualization. We have

[20] Paul Goodman, *Compulsory Mis-education and the Community of Scholars* (New York: Vintage Books, 1964), p. 25.
[21] Paul Goodman, *Growing Up Absurd* (New York: Vintage Books, 1962), pp. 17–18.

already indicated that the means of achieving subgoals, such as literacy, must not be inconsistent with the end or ultimate goal, as it so often is in our current educational system. This suggests that the ultimate goal serves, and should serve, as a criterion for the acceptability of mediate goals, as well as of the means by which they are achieved. One of the difficulties with our present educational system is that we seem to have no criterion for the many things that are included in the educational process, many of which are not ends in themselves. We need such a criterion, and the goal of self-actualization provides it. The question we must ask is: Does this activity contribute to the development of self-actualizing persons?

Another value of the recognition of subgoals, or two levels of goals, is that it provides for recognition of the commonalities of man and of the differences among men. The motivation toward self-actualization is shared by all men—except possibly those, hopefully, relatively few in number, in whom it has been quenched by tragic experiences or inhumane treatment. But the subgoals may, to some extent at least, vary among men. Maslow points out that since no two selves are completely identical, individuals may actualize themselves in somewhat different ways.[22] Thus, there is room for individual differences, for different ways of achieving the goal of self-actualization. The self-actualizing person pushes to make use of and exercise his talents, and achieves satisfaction from developing his potentials, which vary widely from individual to individual.

SUMMARY

Many have long been dissatisfied with the traditional goal of education—the transmission of the culture, the perpetuation of existing society. Some have proposed that the function of education is to foster change, to stimulate the development of a better society. But no one has been able to propose just how this can be done.

The current reforms and innovations in education do not question its goals. They are essentially attempts to remedy deficiencies in achieving the traditional goal. The humanistic critics of education have not clearly defined their goal, nor have they indicated just how education should be changed to meet their criticisms.

This chapter has proposed a goal of education which would meet the criticisms of the humanists. It is a goal which would lead to the development of people who are open to change and to continued learning. It is relevant to the basic problem of society, which is in the area of interper-

[22] Abraham H. Maslow, *Toward a Psychology of Being.* (New York: Van Nostrand, Reinhold, 1962), p. 196.

sonal relations. It is a universal goal, not limited to any culture, place, or time.

This goal is the development of self-actualizing persons. The nature and characteristics of such persons are developed, so that we can determine just what it is that we should be striving for, and can determine and provide the conditions—or the kind of education—which will result in the development of self-actualizing persons.

Early Examples Of
3 Humanistic Education

*The supreme good [is] the end of political science
[which includes education], but the principal care of
this science is to produce a certain disposition in
the citizens, namely to make them good and disposed
to do what is noble.*

—Aristotle, ETHICS

The great and good teachers of all times have exemplified humanistic education. They have respected their students, have treated them as individuals and persons, and have been interested in their feelings and attitudes. They have recognized that in learning the whole person is involved, that learning is not a purely cognitive activity. They have intuitively been aware that teaching does not necessarily and automatically result in learning, and that learning is something more than the acquisition of facts, information, or even knowledge. They have known that learning must involve interest and activity on the part of the learner, not passive submission to the teacher.

ARISTOTLE ON EDUCATION

For the early Greeks, the purpose of education was to develop good citizens. The specific goals and methods varied among the city-states.

Sparta emphasized discipline and strict obedience to the state. Athens emphasized freedom and personal development and encouraged the individual development of one's physical, psychological and artistic capabilities. Education consisted, for the Greeks, of the acquisition and transmission of excellences, or *arete*. *Arete* was more than its narrow translation as virtue; it included intellectual and physical as well as moral excellence.

Even here, differences in method and content existed. The essentialist/humanistic distinction appeared. Plato was an essentialist, placing pure reason as the highest state of knowledge. Aristotle was a humanist, and to the virtue of intellect or reason he added those of the practical, the artistic, and the moral. To him, education was an internal process, assisted by external agents, in which the individual actualized his potentialities.

Aristotle, in his consideration of the goal of education, went beyond the concept of *arete*, since *arete* is a condition which one has or is in without involving action or living. The good, according to Aristotle, is happiness, and happiness is *eudaimonia*, or "living well." This is not just pleasure, but the kind of life or activity that is pleasant because it is desirable. What is desired or desirable is good. The highest or supreme good is that which is sought for its own sake, and, if it is attained, nothing more would be desired. It is thus the ultimate goal of all human striving. It is, in short, self-actualization, or self-actualizing activity.

Aristotle relates this to man's basic human function (or motivation), which is to exercise his highest capacities. The good man is the one who exercises these capacities well or excellently, so that happiness, *eudaimonia*, or the highest good "is an activity of the soul in accordance with excellence." [1] The capacities of man, according to Aristotle, are nutrition, reproduction, sense, locomotion, imagination, desire, emotion, and reason. While reason is the highest, and distinctive of man, the others are important. Activities associated with all of these capacities are excellent if well done, but there are two kinds of activity which are intrinsically excellent—moral and political action, and activities of the intellect. These constitute happiness or *eudaimonia*. Other activities, though good or excellent, do not constitute happiness even though they contribute to it, or are indispensable for it, since happiness must be desirable for its own sake, as the ultimate goal.

While in subhuman organisms the actualization of potentialities proceeds naturally and virtually automatically, in man much of it depends on his own efforts and the cooperation of others. Thus, since this involves education, the ultimate aim of education is the attainment of happiness (*eudaimonia*). Since this cannot be achieved directly, but only by activi-

[1] Aristotle, *Ethics* I, 7, 1098a.

ties, the mediate goal of education is to cultivate the dispositions that will lead people to be ready, able, and willing to engage in the excellent activities that constitute or which lead to happiness. These dispositions are varied, and, while including the intellectual dispositions, also include moral virtues, art and friendship.

Aristotle was in conflict about whether a state system of education should cultivate the excellences of the good man or the good citizen, since these might not be the same. A state's educational system must cultivate the virtues of a good citizen according to its constitution, and promote the excellences of the good man only as they are compatible with the constitution or as they coincide with those of the good citizen. Education may not attempt to foster social reform, according to Aristotle. In the ideal state, however, there would be no conflict.

The actual process of education, as described by Aristotle, would hardly be considered humanistic by today's critics of education, however. While in infancy the child would be free to develop naturally, but from the age of five the educational process would be controlled. Nevertheless, from age five to seven, the child would learn, not by direct instruction, but by observing older children being instructed. And from age seven to puberty, emphasis would be on physical education. Thus it appears that young children would not be pressured. It was only during the three years after puberty that the academic subjects would be emphasized, to be followed by more physical education and military training until the age of twenty-one. But education would not stop at twenty-one. More mathematics, physics, philosophy, and politics would be studied. For Aristotle learning was a serious business, "for learning and play do not go together. Learning is accompanied by pain." [2]

RENAISSANCE AND EARLY MODERN EDUCATORS

Little is known about education during the long period between Aristotle and the Renaissance. Roman education was geared to the Roman state. St. Augustine (354–430) is reminiscent of Plato.

St. Thomas Aquinas (1225–1274) utilized Aristotle's principles of potentiality and actuality for his educational model, which envisions the learner as a striver toward the actualization of his rational and spiritual potentiality.

The early Renaissance produced a group of educators who have been called humanists. This term was coined toward the end of the fifteenth century to refer to a group of educators or teachers who were concerned

2 Aristotle, *Politics* VIII, 3, 1338b.

with literature, the liberal arts, or the humanities. (German scholars of the early nineteenth century used the word humanism to refer to educational theory based on the Greek and Latin classics.) Humanism was an attempt to reverse the professional and clerical emphasis of education in the middle ages—the education of doctors, lawyers, merchants, philosophers and theologians—and to emphasize the education of citizens, or rulers, to make men virtuous and learned. They were, however, not to be pure scholars, but active citizens. Baldassare Castiglione's book, the *Courtier,* published in the fifteenth century presented a model of the universal man, though in somewhat different terms; he described the courtly gentleman as one who could love, fight, paint, compose poetry, and discuss affairs of state with equal ease and skill. Such an education produced perhaps, in modern terms, a well-rounded person. Extreme specialization or excellence in only one area was disapproved of.

Humanism continued to influence education, indeed dominated education until the end of the nineteenth century, and continues as the basis of a liberal education. Note, though, that this is not what the word humanistic refers to in this book. The humanities in this period are concerned with the study of man's productions or creation—languages, literature, history, the arts.

Humanistic, as it is currently used, refers to the more basic aspect of humanity, or human nature. It derives from the adjective humane, which is defined as having feelings and inclinations creditable to man, including kindness and benevolence. In psychology, the movement designated as humanistic psychology extends psychology from behaviorism and psychoanalytic psychology, which view man as an object, to a concern about the person as subject, who is more than the sum of conditional responses, but a person, or self, who thinks, feels, and acts on his own.

Desiderius Erasmus (1466–1536) was influenced by the humanists, and is often labeled a humanist. In "The Education of a Christian Prince" (1503) he emphasized virtue as the "finest quality" to be inculcated. Montaigne (1533–1592) recommended that a tutor should be selected for character, and intelligence, rather than information or knowledge, and that he should not "monopolize the speaking, but . . . listen while the pupil speaks in his turn. . . . *The authority of the teachers is generally prejudicial to those who desire to learn* (Cicero)." [3]

A major figure in the early modern period was John Amos Comenius (1592–1670). In his book *The Great Didactic* (1657), he promised to provide "the whole art of teaching all things to all men, and indeed of teaching them with certainty, so that the result cannot fail to follow;

[3] Michel de Montaigne, *Essays,* excerpted in J. W. Noll & Sam P. Kelly, *Foundations of Education in America: an Anthology of Major Thoughts and Significant Actions* (New York: Harper & Row, 1970), p. 73.

further, of teaching them pleasantly, that is to say, without annoyance or aversion on the part of the teacher or the pupil, but rather with the greatest enjoyment for both . . ." [4] He promised a system of education that "shall be conducted without blows, rigor, or compulsion, as gently and pleasantly as possible, and in the most natural manner (just as a living body increases in size without any straining or forcible extension of the limbs; since if food, care, and exercise are properly supplied, the body grows and becomes strong, gradually, imperceptibly, and of its own accord. In the same way I maintain that nutriment, care, and exercise, prudently supplied to the mind, lead it naturally to wisdom, virtue and piety.)" [5] If one follows the nature of the child, one finds that not only does the child learn easily, but shows a desire to learn which resists any obstacles.

Comenius proposed a system of progressive instruction adjusted to the stage of development of the child, and was thus, as Piaget notes, a precursor of the genetic idea in child psychology.[6] To be sure, the stages were based on speculation rather than scientific knowledge, but he apparently knew children, and recognized the importance of spontaneity for learning and of activity in the child. All teaching would be geared to the child's capacities as he developed. The interest of the pupil must be aroused, and the material presented must be useful, i.e., relevant to the needs of the child. Teaching would involve learning by experience, by doing, before verbal instruction involving generalizations or rules were given. Teaching, in the school, would be limited to four hours a day, with another four hours for individual study.

Comenius obviously recognized that the natural inclination of children is to learn, and that teaching simply must recognize the stage of development of the child in providing appropriate stimuli and materials. Not discipline and the cane, but tender loving care, similar to that of a gardener handling young plants, would lead to learning. The goal would be to educate all men fully to full humanity. Then all men would be wise, free, happy, kind, and would live in peace.

In his emphasis on sense perception, concern with experience, and with practical knowledge, Comenius evidenced the beginning of a revolt against the classic humanist curriculum which was, however, continued by Locke.

John Locke (1632–1704), although a believer in discipline, also had a humane respect for the child as an individual. If the right course were to be taken with children, he said in his book *Some Thoughts On Educa-*

---

[4] John Amos Comenius , *The Great Didactic,* excerpted in Noll & Kelly, *ibid.,* p. 108.

[5] *Ibid.,* p. 109.

[6] Jean Piaget, "The Significance of John Amos Comenius at the Present Time," introduction to *John Amos Comenius on Education* (New York: Bureau of Publications, Teachers College, Columbia University, 1967), p. 10.

tion, there would not be so much need for punishment.[7] It was this, perhaps, which has led many writers to call him the father of the Enlightenment in education.

Some Thoughts on Education was originally written, as was Montaigne's *Essay* on education, in the form of letters to a parent. But, as part of his system of philosophy, it is empirical, based upon his observation of children. He recognized differences in the stages of development in children related to their capacities for learning. Like Comenius, he emphasized learning by practice, or experience, and by imitation, rather than simply by rules or verbal instruction.

The child, according to Locke, is receptive and malleable, his mind being a "tabula rasa," or clean page upon which experience writes. Thus, "of all the men we meet with, nine parts of ten are what they are, good or evil, useful or not, by their education." [8] Yet the child has some innate individual characteristics. The good teacher does not try to force grave children to be gay.[9] Nor is compulsion effective in other respects. Children naturally are active and enjoy freedom, and do not like idleness. They will enjoy learning when it is made enjoyable. "None of the things they are to learn should ever be made a burden to them, or imposed on them as a task." [10]

Locke was a humanitarian. The individual does not exist for the state, but for himself, and the child is an individual, a human being of worth. Learning requires a nonthreatening atmosphere. "It is impossible children should learn any thing, whilst their thoughts are possessed and disturbed with any passion, especially fear, which makes the strongest impression on their tender and weak spirits." The teacher must get and keep the attention of the child. In addition to this, and the method of instruction, the teacher "should add sweetness in his whole carriage, make the child sensible that he loves him, and deigns nothing but his good." [11]

Locke was concerned with more than the intellectual development of the child. In fact, the learning of academic subject matter comes last, following virtue, respect for truth, wisdom, and good breeding as qualities to be cultivated in children. Good breeding consists of a basic rule: "not to think meanly of ourselves, and not to think meanly of others." [12] In other words, one must respect, and accept, himself and others. But, it

[7] John Locke, *Some Thoughts on Education,* in Peter Gay, ed. *John Locke on Education* (New York: Bureau of Publications, Teachers College, Columbia University, 1964), p. 39.
[8] *Ibid.,* p. 20.
[9] *Ibid.,* p. 43.
[10] *Ibid.,* p. 55.
[11] *Ibid.,* pp. 126–127.
[12] *Ibid.,* p. 103.

must be remembered, Locke's book on education was concerned with the education of "gentlemen," and he did not think about universal education, as did Comenius.

ROUSSEAU'S EMILE

Jean Jacques Rousseau (1712–1778) was greatly influenced by Locke. His book, *Emile* (1762) is one of the most influential writings on educational thought and practice. It became a pattern for many people in the education of their children, though it is directly applicable only to education by individual tutors, and is not a systematic treatise but an illustration of principles. Since humanistic education is a personal approach, philosophy and principles are more important than method. Rousseau, influenced by Aristotle as well as Locke, focused upon the learner as naturally good. The purpose of education is therefore to allow, or foster, his natural growth and development and the actualization of his potentials. Learning is natural, and thus should be spontaneous and joyous.

Emile was begun as a brief statement for a mother concerned about the education of her son. It is cast in part as a story, describing the education of a boy, Emile, and his wife-to-be, Sophie. Rousseau was concerned about the lack of knowledge about, and understanding of, children. "Begin then," he says in his Preface, "by studying your pupils better; for assuredly you do not know them." [13]

Man is naturally good, but is corrupted by society and its institutions. Education must prevent this corruption, by following the inclinations of man's nature. Faced with the choice of making a man or making a citizen, Rousseau, unlike Aristotle, does not hesitate in choosing the former. Education must preserve man's original nature unspoiled. The product of such an education must, of course, enter society, but he is a human being true to his own nature, in the world but not of it. Manhood—becoming a man—is the goal of education, not preparation for a specific station or vocation. "All that a man must be he will be when the need arises, as well as anyone else. Whatever the changes of fortune, he will always be able to find a place for himself." [14] In our terminology, the self-actualizing person is adaptable to an existing society, and to changes in it. Education must not simply allow men to survive, but "to make sure they really live. . . . The man who gets the most out of life is not the one who has lived longest, but the one who has felt life most deeply." [15]

---

[13] W. Boyd, *The Emile of Jean Jacques Rousseau* (New York: Bureau of Publications, Teachers College, Columbia University, 1962), p. 6.
[14] *Ibid.,* p. 15.
[15] *Ibid.,* p. 15.

Emile was an imaginary pupil, an ordinary boy, yet rich, "since it is only the rich who have need of the natural education that would fit them to live under all conditions," and an orphan with a tutor, since Rousseau felt that normally the education of the child should be conducted by the father, not by a hired tutor.[16] Yet what he prescribes for the tutor could also be performed by the father.

Rousseau divided childhood into four stages: infancy, boyhood, the approach of adolescence, and adolescence. He deals with infancy, which ends with weaning, briefly and simply. It is with boyhood, which extends to the age of twelve, that Rousseau begins his systematic discussion of education.

Rousseau attempted to suit education to each stage of the child's development, yet he was not overprotective. The child must be allowed to learn from experience. Dependence on things is natural, and leads to the child learning from consequences. Dependence on men restricts freedom and leads to vices. "Our pedantic eagerness to instruct is always leading us to teach children what they can learn better for themselves. . . ."[17] Recognizing the uncertainty of life, Rousseau felt that education which "sacrifices the present to an uncertain future and makes the child miserable in order to prepare him for a remote happiness which he will probably not live to enjoy" is barbarous. *"Your first duty is to be humane."* [18] Humaneness, however, does not include indulgence.

Young children, before the age of twelve, do not have the capacity to reason, except about their present concerns. Thus Rousseau disagrees with Locke's emphasis on reasoning with children. The child should not be taught on the basis of obedience, duty, or obligation, however, but on the basis of what he finds necessary to do, including the necessity of recognizing his weakness and the teacher's power. Lessons should be the lessons of experience, not just verbal. Punishment should not be used because the child cannot, by nature, do anything morally wrong; his wrong actions are mistakes, not intentional wrongs. Wrong actions should be prevented, not forbidden. "Be reasonable and do not reason with your pupil." Early education "consists not in teaching virtue and truth, but in preserving the heart from vice and the mind from error. If you could do nothing and let nothing be done, so that your pupil came to the age of twelve strong and healthy but unable to distinguish his right hand from his left, the eyes of his understanding would be open to reason from your very first lesson." [19] The education of childhood is the exercise of the body and senses, with no pressure on the mind. "Let childhood ripen in children." [20]

[16] *Ibid.,* p. 20.
[17] *Ibid.,* p. 28.
[18] *Ibid.,* p. 33; emphases added.
[19] *Ibid.,* p. 41.
[20] *Ibid.,* p. 42.

Teaching consists of the presenting of good examples, avoiding bad examples, and selecting a good environment insofar as possible. If the child observes undesirable behavior, such as anger, don't lecture to him about it. "Leave the child to come to you. Astounded by the sight of an angry man he will be sure to ask questions. Your answer is simple. It is suggested by the very things which have struck the senses. He sees an inflamed countenance, flashing eyes, threatening gestures, he hears cues: all signs that something is wrong with the body. Tell him quietly: 'The poor man is ill, he has an attack of fever.' Such an idea if given at the proper time will have as salutary effects as the most longwinded discourse, and it will have useful applications later on." [21]

The emphasis on training of the body and the senses precludes the teaching of language, geography, and history, since words and ideas are meaningless without experience. Moreover, "Reading is the greatest plague of childhood. Emile at the age of twelve will scarcely know what a book is. But at least, I will be told, he must be able to read. I agree. He must be able to read when he needs to read. Before that it will only be a bother to him." The principle is that children "will only learn what they feel to be of actual and present advantage, either because they like it or because it is of use to them. Otherwise, what motive would they have for learning." [22] If Emile receives letters or notes from relatives or friends which he must read because no one else is available to read them for him, and if he misses out on something because of inability to read, then he will learn to read without the need of devices such as those suggested by Locke.

Emile at twelve is healthy, bright, eager, care-free, absorbed in his present.

His ideas are limited but precise. If he knows nothing by heart, he knows a great deal by experience. If he is not as good a reader in books as other children, he reads better in the book of nature. His mind is not in his tongue but in his head. He has less memory but more judgment. He only knows one language, but he understands what he says, and if he does not talk as well as other children he can do things better than they can. . . . Work and play are all the same to him. His games are his occupations: he is not aware of any differences. He goes into everything he sees with a pleasing interest and freedom." [23]

At twelve or thirteen the child is strong and self-sufficient. While necessity has been the basis of his education, he is now ready for an understanding of the nature of utility, though not yet for moral notions. The

[21] *Ibid.*, p. 43.
[22] *Ibid.*, p. 51.
[23] *Ibid.*, p. 66.

world, not books, is the focus of attention, but rather than being told about it he is allowed to discover things for himself. Not knowledge, but the stimulation of curiosity and seeking is the objective. As in the preceding stage, only what the child is ready for will be learned; if it be questioned whether there will be time for him to learn what he ought to know later, when he needs it, one can only answer that he cannot and should not learn it sooner.

At fifteen, Emile has limited knowledge, but a mind open, intelligent, responsive, and capable of acquiring more knowledge. His knowledge is limited to the relations between man and things, and does not include knowledge between man and man. He has the personal virtues but not the social virtues. "We have made him an efficient thinking being and nothing further remains for us in the production of a complete man but to make him a loving, sensitive being." [24]

Education in adolescence is concerned with man as a moral being in relationships with others. The adolescent becomes aware of other people, experiences compassion for those who suffer, feels his need for other people, and develops friendships. He broadens from friendship to a concern for humanity through the study of great men and history. He enters society.

PESTALOZZI AND NATURAL EDUCATION

Johann Heinrich Pestalozzi (1746–1827), like Rousseau born in Switzerland, built upon the work and insights of Comenius and Rousseau. His emphasis was the same—the total development of the child, with education based upon the child's natural development. He was more concrete in his recommended practices, and was concerned about the psychology of learning and instruction. And in contrast to Rousseau's focusing upon the education of the children of the rich or well-to-do, Pestalozzi was concerned about the education of poor children.

In 1782 he published *Leonard and Gertrude,* a successful novel which portrayed the benign influences of a mother on her children in spite of their poverty and a drunken father. *How Gertrude Teaches Her Children* was published in 1801. It is in the form of fourteen letters to his publisher in Zurich, and contains his theory of education.

In contrast to Locke and Rousseau, who were philosophers, Pestalozzi was an educator, but he was concerned about placing his practice upon a theoretical base. In *Leonard and Gertrude* he declared that man is good, and the source of evil is in his environment. Though ignorant, man is capable of learning, and education is the development of man's moral, intellectual and physical potentialities. These powers must be exercised for men to grow. They are present in all men, and each man has the right to develop his potentialities, and the obligation to allow other men the same freedom. Man makes use of his self-activity to exercise his natural powers. Man's happiness lies in the cultivation of his powers to the end of self-perfection.

Education begins in the home with the mother. In *Researches Into the Course of Nature in the Development of the Human Race* (1797) he developed the thesis that knowledge of the natural processes of development would provide a basis for education. Natural development is continuing and gradual, each phase built upon the last. Education must co-operate with the natural laws of growth and development.

> All instruction of man is then only the art of helping nature to develop in her own way; and this art rests essentially on the relation and harmony between the impressions received by the child and the exact degree of his developed powers. It is also necessary, in the impressions that are brought to the child by instruction, that there should be sequence, so that beginning and progress should keep pace with the beginning and progress of the powers to be developed in the child.[25]

Pestalozzi likened man to a tree, in that the seed holds the potential for its growth, given the proper environment. Man needs organized instruction in order to develop because without it he is unable to apprehend reality clearly. The art of instruction is to provide a balanced environment so that man's growth will not be distorted, as a tree which has inadequate light will develop a tropism. The moral, intellectual and physical powers must be developed and harmoniously integrated in balance.

Pestalozzi objected to the system of education then practiced, in which children, after five years of freedom, were penned up "like sheep, whole flocks huddled together, in stinking rooms; piteously chain[ed] . . . for hours, days, weeks, years, to the contemplation of unattractive and monotonous letters (and, contrasted with their former condition) to a maddening course of life." [26]

Pestalozzi recommended changes in the curriculum, including going from abstract verbal teaching to learning by direct experience. But in addition to his concern with content, its organization and its presentation, he was concerned with the environment or atmosphere of education.

Pestalozzi was a humanitarian, a gentle person, whose theory or philoso-

---

[25] Johann H. Pestalozzi, *How Gertrude Teaches Her Children* (Syracuse: Bardeen, 1900), p. 26. Quoted in G. L. Gutek, *Pestalozzi and Education* (New York: Random House, 1968), p. 86.
[26] *Ibid.*, p. 28, quoted in G. L. Gutek, *ibid.*, p. 102.

phy held that in everyone there is, at birth, the germinal quality of benevolence or love. This hidden quality depends upon an appropriate environment for its development or expression. If the child is given love, he will respond, reciprocally, with love. Pestalozzi's general method of teaching was to provide an atmosphere of love, an environment of emotional security, which depended on a love relationship between the teacher and the student. The natural goodness of the child is brought out by love rather than by coercion. If children are disorderly, it is because they have come from homes in which they have been deprived of love. The remedy is not disciplining the child, but changing his environment. The parents, especially the mother, are first responsible for stimulating the love of the child. But the school must extend the familial relationship to create a climate of emotional security and give the child experience with a larger range of persons. The schools which Pestalozzi conducted resembled homes, with many children, rather than schools.

In *Christopher and Elizabeth* (1782), Pestalozzi described the schoolmaster as follows: he

should, at least, be an openhearted cheerful, affectionate, and kind man, who would be as a father to the children; a man made on purpose to open children's hearts, and their mouths, and to draw forth their understandings, as it were, from the hindermost corner. In most schools, however, it is just the contrary; the schoolmaster seems as if he were made on purpose to shut up children's mouths and hearts, and to bury their good understandings ever so deep in the ground. That is the reason why healthy and cheerful children, whose hearts are full of joy and gladness, hardly ever like school.[27]

The result of education should be, as indicated above, a man in whom the moral, intellectual, and physical powers are balanced and integrated. Such a man—the good hearted man—would be a person who was emotionally secure, capable of loving others and accepting love in return, and aware of his moral duties and responsibilities. He would be a man who could trust his senses, and his senses would reveal reality accurately and clearly. In short, he would be a fully-functioning or self-actualizing person.

SUMMARY

The origins of humanistic education go back a long way—at least to Aristotle, whose goal for education was the exercise of man's highest capacities. Aristotle influenced many of those who later wrote about

---

[27] Quoted in G. L. Gutek, *ibid.,* pp. 124–125.

education, including Erasmus, Aquinas, Comenius, Locke, and Rousseau. Comenius recognized the importance of adjusting instruction to the child's stage of development, and Locke, Rousseau, and Pestalozzi continued this emphasis. That the natural activity of the child is to learn was also recognized by these writers, who believed that education should fit into this natural process of learning, and thus be enjoyable to the child. Man is basically good, but he can be spoiled or corrupted by society. "The child does not become good or intelligent by having the habits or opinions of society imposed upon him. What he does or knows should be the outcome of a personal reaction on life situations. The truth for me is what I have convinced myself is true." [28] Learning is through experience, not through being told.

Locke, Rousseau and Pestalozzi also realized that the child is not a miniature adult, but a child, and must be treated as a child, but also with respect as a person. The purpose of education, they agreed, is not the development of a scholar, nor even a citizen of a state, but a "gentleman" (Locke), a man (Rousseau), an integrated, balanced whole man (Pestalozzi).

The teacher is a person, one who is humane (Rousseau). He must be patient, interested, concerned—in short, he must love the child (Pestalozzi). Pestalozzi saw all men as alike, with the same potentials to be developed or actualized, but he knew that men also differed in the ways in which they would use their potentials in society, occupying different social positions and occupations.

The basic and essential principles of humanistic education were thus clearly enunciated some two hundred years ago. They may be stated simply as (1) the purpose of education is to develop the potentials—all the potentials—of man as a whole; (2) the essential method for achieving this is the providing of a good human relationship between the teacher and the student—or, as Pestalozzi put it, a love relationship.

The ideas of Locke, Rousseau and Pestalozzi had very little influence on the education of their times or immediately afterwards. Authoritarian discipline and memorization dominated education. Comenius called the schools "the slaughterhouses of the mind." But why is it that we have not yet applied these principles in our educational system? There are, to be sure, some current attempts to do this, and we now turn to a consideration of some of these.

[28] W. Boyd, *op. cit.*, p. 172.

4

Some Recent Humanistic Developments In Education

The bestowal of freedom is the bestowal of love.
. . . Children do not need teaching as much as they
need love and understanding. They need approval
and freedom to be naturally good.

—A. S. Neill, SUMMERHILL *

For three hundred years or more, schools have been
denounced for their capacity to destroy children's
spontaneity, curiosity, and love of learning, and for
their tendency to mutilate childhood itself. To
create and operate schools that cultivate and nurture
all these qualities without reducing children's aca-
demic attainment—this is a magnificent achievement.

—Charles E. Silberman, CRISIS IN THE CLASSROOM †

Examples of a humanistic approach to education exist today. Perhaps the best known is Summerhill, but the English infant and junior schools are also becoming well known. Less well known are the Danish Folk Schools. These, and some other examples will be briefly summarized in

* From pp. 92, 118, of *Summerhill: A Radical Approach to Child Rearing,* by A. S. Neill, copyright 1960 Hart Publishing Company, Inc., New York.
† (New York: Random House, 1970), p. 262, comment on the new English Primary Schools.

this chapter, but more detailed discussions will be found in the references cited.

SUMMERHILL

Perhaps the most radical attempt to implement the concept of learning as natural development in an atmosphere of love, understanding, and responsible freedom is Summerhill.

Summerhill is the creation of A. S. Neill, and was founded in England (about a hundred miles from London) in 1921. The school accepts boys and girls, from the age of four or five years on, the age of leaving being from about fifteen to seventeen or eighteen. The total of about forty-five or fifty children live by age groups, each with a house mother.

There is no requirement for attendance at classes. Classes are held according to age, and sometimes on the basis of interests. There are no examinations. There is no moral or religious instruction. Yet the children attend classes, study and learn. They may not always be successful in passing the university examinations because they may not know the right things, but they are usually successful in life. Like Rousseau's Emile, they are not educated for the world, but they are able to adapt to the world. As Fromm notes, "they will have acquired a sense of genuineness which will prevent their becoming misfits or starving beggars. [Neill] has made a decision between full human development and full market-place success . . ." [1]

Neill writes: "My view is that a child is innately wise and realistic. If left to himself without adult suggestion of any kind, he will develop as far as he is capable of developing. . . . The function of the child is to live his own life—not the life that his anxious parents think he should live, nor a life according to the purpose of the educator who thinks he knows what is best. All this interference and guidance on the part of adults only produces a generation of robots." [2]

The child is naturally good, and progresses through natural stages of development. He cannot be forced in his development, for to do so leads to psychological disturbance. The young child is normally an egoist or self-centered. To force him to share, for example with a younger brother, leads to the development of hatred for the brother. But, if the child is not prematurely taught to be unselfish, altruism comes naturally later. Children will learn moral values from their environment when they are capable

---

[1] Erich Fromm, Foreword to A. S. Neill, *Summerhill: a Radical Approach to Child Rearing* (New York: Hart Publishing Co., 1960), pp. xiv–xv.
[2] A. S. Neill, *Summerhill: a Radical Approach to Child Rearing* (New York: Hart Publishing Co., 1960), pp. 4, 12.

of doing so. Patience, rather than pressure, will facilitate natural development.

Classes are held from 9:30 to 1:30. Although attendance is not required, most children want to attend, and banishment from lessons is a punishment which may be imposed by the General School Meeting (of staff and pupils), though such punishment is considered severe. The afternoons, and some evenings, are filled with various activities according to the interests of the children—sports, games, hobbies, dramatics, art work, pottery, metalwork, and woodwork.

Freedom is not absolute. There are rules for the protection of the children, but the rules are made by the General School Meeting. The rights of others must be respected. Thus, if a student does not want to attend class regularly, and/or interferes with the learning of others in class, he is not permitted to attend class. Freedom is not license.

For Neill, the aim of life is to find happiness, that is inner happiness, which is life's natural fulfillment. Education is preparation for life, and should be happy. In the past many have said that children should learn through doing—which usually means doing things which are required. Now some are saying that children should learn through playing, with playing considered as a means to an end. Neill simply says that children should play. This is not organized play or athletics, but imaginative or fantasy play, since reality and fantasy merge in children. "One could, with some truth, claim that the evils of civilization are due to the fact that no child has ever had enough play. To put it differently, every child has been hothoused into an adult long before he has reached adulthood." [3]

Adults are afraid that if children play all day, they will never be able to pass the examinations for admission to the University. At Summerhill, students are able, if they want to, to pass the exams after two or three years of intensive study.

Neill's idea of happiness is not simply pleasure, nor is it assured by wealth. It is "an inner feeling of well-being, a sense of balance, a feeling of being contented with life. . . . Happiness always means goodness. The evil of life is all that limits or destroys happiness." [4] It is not absolutely necessary for happiness—or for success in life—that a person be able to read well. The happy person is not afraid, and therefore is at peace with others, does not hate but loves others, and is sincere and honest. In other words, it would appear that the happy person, as described by Neill, is a fully functioning or self-actualizing person.

Happiness requires freedom, and freedom leads to the development of self-regulation. Freedom is not to be confused with complete permissiveness, which ignores the rights of others. There are limits to the child's

[3] *Ibid.,* p. 64.
[4] *Ibid.,* pp. 111, 356.

rights; but he does have rights. Social laws are necessary and are accepted by children.

The child who is free discovers his interests; he can be himself—a real person—natural. Freedom leads to sincerity, charity, lack of fear and lessening of aggression. Neill reports that in thirty-eight years there has never been a fight with bloody noses at Summerhill, even though there have been children from bad homes. "To give freedom is to allow the child to live his own life." [5] Self-interest will lead to his learning what and when he needs to. "Every child under freedom plays most of the time for years, but when the time comes, the bright ones will sit down and tackle the work necessary to master the subjects covered by the government exams." [6] Free children do learn the academic subjects which interest them, even though they spend most of their time in other activities.

Allowing children to be free is difficult, for it means avoiding imposing our religion, politics and social values on them. Fear keeps adults from giving freedom to the young. "The adult fears to give freedom to the young because he fears that the young may do indeed all the things that he, the adult, has wanted to do." [7] Giving freedom to children who have not had it for years does lead to problems, though. The child who has hated school but has been forced to attend may, when free not to attend, refuse to do so for some time. Freedom works slowly, even when started early. It requires patience. It also requires trust.

Freedom encourages responsibility. But as freedom is not absolute, and children need to be protected, so responsibility should be adjusted to the child's age or ability to accept the responsibility. Allowing too little responsibility, though, is retarding. The child should be given enough responsibility so that he can grow, but not so much that he loses his self-assurance.

Happiness also requires love and approval. This is not possessive or sentimental love, which does not let the child live his own life. Parents who really love their children are not always asking the school about the child's progress. "It is all a matter of faith in children. Some have it; most haven't it. And if you do not have this faith, the children feel it. They feel that your love cannot be very deep, or you would trust them more." [8]

Approval of the child does not mean acceptance or approval of all his behavior, or not expressing one's feelings about undesirable behavior. "The strange thing is that you can be on the child's side even though you sometimes swear at him. If you are on the side of the child he realizes it. . . . *It doesn't matter what you do to a child if your attitude toward that child is right.*" [9]

[5] *Ibid.*, p. 113.
[6] *Ibid.*, p. 116.
[7] *Ibid.*, p. 113.
[8] *Ibid.*, p. 117.
[9] *Ibid.*, pp. 119–120, 144. Italics in original.

Strong discipline and authority depend on fear, and fear is inimical to happiness. It leads to lying and hate. Freedom encourages fearlessness. Ruling by love, not through fear, leads to genuine respect. If there is love, discipline is not necessary. The child who loves and trusts in return, responds to reasonable requests. Punishment is unnecessary. *"Punishment is always an act of hate.* In the act of punishing, the teacher or parent is hating the child—and the child realizes it." [10] Punishment leads to hate, though the hate may be covered by apparent remorse or love. Rewards are bribes, involving an admission that the behavior is not worth doing for its own sake. "Rewards and punishment tend to pressure the child into interest. But true interest is the life force of the whole personality, and such interest is completely spontaneous. . . . Though one can compel attention, one cannot compel interest." [11]

It is clear that at Summerhill the total development of the child is the focus. The purpose of education is to facilitate the development of people —happy people. Academic or intellectual development is subordinated to affective or emotional development. But, as a 16 year old former student notes, "one is learning all the time. What a kid wants to learn may be entirely different from what his parents want him to know, but doesn't it seem logical that the person who has to do the learning should have the choice?" [12] The students are restricted, however, by the need to meet the requirements of society and its institutions for courses, credits and diplomas.

Learning—not only or simply academic, but social and emotional—takes place at Summerhill not because of its extensive library, its well equipped laboratories, its modern classrooms, its highly qualified teaching staff, or its extensive teaching materials. In fact, it has none of these, and there is no consideration given to these, or to its curriculum, in describing Summerhill. Its success with children is the result of the kinds of persons who make up the staff, and the atmosphere of love, respect, understanding, patience, kindness and basic humanity which is created and maintained.

THE DANISH FOLK HIGHSCHOOL

The Danish folk highschool is not new. The first one was established in 1844. From one school with twenty students they grew to eighty-three schools with 5600 students in 1910. Now there are about seventy with more than 8500 students, or about ten percent of all Danish twenty-year-old's.[13] The persistence of these schools makes them particularly significant, since the schools have obviously met a continuing need. Although they originated through the idea of an individual, they have had government support since 1852. Under the Danish Folk Highschool Act of 1942, students are supported on the basis of need. In addition, the school receives support for teachers' salaries and operating expenses.

The man whose idea led to the schools was Bishop N.E.S. Grundtvig (1783–1873), who, in his speeches and writings, fought for freedom and democracy for the common man. The folk highschool "was intended to be a means through which the common man could be helped to learn his own value and his strength-giving ties with his country's past and the mother tongue," [14] at a time when Latin and German were the language of the schools and of the educated classes.

His school was for young men of about eighteen or older, since Grundtvig felt that younger children should not be pressed intellectually, since they were not ready; children should be allowed to play, experiment and be active, until their bodies and brains became fully developed. Then they would have questions, and experience the need to learn. In addition, the developing democracy in government in Denmark required that the common people, the sons of peasants, be better educated. The core of the curriculum of the early highschools was Danish language, history, and culture.

The current highschools vary somewhat in type. The Workers Education Association operates two residential schools for the children of workers, including farmers; the curriculum is comprehensive. Other schools have specialized curriculums: There are gymnastic high schools, nursing highschools, preparatory schools for teacher training seminaries, schools for child welfare workers, and schools for the disabled. Two schools prepare handicapped students for work in public administration and technical work. There is some conflict about introducing vocational courses into the schools, since the tradition has been to emphasize the development of the person rather than the worker.

The folk highschools are of course not compulsory. They have no entrance requirements, but women were not admitted until 1945. There are no grades, examinations or diplomas. They are boarding schools. There is thus a closeness among students and staff, a sense of community which is perhaps fostered in part by activities such as group singing. There are no strict requirements or standards set by the government. All that is required is that they be boarding schools, that they offer at least one five-month course, or two three-month courses, annually, that there

13 David C. L. Davis, *Model for Humanistic Education: the Danish Folk High-School* (Columbus, Ohio: C. E. Merrill, 1971), p. 6.
14 *Ibid.*, p. 27.

be no educational prerequisites, and that at least half the curriculum be nonvocational, or concerned with cultural and social problems. The term of five months, during the winter, originated with the intention to serve a farming population. Although a few schools offer two-year courses, the program is limited to one term.

The teachers are not required to hold credentials, but they must have ability or experience in one of the areas included in the curriculum, a desire to teach, and a willingness to be a part of the community, not limiting their contact with students to scheduled classes.

The lack of grades and examinations allows freedom in teaching. The communal living facilitates social and emotional growth and development, which is not subordinated to intellectual progress. While students at a University live together, it is an entirely different experience in the small folk highschool. In the University social interaction is limited and, between teachers and students, is formal, and the emphasis is upon standard courses and subject matter. In the highschools there develops a personal closeness among students, a closeness to one another, a caring for each other, and an openness and trust, so that discussions are personally meaningful, not simply academically or intellectually stimulating.

The schools vary in the freedom allowed students, and in the democracy of their operation. Both are being extended, even though there is resistance from some principals. Democracy is expanding. Yet probably few of the folk highschools are as democratic as Summerhill.

The folk highschool idea has been extended to the continuation schools, for children from age fourteen to eighteen. Some of thsee are more democratic than the highschools, though some have met resistance from boards of trustees.

Many believe that the folk highschools have influenced Danish society, e.g., in raising the level of literacy, in developing the cooperative movement, and in advanced social legislation.[15] The schools have been a success—demonstrated by one hundred and twenty years of existence.

In summary, what have they done? They have incorporated a humanistic approach to students and their education. They have shown that people are interested in learning, without the need of credits and diplomas, that when they are interested they learn, without the stimulus—or goad— of examinations, and that they become involved in learning through living together.

The Danish folk highschool seems to have demonstrated that with freedom to attend or not, and a curriculum related to the interests and needs of students, and staff, the school will be a place of real learning. "The folk highschool experience has shown that when students wanting to find

[15] *Ibid.,* p. 18.

out come together with teachers who want to help them find out, there is purpose and commitment." [16]

One of the problems seems to be to extend the benefits of residential schools to nonresidential schools in urban environments. The day and night community school, including recreational facilities, may be at least a partial answer.

THE BRITISH INFANT AND JUNIOR SCHOOLS

One of the criticisms of Summerhill is that it is too extreme in its lack of emphasis on or concern for academic and intellectual development. In addition, Summerhill is a residential program; nonresidential schools cannot operate in the same way, since they cannot control the total environment of the child. The British infant and junior schools incorporate aspects of Summerhill in a nonresidential, more academically oriented educational program.

A major characteristic of the traditional school is its emphasis upon order and control. The classrooms are regimented, with students glued to seats which are bolted to the floor. Silence is maintained, with students speaking only when called upon. They are teacher dominated—the teacher lectures or talks most of the time. All students are (supposedly) engaged in the same activity at the same time under the teacher's control. At set times, when a bell rings, the subject of study suddenly changes. It is an arbitrary, regimented routine.

Not all schools are or have been like this, of course. In England, especially, and particularly since World War II, there are schools which do not fit this description, variously referred to by terms such as the free school, the free day, the open school, the integrated day, and informal education. In these schools childhood and children are respected, and the school experience is recognized as important in itself, not simply as preparation for the future. The so-called Plowden Report, in 1967, publicizing and urging extension of this approach, stated: "Children need to be themselves, to live with other children and grownups, to learn from their environment, to enjoy the present, to get ready for the future, to create and to love, to learn to face adversity, to behave responsibly, in a word, to be human beings." [17]

---

[16] *Ibid.*, p. 104.

[17] Central Advisory Council for Education (England), *Children and Their Primary Schools* (London: Her Majesty's Stationery Office, 1967), (2 vols.) Generally referred to as the Plowden Report after Lady Bridget Plowden, the Chairman of the Central Advisory Council for Education. Quoted in Charles E. Silberman, *Crisis in the Classroom* (New York: Random House, 1970), p. 209.

These schools are not new, but have been developing over the last fifty years or more. Silberman suggests that their roots go back to Robert Owen's infant school in New Lanark in 1816.[18] Apparently humanistic teachers in different schools began to function instinctively in ways which respected the child and his interests. At present Silberman estimates that about 25 per cent of the English primary (i.e., infant and junior) schools are operating as "open" or "free" schools, with another third of the total moving in this direction.[19] More of the infant schools than the junior schools are open or free. In England children enter the infant schools at age five, continuing until age seven or eight, when they move to a junior school. At eleven they go on to secondary school.

Joseph Featherstone has described the British schools on the basis of a month's visit to England.[20] Silberman [21] also observed a number of the English infant and junior schools. His excellent discussion, based upon considerable investigation of the literature as well as consultation with authorities in addition to his own observations, is drawn upon here.

The informal English classroom resembles an American kindergarten, but continues it beyond the preschool year. In addition, the English classroom has many more resources available. Besides reading and arithmetic materials, there are toys, a playhouse, household utensils and equipment, a sand table, a water table, painting equipment and materials, a musical area, and a science area, including animals. Although there may be as many as forty children in a room, there are no desks, and not enough chairs for each child—the children are seldom seated all at once, and if they are, some sit on the floor.

The classroom is a hive of noisy activity of various kinds all at once. The teacher moves around, from group to group. The children move from activity to activity, often out of the room and into the "hall," or large central room which serves as auditorium, cafeteria, and gymnasium.

Though the first impression may be one of chaos, there is a difference between the noise of aimless activity and that of purposeful activity. The teacher is not just there, passively, but is actively involved, as well as observing and recording the progress of individual children. She talks with the children about their activities, introducing relevant words and concepts. The teacher guides the activity when it seems to be desirable, such as keeping children from flitting from one thing to another without completing anything. But it is an informal, quiet guidance, with the teacher

[18] *Crisis, ibid.,* p. 213.

[19] *Ibid.,* p. 211.

[20] Joseph Featherstone, *The Primary School Revolution in Britain* (New York: Pitman, 1967). Originally published in *The New Republic,* August 10, September 2, and September 9, 1967.

[21] Charles E. Silberman, *op. cit.*

speaking in a normal conversational tone, with respect for the child. There is structure, but it is flexible and adapted to the child.

"What impresses the American observer the most, however, is the combination of great joy and spontaneity and activity with equally great self-control and order. The joyfulness is pervasive: in almost every classroom visited, virtually every child appeared happy and engaged. One simply does not see bored or restless or unhappy youngsters, or youngsters with the glazed look so common in American schools. The joy is matched by an equally impressive self-discipline and relaxed self-confidence. There seem not to be any disruptive youngsters or even restless youngsters in informal classrooms—indeed, few of the behavior problems with which American teachers are almost always coping." [22]

This is not a difference between English and American children, because English formal classrooms are like those in America. The primary schools are child-centered. They are the children's schools. Their lack of disciplinary problems is related to the fact that, as the Plowden Report states it, the schools are "ideally suited to the needs and nature of young children and to their development as human beings." [23] Children are treated as children, but with the expectation that they will grow and develop and learn.

Although there is a great deal of freedom and informality, the children's activity is not entirely free play or random activity. Materials are selected, experiences are planned, discussions of experiences are conducted, and some direct instruction and even drill in reading and writing are given.

A unique aspect of the English schools is what is called movement. "In its most fundamental sense, movement is an attempt to educate children in the use of their bodies—to provide them with an ease, grace, and agility of body movement that can carry over into sports, crafts, and dance." [24] But it is not physical education, or dance instruction. Usually the entire class participates under the teacher's direction, but what is done varies with the teacher and the child's interpretation. "There is, after all, no right way or wrong way to move as if you were a snowflake, or a leaf fluttering down from a tree . . ." [25] It is not a stylized, prescribed form of exercise, but expressive movement. It unites the body with the feelings and thoughts in an integrated, total person.

It has been indicated that the change in primary education in English schools developed on the basis of the instincts of humanistic teachers, rather than on the basis of any theory of child development. But the practices find theoretical support in the work of philosophers and edu-

22 *Ibid.*, p. 228.
23 *Ibid.*, p. 229.
24 *Ibid.*, p. 253.
25 *Ibid.*, p. 254.

cators, some of whom have been included in the last chapter—Rousseau, Pestalozzi, Froebel, Montessori and Dewey. Silberman notes also that the work of Jean Piaget supports the English informal approach. Piaget emphasizes the activity of the child in assimilating his experiences and accommodating to them. The child proceeds through a series of stages in his development, each stage opening up new possibilities which the child actualizes through his own activities, leading to progress to the next stage. The problem of education is to present the child with situations which are appropriate to his level of development, and which challenge without threatening, so that he can explore, experiment, experience and grow— at his own rate. The provision of a wealth of resources and materials, as in the English infant and junior schools, allows children at different stages to make use of those he is ready for, and to progress normally.

"The informal English schools demonstrate in practice what Dewey argued in theory: that a deep and genuine concern for individual growth and fulfillment not only is compatible with but indeed demands an equally genuine concern for cognitive growth and intellectual discipline, for transmitting the cultural heritage of the society. And the intellectual disciplines of language, arithmetic, history, music, science, et al., Dewey also agreed, 'are themselves experience,' experience that embodies 'the cumulative outcome of the efforts, the strivings, and the successes of the human race generation after generation.' " [26]

THE FIRST STREET SCHOOL

The First Street School consisted of twenty-three black, white and Puerto Rican children, ages five to thirteen, from low-income families in the lower East Side of New York City; their three full-time teachers; and a part-time teacher, George Dennison, who has described the school.[27] The school was supported by a private grant. It was influenced by the writings of Neill on Summerhill.

The school was conceived of not simply as a place for instruction, but as an environment for growth, which takes place in relationships, relationships between children and adults, adults and adults, and children and other children. There were no grades or report cards, no standardized tests, no conventional schedules or routines, no homework, no administrators, but just teachers. Attendance was not compulsory.

The school offered freedom: "1) we trusted that some true organic bond existed between the wishes of the children and their actual needs,

[26] *Ibid.,* p. 220.

[27] From *The Lives of Children,* by George Dennison (New York: Vintage Books, 1969). Copyright © 1969 by George Dennison. Reprinted by permission of Random House, Inc., and by permission of Penguin Books, Ltd.

and 2) we acceded to their wishes (though certainly not to all of them), and thus encouraged their childish desiring to take on the qualities of decision-making." [28] Schedules and routines did not take precedence over the interests of children in spontaneous events.

Many of the older children were "problem children." An effort was made not to force them to learn, or to impose instruction on them. Opportunities offered through their free play were sometimes taken advantage of, but essentially they were offered relationships with adults, adults who accepted and who respected and liked them, and who did not play roles —teacher roles—but were themselves. And part of being themselves and being concerned about the children consisted in wanting the children to learn, and offering them opportunities to learn. The offering was active, not a passive waiting for the children to ask for or demand help, but it was not imposed, and could be refused. At times the desire to teach led to attempts to impose instruction, but the children resisted and rejected these attempts.

Their play was not supervised, forcing the children to face the problems of accepting and enforcing rules and of fairness and ethics themselves, so that they experienced responsibility for their own activities. Adults intervened only to protect a child from injury—as when a heated fight led to one boy producing a knife. The children learned from their interaction with each other—not only in the areas of socialization, morality and ethics, but academically.

And the children gradually became less rebellious, less overactive and resistant, and began to learn. They were intelligent, but, at the beginning, behind their age levels academically. Almost all improved markedly, and some spectacularly. At the end of the year many of them were reading beyond their age levels. They found, when they were not treated as failures, and not pressured to compete—with standards or with other children —that they could succeed, and that learning was interesting. They also changed in their behavior—from being problems to being "normal" children. The respect, confidence and trust shown by the teachers led to self-respect, confidence and trust, and the reduction of self-contempt, shame, and hostility.

Dennison does not suggest that the First Street School be *the* model for education; it is a first step, limited by circumstances and its newness. But he says: "I do propose the kinds of relationships we established at First, the kinds of freedom enjoyed by teachers and children and parents, the respect for experience, the absence of compulsion, the faith in the inherent sociability of children; I do propose all these as the environmental model

[28] *Ibid.,* p. 21.

for an entire system, for they belong intrinsically to the educational experience, and not just to the rationale of a school." [29]

SOME OTHER EXAMPLES

At the same time that the informal schools were beginning to gain acceptance in England, child-centered or progressive education reached its height in America. Many of the progressive schools of the 1920's and 1930's which were close to John Dewey's philosophy were very similar to the new English schools, as evidenced by the descriptions of these schools by Harold Rugg and Ann Schumaker.[30] The progressive education movement declined amidst public disfavor when its ideas and principles were misunderstood, distorted and misapplied.

Rather than turning to Dewey and the examples of good progressive education, however, American education is turning toward the English schools, perhaps because they are currently existing models. Beginning in 1968, North Dakota, following an intensive study of its elementary school system, adopted a program of informal education influenced by the English schools. By early 1971, seventy of the state's 650 elementary schools were involved in the new approach.

The children have in most cases reacted positively to the change in the schools, and attendance has risen. Most parents have accepted the change, although many are concerned about their children's academic achievement. There is more emphasis on formal academic instruction, particularly in reading, than in the English schools.

In spite of the changes, and the glowing reports about the North Dakota schools, most of the schools are a long way from the English schools. One observer writes that "anyone going to North Dakota expecting to find a fully developed model of change for schools throughout the nation is bound to be disappointed. Rarely are the actual changes in the schools as radical or as extensive as the impression of them conveyed by the media" [31]—or by Silberman. Not only the parents, but most of the teachers, are concerned about teaching the traditional basics, though attempts are made to individualize the instruction, and to encourage informality. But as one undergraduate student in the new School for the Behavioral Sciences at the University of North Dakota (where the teachers for the new

[29] *Ibid.,* pp. 260–261.
[30] Harold Rugg and Ann Schumaker, *The Child-centered School: An Appraisal of the New Education* (New York: World, 1928). Quoted in C. E. Silberman, *op. cit.*
[31] Henry S. Resnik, "Promise of Change in North Dakota," *Saturday Review,* April 17, 1971, pp. 67–69, 79–80.

program are prepared) commented: "There's a big difference between individualized instruction and instruction of the individual." [32]

The difficulties of developing really open classrooms and open schools in America lie in a basic conflict between the philosophy and goals of the humanistic approach to education and the philosophy and goals of the traditional American school. It appears that in North Dakota the methods of the open classroom and the free school movement are being introduced in a system whose goals are inconsistent with those of the open school. Informal teaching, even personalized teaching, with a standard, graded, imposed curriculum, even individualized, as a technique to get the student to progress through the formal curriculum step by step, ignores the learner. Real humanistic education involves personalization and teacher concern for the individual as a person whose stage of development and interests lead to the creation or development of his own curriculum.

In New York City in 1968 Dr. Lillian Weber of City College, after returning from an eighteen month study of the English informal schools, began to introduce informal education in a public school where her students were assigned for student teaching. The materials were set up in the school corridor, and children were permitted to leave their classrooms to use them three hours a week. The response of the children, and of the teachers, was favorable. The project was extended the next year to another school, using space in the classrooms instead of the corridor. The next year, three more schools were involved.[33]

There are other schools which are developing changes along the lines of open schools, often independently. Silberman describes those in Philadelphia, and Tucson.[34]

There are no doubt many which have received no publicity. The increasing number of attempts, some by individual teachers, to break out of the prison of the traditional classroom and school indicates that the process of change in American education has begun—a change greater than the introduction of technology only to do better what the schools are now doing.

SUMMARY

Here in this chapter, as in the last chapter, we have seen that the process of education is essentially a relationship between the teacher and the student. Neill's Summerhill demonstrates the results of a relationship characterized by freedom and love. It proves what most of us know in-

[32] Ibid.
[33] Silberman, pp. 297–306.
[34] Ibid., pp. 306–318.

tuitively and from experience—when the child is interested and motivated he learns easily, quickly and joyously what it takes years to drill into children in a traditional school. The English infant and junior schools illustrate the effects of respect for children and childhood and the importance of expectations on behavior. The First Street school also, in a sort of combination of Summerhill and the English open school, shows us the same thing.

The English primary schools introduce more structure and more cognitive activity than Summerhill has—although Summerhill is not as devoid of adult influence and cognitive activity as may appear or as its critics charge. The children interact extensively with adults, who teach informally as well as serve as models for personal-social and moral-ethical behavior.

A number of writers point out that there are differences among the various attempts to develop informal schools and open classrooms—differences related to countries and cultures as well as types of students. Silberman, for example, states that the English approach could not be transplanted to America. Perhaps it couldn't immediately in its current form, but it did not appear suddenly in its present form in England. In fact, the development of the English infant and primary schools has been slow. No doubt this should be expected in a society which is more tied to tradition than America. One might expect that the progress of the movement toward informal education and open classrooms would be more rapid in America. However, as indicated above, there is a strong resistance, among parents, as well as many teachers and administrators. The tendency of some to go to extremes (remember progressive education) also can lead to a reaction against the movement, slowing its progress.[35]

There are, of course, differences among the new programs. But, more important, there is also a basic and fundamental similarity—the teacher is a facilitator, a human being living with children or students who learn naturally, at their own rate, with little or no direct instruction involving a set and structured curriculum. It is this basic concept, which also involves a change in the goal of education, which appears not to have been recognized or incorporated into the North Dakota program.

American education has been obsessed with narrow, limited, specific, concrete, measurable—and almost always short-term—objectives. This obsession is manifested in the work of the curriculum reformers and the behaviorists and technologists whose work was discussed in Chapter 1, an approach inconsistent, as we have seen, with the naturalistic, humanistic approach to education. It emphasizes and focuses upon techniques,

[35] See, for example, Marilyn Hapgood, "The Open Classroom: Protect It from its Friends." *Saturday Review,* September 18, 1971, pp. 66–69, 75.

gimmicks, curriculum resources and materials (including teaching machines and other hardware) which are limited to achieving specific objectives. This obsession with technology characterizes, for example, the report of the Committee for Economic Development on *Innovation in Education.*[36]

These objectives are not concerned with the total child as a person, but with specific attributes or characteristics, which have been abstracted from the person. This seems to be a difficulty in the North Dakota program, and is illustrated, in a less obvious way, in the Tucson, Arizona, program as described by Silberman. In this program there are objectives, including "developing a positive attitude toward learning" and "developing an intellectual base," the latter including some twenty different activities. These long lists of categories and subcategories of objectives lead to concern with techniques for achieving them, but by what techniques does one induce a "positive attitude toward learning"? Positive attitudes toward learning are inherent in the child until they are killed by teaching techniques, and so are all the other objectives. They are *there*—they don't have to be achieved or developed. They must only be preserved, and this is not done by techniques or teaching methods. In formalizing objectives and devising techniques for achieving them (the favorite pastime of educational writers and writers of proposals for financial support from the U.S. Office of Education) we miss the whole essence of education. This essence is the providing of a relationship which allows the child's natural learning to occur. "The educational function does not rest upon our ability to control, or our will to instruct, but upon our human nature and the nature of experience. . . . The task of education is to provide experience. In order to do this, he [the teacher] must *interact* with his students, not as a teacher, but as a person."[37]

We turn then, in the next chapter, to the nature of this relationship or interaction, to the conditions for learning and personal development.

---

[36] Committee for Economic Development, *Innovation in Education: New Directions for the American School.* (New York: The Committee, 1968).
[37] George Dennison, *op. cit.,* pp. 246, 256.

5 The Conditions For Learning And Self-Actualization

The basic nature of the human being, when functioning freely, is constructive and trustworthy. . . . When we are able to free the individual from defensiveness, so that he is open to the wide range of his own needs, as well as the wide range of environmental and social demands, his reactions may be trusted to be positive, forward moving, constructive.

—Carl R. Rogers, FREEDOM TO LEARN *

In Chapter 2 we proposed the development of self-actualizing persons as the goal of education, and defined the self-actualizing person, including his characteristics. Chapters 3 and 4 presented evidence that this goal of education has been accepted by, or is inherent in those approaches to education which may be designated by the word humanistic. However, nowhere has there been attempted a systematic analysis of the conditions for the development of self-actualizing persons. Humanistic approaches to education have emphasized the importance of the person of the teacher and the relationship between the teacher and the student, thus indicating that the essential conditions for learning reside in the person of the teacher and the relationship with the student. What are the characteristics

* (Columbus, Ohio: Merrill, 1969), pp. 290–291.

61

of the good teacher, and what is the nature of the human relationship that leads to learning, and thus self-actualization? Before considering this question specifically, it is desirable that we look first at some concepts of the nature of man.

THE NATURE OF MAN

Man Is an Active as Well as a Reactive Being

Gordon Allport, the psychologist, describes three concepts of man, or, as he puts it, three images.[1] The first, the traditional or so-called scientific approach to man, or of stimulus-response psychology, sees man as a reactive being. Man is an object, a biological organism, responding to the stimuli in his environment. He is determined by his past experiences, or conditioning; his present and future are determined by potential conditioning. He is thus not free, or capable of determining his own behavior. His behavior is reflexive, reactive, responsive, to outside stimuli, to rewards or reinforcements. Consciousness—thinking and feeling—is irrelevant in the study of man's behavior. This is the behavioristic view of man, the view of John B. Watson and B. F. Skinner.

A second image of man is that of man as a reactive being in depth. Though man is still determined by his past, and is not free, the determining factors in his behavior are internal, consisting of his drives, chiefly the sex or libido drive and the death or aggressive drive. This is the view of Freud and of psychoanalysis and other depth psychologies.

Contrasted with these two views of man is a third, what Allport calls that of man as a being in the process of becoming. This model sees man as personal, conscious, future oriented, in control of his behavior and his destiny. It is the model often labeled existentialism, or humanistic psychology.

These three images may be reduced to two opposing models. One sees man as a reactive being, whether in response to his environment or to his innate drives, motives, or needs. In one case he reacts (mainly, rather than exclusively) to stimuli from without; in the other he reacts (mainly) to stimuli from within. In either case he is controlled by stimuli, a victim of his environment or of his innate needs and drives, or of both. The second model, that of man in the process of becoming, sees man as a determiner. He is not controlled but controls; he has something to say

[1] Gordon W. Allport, "Psychological Models for Guidance," *Harvard Educational Review*, 1962, 32, 373–381. Reprinted in C. H. Patterson, Ed., *The Counselor in the School: Selected Readings* (New York: McGraw-Hill, 1967), pp. 39–47.

about what he shall do or become. Rather than being manipulated by his environment he manipulates his environment. Man is an active being. He creates, to some extent at least, his own world. He is free, within limits, of course, and since he is free he is able to make choices. And since he is free to choose, he is responsible for his actions and behavior.

These two views of man are in conflict. They appear to be antithetical, and the tendency is to accept one or the other. The prevailing view of man, the one that is fostered by our current scientific approach, is that of man as a reactive being, as determined. The concept of freedom appears to be inconsistent with the assumption of determinism required by science. The whole approach to education represented by teaching machines, computer assisted instruction, behavior control and modification through reward and reinforcement, is based upon this model of man. The effectiveness of these methods of influencing behavior is evidence of its validity. There is overwhelming support for the view that man is a reactive being, and we cannot reject it. Are we then in a position where we must reject the humanistic view, as the behaviorists do, and insist that everyone must do?

The difficulty inheres in stating the problem as an either/or choice. This way of stating problems is one of the basic fallacies in reasoning. It is not necessary to accept one point of view and to reject the other. The solution is to recognize that neither model alone is a complete model of man, that each, by itself, gives us only a partial view. The reactive model of man is a "nothing but" model, but man is this and "something more." This something more is significant, even crucial, in understanding man and his behavior and in providing an adequate theory of human behavior.

A major difficulty in accepting a humanistic view of man is the freedom-determinism dilemma. Science accepts determinism—it is a necessary assumption. But science also must recognize and deal with human experience and the influence of beliefs—or assumptions—on behavior. There are two such factors which must be recognized in regard to the freedom-determinism dilemma. First is the psychological fact of the existence of the feeling or experience of freedom and of choice in the individual, the existence of which must be recognized and included in a theory of human behavior. Second, and of more importance, it makes a tremendous difference in our conception of man and in the way we deal with human beings whether we accept the assumption of determinism or of freedom. To view man as free means that we treat him differently than if we view him as completely determined, and this difference is a real factor in human relationships. This is an illustration of the crucial influence of a theory or assumption about the nature of man in human relationships. An example of this influence is the effect of expectations, or the self-fulfilling prophecy, which will be considered in another place.

Man Is Inherently Good

One of the differences in views of man is whether man is innately bad or innately good. Many, if not most, religions accept the innate depravity of man. Freud also was pessimistic in his view of man. Feeling that the individual's instincts must be controlled by culture, he stated that "it does not appear certain that without coercion the majority of human individuals would be ready to submit to the labour necessary for acquiring new means of supporting life. One has, I think, to reckon with the fact that there are present in all men destructive, and therefore anti-social and anti-cultural, tendencies, and that with a great number of people these are strong enough to determine their behavior in society." [2] Man is not only anti-social, but hostile to others, according to Freud. "Civilized society is perpetually menaced with disintegration through this primary hostility of men toward one another. . . . Culture has to call up every possible reinforcement in order to erect barriers against the aggressive instinct of man." [3]

Aggression has long been considered an instinct, and its strength and practical universality have supported this view. But there are many who question the existence of aggression as an instinct. Ashley Montagu, the anthropologist, writes: "My own interpretation of the evidence, strictly within the domain of science, leads me to the conclusion that man is born good and is organized in such a manner from birth as to need to grow and develop in his potentialities for goodness. . . . [The view that aggressiveness is inherited] is not scientifically corroborated. In fact, *all* the available evidence gathered by competent investigators indicates that man is born without a trace of aggressiveness." [4]

He cites the psychologist Lauretta Bender's finding that hostility in the child is a symptom complex resulting from deprivations in development. Charlotte Buhler, a child psychologist, in her studies of infants also found that "they give evidence of a primary orientation toward 'reality' into which the baby moves with a positive anticipation of good things to be found. Only when this reality appears to be hurtful or overwhelming

---

[2] Sigmund Freud, *The Future of an Illusion* (London: Hogarth Press, 1949), pp. 10–11. Quoted in D. E. Walker, "Carl Rogers and the Nature of Man," *Journal of Counseling Psychology*, 1956, 3, 89–92. Reprinted in C. H. Patterson (Ed.), *op. cit.,* pp. 47–50.

[3] Sigmund Freud. *Civilization and its Discontents* (New York: Jonathan Cape & Harrison Smith, n.d.). Quoted in Walker, *ibid.,* reprinted in Patterson, op. cit., pp. 49–50.

[4] Ashley Montagu, *The Humanization of Man* (Cleveland, Ohio: World Publishing Co., 1962).

does the reaction become one of withdrawal or defense."[5] Maslow as well declares that impulses of hate, jealousy, hostility, etc., are acquired. "More and more," he writes, "aggression is coming to be regarded as a technique or mode of compelling attention to a satisfaction of one's needs."[6]

In other words, aggression is a reaction to deprivation, or frustration. This was the thesis of the frustration-aggression hypothesis put forward by the anthropologist Dollard of Yale and his psychological associates in 1939.[7] More generally, aggression is a reaction to threat, a behavior which is universal because threat, in some form or other, is universal. Bibring, a psychoanalyst, in criticizing Freud's theories, questions "whether there are any phenomena of aggression at all outside the field of the ego-preservative functions," noting "the empirical fact that aggressiveness appears only or almost only when the life instincts or the ego instincts are exposed to harm."[8] A widely read novel purporting to depict the horrible results of the innate aggressiveness of man inadvertently supports the view that aggression is the result of threat, since its development occurred under conditions of fear and threat.[9]

There is evidence that man is inherently good in the continual striving towards an ideal society, with the repeated and independent development of religious and ethical systems, whose ideals have withstood the test of time. In spite of conditions of deprivation and of threat these ideals have been held and practiced by many individuals. We have developed systems of government and law which, though imperfectly, especially in their applications, represent these ideals. In Chapter 2, in another context, we argued that goodness has a survival value. If there were not an inherent drive toward good in man, it is difficult to understand how the human race could have continued to survive; men would long ago have killed each other off. It is perhaps even arguable that the process of evolution has resulted in the survival of those more positively oriented to others—or the converse, that those with the lesser potentialities for good or the greater potentialities for destructiveness have less often survived, perhaps destroying each other. While this may appear to be a more optimistic view than is warranted by the devastating wars of this century, it does

[5] Charlotte Buhler, *Values in Psychotherapy* (New York: Free Press, 1961), p. 71.
[6] Abraham Maslow, "Our Maligned Animal Nature," *Journal of Psychology,* 1949, 28, 273–278.
[7] John Dollard, Leonard W. Doob, Neal E. Miller, O. Hobart Mowrer & Robert R. Sears, *Frustration and Aggression* (New Haven: Yale University Press, 1939).
[8] E. Bibring, "The Development and Problems of the Theory of Instincts," in C. L. Stacy & M. F. Martino (Eds.) *Understanding Human Motivation* (Cleveland, Ohio: Howard Allen, 1958), pp. 474–498.
[9] William Golding, *Lord of the Flies* (New York: Coward McCann, 1955), (Capricorn Books, 1959).

appear that there is a changing attitude about the necessity and inevitability of war, especially among the young. And the technological potential for destroying the human race appears to be leading statesmen to take steps to reduce threat and thus the possibility of such a catastrophe. Thus the potential for good has survived, and when we can further still reduce deprivation and threat it will become more evident and effective.

Man Has a Single Basic Motivation

In Chapter 2 we stated that the single basic motivation of all human beings is the actualization of one's potentials. A number of psychologists have reached this conclusion, apparently independently. Goldstein was perhaps the first to use the term self-actualization. He wrote: "We can say, an organism is governed by a tendency to actualize, as much as possible, its individual capacities, its nature in the world." [10] Angyal speaks of self-realization as being the intrinsic purpose of life.[11] Rogers states that "The organism has one basic tendency and striving—to actualize, maintain, and enhance the experiencing organism." [12] Self-actualization is a part of Rogers' general, organismic actualizing tendency. Combs and Snygg write: "From birth to death the maintenance of the phenomenal self is the most pressing, the most crucial, if not the only task of existence. . . . Man seeks not merely the maintenance of a self. . . . man seeks both to maintain and enhance his perceived self." [13]

A question might be raised as to whether the maintenance and enhancement of the self are not two independent motives, rather than a single one, and that they may even oppose each other at times. Preservation of the physical organism may mean the sacrifice of the psychological self. Conversely, preservation of the psychological self may require the sacrifice of the physical organism. Maslow apparently was influenced by some such considerations in his concept of deficiency motivation and growth motivation.[14]

But preservation or maintenance, and enhancement or actualization may be seen as two aspects of the same motive, operating in different

[10] Kurt Goldstein, *The Organism* (New York: World Book, 1939), p. 196.

[11] Andras Angyal, *Foundations for a Science of Personality* (New York: Commonwealth Fund, 1941), p. 354.

[12] Carl R. Rogers, *Client-centered Therapy* (Boston: Houghton Mifflin, 1951), p. 487.

[13] Arthur W. Combs & Donald Snygg, *Individual Behavior* (New York: Harper & Row, 1959), p. 45.

[14] Abraham H. Maslow, "Deficiency Motivation and Growth Motivation," in M. R. Jones (Ed.) *Nebraska Symposium on Motivation,* 1955. (Lincoln, Nebraska: University of Nebraska Press, 1955), pp. 1–30.

situations. Adler recognized the different expression of the same basic motive in neurotics and normals. The neurotic, threatened and compensating for a deep feeling of inferiority, reacts to preserve or restore his self-esteem, to overcome his inferiority with superiority through the striving for power.[15] The normal individual, on the other hand, free of threat, can strive for completeness or perfection. In the unhealthy individual, in the individual under stress, or the individual who is threatened, enhancement or positive striving is impossible. He must defend himself against attack or threat of attack, and strive to safeguard, defend or secure what he has. His energies are absorbed in preservation. Goldstein makes the same point. He considers the drive for self-preservation a pathological phenomenon. The drive for self-actualization, he suggests, undergoes a change in the sick (or threatened) individual in whom the scope of life is reduced, and he is driven to maintain (or defend) a limited state of existence.[16] Preservation or maintenance of the self is thus a pathological form of self-actualization, the only form of self-actualization left to the threatened individual.

A more serious question is raised by those who believe that man has many motives and who propose various hierarchical orderings of them. The most influential proposal of this kind is Maslow's, whose hierarchy starts with the basic physical needs, which are prepotent, and which take precedence, when they are unmet, over all other needs. When these are satisfied, the safety needs emerge. Then come the belongingness and love needs, followed by the esteem needs, and then by the need for self-actualization.[17] The problem arises that the order is not invariant, as Maslow himself recognizes. It is not always true that the lower, more basic physiological needs take precedence over the higher, less prepotent needs. A man may sacrifice his life for honor. We need, therefore some organizing principle to explain this apparent inconsistency.

The concept of self-actualization as the single basic need provides this principle. The individual's specific needs are organized and assume temporary priority in terms of their relationship to the basic need for self-actualization. That specific need which is momentarily most relevant assumes priority or prepotence, or to use Gestalt terminology, becomes the figure against the ground of other needs. When it is satisfied, the next most relevant need assumes prepotence, or figure, while the others recede into the ground. All are organized by the basic need for self-actualization, and their significance or relevance is determined by this basic need.

[15] H. L. & Rowena R. Ansbacher, *The Individual Psychology of Alfred Adler* (New York: Basic Books, 1956), p. 114.

[16] *Op. cit.*

[17] Abraham H. Maslow, *Motivation and Personality* Sec. Ed. (New York: Harper & Row, 1970), pp. 35–47.

Behavior is Determined by the Individual's Perceptions

Behaviorism assumes that behavior is determined by external stimuli; depth psychology assumes that behavior is determined by internal stimuli. Neither is true. Stimuli influence but do not determine behavior. We react to stimuli, both external and internal, in terms of our perceptions of them, how they appear to us, what they mean to us. The same objective stimuli are perceived differently by different individuals. In this sense, we do not react to "reality", but to what we perceive. We can only know the world through our perceptions, and reality is what we perceive and what we believe. Our perceptions are our only reality; we cannot react to what we do not perceive. This theory of human behavior is known as phenomenology. "What is perceived is not what exists, but what one believes exists, . . . what we have learned to perceive as a result of our past opportunities and experiences." [18]

This is a simple, common sense theory of human behavior. It is also a very useful one, in that it helps us understand the apparently unreasonable behavior of others. For a simple example, take the case of an automobile driver who stops at a stop sign, then immediately starts up again going right into the path of a car coming into the intersection from his left. "He must be blind" is perhaps one of the most charitable reactions of an onlooker. The driver of the other car will no doubt have a much more derogatory reaction. The driver's behavior seems ununderstandable. But, if one simply assumes that the driver perceived the intersection as a four-way stop, his behavior is at once clear and understandable.

The Perception of the Self or the Self-Concept Is the Most Important Determiner of Behavior

Perceptions are influenced by our needs and our beliefs. Our perceptions of others and of the world are influenced by our perceptions of ourselves. The self is the most significant part of the individual's phenomenal field, the center around which all other perceptions are organized. Other perceptions take their meaning or significance from their relevance to the self-concept, in terms of their contribution to the maintenance and enhancement of the self, or to self-actualization. The person who sees himself as a failure expresses this in his perceptions of the behavior of others and in his own behavior in response to the behavior of others. The

[18] Arthur W. Combs and Donald Snygg, *op. cit.*, pp. 84, 85.

child who perceives himself as a nonreader does not read. Many children do not learn to read because they are convinced that they can't read. With this conviction they do not attempt to read, and thus do not learn. This vicious circle operates in the case of children who believe they are failures in other areas, or indeed that they are failures in all areas.

If all behavior is determined by the behaver's perceptions, or phenomenal field, including his perception of himself or his self-concept, then it should be clear that in order to understand and to predict another's behavior one must know his phenomenal field. That is, it is not what we know *about* the individual and his environment which is important, but whether we are able to put ourselves in his place to perceive him and the world as he perceives them. In other words, we must be able to take the internal frame of reference rather than the external frame of reference if we are going to understand people.

To Change Behavior We Must Change Perceptions

If perceptions, particularly perceptions of the self, determine behavior, then we must change perceptions in order to change behavior. Perceptions change under those conditions which have relevance to the basic need for the preservation and enhancement of the self. Other conditions are simply not perceived. This is why much of what children are exposed to in school has no effect. It is not seen as relevant; it is simply not perceived.

The first condition for perceptual change is an experience which is relevant to the self and the self-concept. If the experience is consistent with the self-concept, there will be no change. An experience which is consistent with a self-concept of failure does not change this perception of oneself. The experience must be inconsistent with the existing self-perception, and must raise a question or pose a problem. But, since one naturally attempts to preserve the existing self-concept there is resistance to change, and experiences which are inconsistent may be rejected, resisted, misinterpreted, distorted, or denied.

The reaction of preservation is the characteristic reaction to threat. An individual under threat does not easily change his perceptions, but becomes defensive and resistant to change. Thus the experience which leads to change must raise a question, pose a problem, but in a challenging rather than a threatening way. This distinction between challenge or threat is important in learning or behavior change, since what is one child's challenge is another child's threat. The teacher of a large class is in the situation where attempts to challenge some children are threatening to others.

Disturbances in Learning and Behavior
Are the Result of Threat

The concept of threat is therefore very important in learning. Threat leads to resistance to change, to self-preservative rather than self-enhancing behavior. The person under threat restricts his perception, becomes defensive, withdraws, narrows and restricts his range of activity. The individual doesn't "see" all aspects of the situation, such as alternative solutions to a problem, and manifesting what is referred to as "tunnel vision," ceases exploration, and engages in stereotyped behavior. As Combs and Snygg put it, "Under threat the impulse of the organism is to protect its organization and its concepts become more strongly defended than ever. . . . A self under threat has no choice but to defend itself in one form or another." [19] It may attempt to overcome or avoid the threat, or if neither of these methods is successful in eliminating it, the self may distort or deny the situation. In any case, learning or positive change in behavior does not occur.

THE CONDITIONS FOR
SELF-ACTUALIZING BEHAVIOR

It is apparent that if learning, or the development of self-actualizing behavior, is to occur, then threat must be minimized. It is thus necessary to consider those conditions which minimize threat in interpersonal relationships, and which furthermore, lead to the positive changes in behavior which were described in Chapter 2 as the characteristics of self-actualizing persons.

Recent research in counseling or psychotherapy has confirmed the existence of several conditions, or aspects of a personal relationship, which have been included, implicitly if not explicitly, in every major theory or approach to counseling or psychotherapy, though differing terminology has been used. Three of the basic conditions which have been identified are empathic understanding, respect, and genuineness.

Empathic Understanding

By emphatic understanding is meant understanding of another from an internal frame of reference, achieved by putting oneself in the place of

[19] *Ibid.*, pp. 91, 135.

the other, so that one sees him and the world, as closely as possible, as he does. A simple illustration relates to the situation mentioned above, where the automobile driver perceived an intersection as a four-way stop. If an observer can put himself in the place of the driver, he may quickly understand his behavior. Rogers' definition perhaps expresses it as well as any: "an accurate, emphatic understanding of the [other's] world as seen from the inside. To sense the [other's] private world as if it were your own, but without losing the 'as if' quality—this is empathy. . . ." [20] There seem to be no synonyms for emphatic understanding. Unlike other languages, English does not have two words to designate the two kinds of understanding or knowing: knowing about, and the knowing which is empathy. Some American Indian languages apparently had this concept, indicated by the phrase "to walk in his moccasins." The theme of the novel *To Kill a Mockingbird* is dependent on the concept of empathy. At one point the lawyer Atticus Finch, trying to help his children understand people's behavior, said: "if . . . you can learn a simple trick . . . you'll get along a lot better with all kinds of folks. You never really understand a person until you consider things from his point of view—until you climb into his skin and walk around in it." [21] However, this is not a trick, nor is it simple.

Respect or Nonpossessive Warmth

The second condition is a deep respect for another, an acceptance of him as a person of worth, as he is, without judgment or condemnation, criticism, ridicule, or depreciation. It is a respect which includes a warmth and liking for another as a person, with all his faults, deficiencies, or undesirable or unacceptable behavior. It is a deep interest and concern for him and his development. It is the warmth of a parent who may still reject, or not accept, particular behaviors of the child. Thus one may accept and respect a person as a person, but still not agree with or condone all of his behaviors.

Genuineness

Genuineness is the congruence or integration of the therapist in the relationship: "It means that within the relationship he is freely and deeply

[20] Carl R. Rogers, *On Becoming a Person* (Boston: Hougton Mifflin, 1961), p. 284.
[21] From the book *To Kill a Mockingbird,* by Harper Lee. Copyright, © 1960 by Harper Lee. Reprinted as abridged by permission of J. B. Lippincott Company, p. 24.

himself, with his actual experience accurately represented by his awareness of himself."[22] The therapist is not thinking or feeling one thing and saying another. He is open, honest, sincere. He is freely and deeply himself, without a facade, and not playing a role. He is, as the existentialists term it, authentic, or, to use Jourard's term, transparent.[23]

These conditions are not new, and there would appear to be nothing revolutionary about them. Yet their consistent application in interpersonal relations might well be revolutionary. They have, however, been known for centuries, and their effectiveness has been demonstrated by over 2,000 years of experience. Experience, however, is discounted by the provincialness of western science. A one-hour experiment in a laboratory—from which actually little if any generalization to everyday life may be possible —is given more weight than the thousands of years of experience of the human race.

If one considers the totality of the facilitative conditions—understanding, empathy, concern, liking, prizing, acceptance, respect, warmth, sincerity, openness, authenticity, transparency, intimacy—they add up to a concept which has long been recognized as basic to good human relationships. The Greeks had a word for it: agape. St. Paul called it love. His letter to the Corinthians (I Cor. 13: 4-8) might be rewritten in the language of these conditions. Love is the therapy for all disorders of the human mind and spirit and of disturbed interpersonal relationships. We do not need to wait for a breakthrough, for the discovery of new methods or techniques. Good human relationships provide the answer to all our social and psychological problems. Caroline Pomodoro, a student, stated the situation well: "No matter how great the strides of future advancement, it is highly unlikely that there ever will be discovered a synthetic substitute for social feeling. The experiencing of positive relationships is the prerequisite for healthy adjustment and growth." Bettelheim speaks of the "unique gratifying experience that only a genuine human relationship can offer."[24] The condition for self-actualizing persons is love.

Not only is this condition for good human relationships not new; recognition of its importance for self-actualization and self-preservation is recognized in folklore and popular music, as witness the titles and lyrics of popular songs: "What the world needs now is love, sweet love," and "You're nobody until somebody loves you," for example.

The basic criticism of our schools, by those who are concerned about more than simple academic achievement, is that in many if not most of

---

[22] Carl R. Rogers, "The Necessary and Sufficient Conditions of Therapeutic Personality Change," *Journal of Consulting Psychology,* 1957, 21, 95–103.

[23] Sidney Jourard, *The Transparent Self* (New York: Reinhard, Van Nostrand, 1964).

[24] Bruno Bettelheim, *Love Is Not Enough* (New York: Free Press, 1950), p. 28.

our schools these conditions do not exist. Children are not respected, they are not liked by teachers or administrators, they are not understood, they are not treated as human beings. On the other hand, in those schools which are humanistic—in Summerhill and the other schools described in Chapters 3 and 4—these conditions are present.

The observant reader, recalling the definition of self-actualization from Chapter 2, will recognize that the conditions for the development of self-actualizing persons are also the characteristics of such persons. *The conditions and the goal are the same.* It thus appears that if one wishes to facilitate the development of self-actualizing persons, one must oneself be a self-actualizing person. The manner in which the conditions operate is complex, but one aspect of the nature of the influence is what is called modeling. One becomes like those with whom one associates or engages in close interpersonal relationships.

A relationship which consists of, or includes, these conditions is nonthreatening. It provides an atmosphere in which learning is facilitated, with a minimum of anxiety and without the restrictions and inhibitions related to threat.

This kind of relationship is also conducive to or facilitative of personal development. The person is free to change, to grow, because he is not threatened and does not have to focus on defending himself. Under the influence of these conditions, with their absence of threat, one can become aware of inconsistencies between his experiences and his self-concept. He is able to see himself as he is, and compare this with the self he would like to be, and become aware of and face up to the discrepancies. In an accepting, nonthreatening environment the person can be himself, and, not feeling it necessary to conceal or defend the self that he is, becomes free to change that self, i.e., to become a more self-actualizing person. Not only do these conditions lead to the development of the characteristics themselves, as well as other characteristics of self-actualizing persons, in those who experience them; they also lead to many other specific behaviors—better grades for college students, better interpersonal relations for counseling center clients, adequate personality functioning for the severely disturbed mental patient, acceptable behavior for the juvenile delinquent, or greater reading ability for the third grade child.[25] The nonreader exposed to these conditions in school may begin to read, or ask for help in reading, without necessarily any urging or remedial instruction.[26] These kinds of behaviors include those referred to as subgoals, or mediate goals, in Chapter 2. It appears that if

---

[25] Charles B. Truax & Robert R. Carkhuff, *Toward Effective Counseling and Psychotherapy: Training and Practice* (Chicago: Aldine, 1967), pp. 116–117.
[26] See, for example, George Dennison, *The Lives of Children* (New York: Vintage Books, 1969).

we are successful in creating these conditions, the recipient, in developing his potentials for self-actualization, will determine or recognize relevant subgoals and work toward achieving them, or seek and obtain specific help in doing so.

DEHUMANIZATION

The absence of these conditions is dehumanizing. A child who was deprived of these conditions would not become a human being. Such deprivation is more devastating psychologically than deprivation of material things. Occasionally we read in the newspapers about the discovery of a child, or an adult, who has been extremely neglected, isolated from human society, treated worse than an animal. Such persons, if they have been treated this way for a long time, seem hardly human. There are stories, some of them documented, of children who, though lost for a long time, have managed to survive. But when they have been found they are no longer human. The "wild boy of Aveyron," discovered in a forest in France in the early 1800's, never became human even though the French physician Itard spent much time and effort with him. Infants and young children brought up in institutions with little human attention suffer from this lack. Patients in mental institutions often deteriorate when they are not treated as persons or human beings. And, as we indicated in Chapter 1 in the quotation from Leonard's "Education and Ecstasy," children deteriorate from the first grade on in a school environment where these conditions are lacking.

A case can thus be made that it is the lack of, or an inadequate amount of, these conditions which results in learning problems, behavior problems, emotional disturbance, juvenile delinquency and criminology—the major problems of our society. There are of course other causes of these problems—sensory deficits and neurological and physiological abnormalities—but these causes affect a relatively small number of disturbed people compared to the psychological factors.

The absence of these conditions leads to the loss of, or the failure to develop, self-esteem or self-respect. A negative self-concept is the result. The individual sees himself as, and feels, inadequate, unworthy, unwanted, unacceptable, and unable. Acceptance of oneself, and the development of an adequate self-concept, require the presence of these conditions. In order for one to accept and respect oneself, one must be accepted and respected by others.

When one sees the faces of little children, expressive of openness, interest, curiosity, energy, love and concern for others, and then watches the change as they grow up, one becomes disturbed and dismayed at this loss of potential and hope for humanity. To be sure, the school is not responsible for all of this loss, but certainly it must accept responsibility for much of it. Dennison writes of the change in children from eagerness in their first classes to "puzzled and anxious faces, faces which harden in two or three years into the sullen resentment which reflects the progressive loss of intelligence several studies have shown to be a feature of school life in the slums. No school at all is better than a bad school. Nothing else in the child's environment is capable of such systematic destruction." [27]

SUMMARY

The view of man or of human nature which a teacher holds is a determining influence in his teaching. It thus is essential that every teacher be aware of his attitudes, feelings and assumptions about man. In this chapter two major contemporary views of man are described—the reactive view and the humanistic view.

The humanistic view sees man as inherently good, not as evil, nor simply as having the potential for good or evil. Man is an active as well as a reactive being, whose single basic motivation is the maintenance and enhancement of the self, or self-actualization. His behavior is not determined by innate drives or instincts, nor by environmental stimuli, though these influence his behavior. His behavior is determined by his perceptions, of his environment and especially of himself, and his drive toward self-actualization.

Changes in behavior are thus dependent on changes in perception, particularly on changes in perception of the self. The conditions for such change, for learning, or for progress toward self-actualization, have been identified by research in counseling or psychotherapy. Three of these basic conditions, empathic understanding, respect or nonpossessive warmth, and genuineness, have been discussed. It is apparent that these are also characteristics of self-actualizing persons.

With our understanding of the goal of education, and of the conditions necessary for achieving this goal, we now turn to a consideration of their implications for the nature of education.

[27] George Dennison, *The Lives of Children* (New York: Vintage Books, 1969), p. 213.

6 Some Necessary Changes In Educational Practices

Any curriculum set up in advance is bound to fail,
because education is a continuing process . . .
Planning what you are going to do is essential if you
are to follow your own purposes. If you are going
to pursue the purposes of another, you do not
need to plan.

—Earl C. Kelley, EDUCATION FOR WHAT IS REAL *

One would expect that in education, which is concerned with learning, or behavior change, the basic conditions of learning or of change would be applied, but the evidence is that they are not. This is the tragedy of education, as summarized in Chapter 1, and as so extensively documented by the numerous humanistic critics of education.

Since schools are not humanistic, they are not fostering learning or behavior change of a self-actualizing nature. What are some of the ways in which the school must be changed to foster learning and self-actualization? We shall now consider some of the necessary changes in the concepts of education and the structure of the school and the curriculum, and the place of the teacher in humanistic education. But first we must consider a prior question.

* (New York: Harper & Row, 1947), pp. 83, 86.

ARE SCHOOLS NECESSARY?

Several critics of education have questioned whether schools are necessary. As noted in Chapter 1, Goodman has suggested that school be omitted from the lives of some children, as an experiment.[1] Leonard devotes a chapter to no school as a true educational alternative, since school itself appears to be the greatest barrier to the development of the potentials of children. "Practically everything that is *presently* being accomplished in the schools can be accomplished more effectively and with less pain in the average child's home and neighborhood playground." [2] Programmed textbooks, audiotapes, and eventually teaching machines, could be placed in each home.

If schools are so bad for children, having negative effects rather than positive, or not even being neutral, then it would seem logical that schools should be abandoned. Dennison, who does not advocate no school, nevertheless states: "No school at all is better than a bad school. Nothing else in the child's environment is capable of such systematic destruction." [3] But how, then, would children develop and grow? Even Rousseau, who believed that children are innately good and will grow and develop if protected from noxious or harmful influences, did not let Emile learn entirely on his own.

Early and primitive societies had no schools. Schools are a relatively recent institution. In most societies children have learned informally and mainly incidentally from observation and personal interaction with adults.

But children can no longer learn directly from the culture, for it, and society, is now so extensive and complex that any child is exposed to only a small part of it. The concept of the "school without walls" is useful to incorporate direct observation and interaction with people into formal education, but it is not sufficient. Much of the culture must be brought to the child in indirect ways, through books, films, and tape, and it is efficient to provide many of the simple basic experiences in a setting where children can be brought together, as in the English primary schools.

Emile did not attend school, and neither did the child who was the subject of Locke's essay, but they had tutors. To eliminate school in our society would require a tutor for each child, or for no more than a handful of children. The cost would be prohibitive.

[1] Reprinted from p. 32 of *Compulsory Miseducation and the Community of Scholars,* by Paul Goodman, (New York: Vintage Books, 1962) , copyright 1964, by permission of the publisher Horizon Press, New York. See also Paul Goodman, "Freedom and Learning: the Need for Choice," *Saturday Review,* May 18, 1968.

[2] George B. Leonard, *Education and Ecstasy* (New York: Dell, 1968), p. 102.

[3] George Dennison, *The Lives of Children* (New York: Vintage Books, 1969), p. 213.

The solution is not to eliminate schools, but to change the schools so that they in fact become educational institutions. It is impossible to expect that the present educational system, with its investment in buildings and people, will be suddenly abandoned, especially for some untested alternative. It is reasonable to expect, however, that the school should change to meet the needs of children, which are not inimical to the needs of society. It is reasonable to expect that the school should be altered in the direction of humanization so that it will produce the kind of persons our society needs, that is, self-actualizing persons.

What are the changes which a humanistic approach to education would require? We shall examine some of these in terms of alternatives to existing characteristics of schools.

NECESSARY CHANGES IN THE SCHOOL

Closed Versus Open Class Scheduling

Teaching in our schools is controlled by the clock, not by the needs of students. At the ringing of a bell, the study of one subject stops and that of another begins. It doesn't matter if the children are ready or not, or if an ongoing activity in which the children are absorbed is finished or not. The basic psychological principle that interrupted activities leave a need for completion is ignored. The expression of this need by children in the next class—manifested by talking and restlessness—is squelched. The time schedule is law. Even in some progressive schools where bells are not rung, the schedule is inexorable. Silberman describes a private progressive school where a technique for quick multiplication is being taught. The students are struggling to understand. "Just as they are beginning to catch on—'oohs' and 'ahs' and mutterings of 'I think I see, I think I see,' 'I think I have it,' 'Oh, that's how it works' can be heard all over the classroom—the lesson ends." It is time to take up the next subject.[4] Thus lessons begin before interest is aroused, and end before interest dies. Worse, perhaps, is that the lesson ends before many or most students have learned the material, and there will be no further opportunity to learn it; the next class begins with a new lesson.

Teachers complain that students are not interested, but when they become interested, the activity ends arbitrarily by the clock. There is perhaps no better way to discourage interest.

Holt says that "We act as if children were railroad trains running on a

---

[4] Charles E. Silberman, *Crisis in the Classroom* (New York: Random House, 1970), p. 124.

schedule," and try to control them by timetables.[5] The obsession with scheduling goes beyond class periods—it controls the curriculum through the prescription of subject matter to be covered each week, each semester, each year throughout the child's educational career.

Time scheduling is an aspect of the total control of children in the school. No time must be left free or something might happen. Time between classes is kept to a minimum, and passing from one class to another is closely monitored. The more the school resembles a military organization, the better it is in the eyes of many administrators. To change the metaphor, the goal of such administrators is to "run a tight ship." Efficiency is more important than learning. Discipline is more important than learning.

The inconsistency between the stated goals of education, and the goals implicit in the operation of schools is not even recognized in many instances. The National Education Association has published a monograph on humanizing education which emphasizes the importance of respect and concern for the person of the student.[6] Yet, another publication of the Association on discipline advises teachers to "be ready to use the first minute of class time. If you get Johnny busy right away, he has no time to cook up interesting ideas that do not fit into the class situation." [7]

Education cannot be broken up into arbitrary time units, each 40 or 50 minutes, a week, or a semester in length—or into "modules," which is simply a new package for old materials. Interests can't be turned on and off by the clock. "If human beings are individual and unique, then any system of fixed scheduling and mass instruction must seem insanely inefficient." [8] Learning does not occur on preplanned schedules. "We cannot organize the educational event in advance. Certainly we can plan and prepare, but we cannot organize it until we are in it and the students themselves have brought their unique contributions." [9] This obviously is demanding of the teacher. Teaching is not simply the use of prepared lesson plans, rigidly adhered to no matter what. The teacher must be free and flexible to take advantage of developing interests as they are expressed in the classroom.

Certainly it will be difficult to change this system, but it can be done. It has been done in a number of the new humanistic schools—in Summerhill, in the First Street School, in the English primary schools, but it

[5] John Holt, *How Children Learn* (New York: Pitman Publishing Corporation, 1967), p. 107.

[6] Robert R. Leeper, (Ed.) *Humanizing Education: The Person in the Process.* Washington, D. C.: National Education Association, 1967.

[7] Martha W. Hunt, "Tips for Beginning Teachers," in *Discipline in the Classroom: Selected Articles of Continuing Value to Elementary and Secondary School Teachers.* (Washington, D.C.: National Education Association, 1969).

[8] George B. Leonard, *op. cit.,* p. 181.

[9] George Dennison, *op. cit.,* p. 258.

requires a basic change in the orientation of the school. Currently, schools, like other institutions, are operated for the convenience of the staffs, not in the best interests of the students. The reversal of this will be necessary if schools are not to continue to straitjacket children and discourage their interest by adhering to fixed, rigid schedules.

Quiet, Passive Learning Versus Noisy, Active Learning

Related to fixed scheduling and its control aspects is the insistence on silence and immobility in the classroom. Teachers are judged mainly on their ability to maintain quiet. Movement in and out of, and between, classes must also be silent. Kaufman, in the novel, "Up the Down Staircase," describes a typical situation. The class was so interesting that the students groaned when the bell rang. They continued talking as they left the room, and the administrative assistant to the principal appeared and said:

> "What is the meaning of this noise?"
> The teacher replied: "It is the sound of thinking, Mr. McHabe."
> That afternoon the teacher received a note (copies of which went to the principal and department chairman), which read:
> "I have observed that in your class the class entering your room is held up because pupils exiting from your room are exiting in a disorganized fashion, blocking the doorway unnecessarily and *talking*. An orderly flow of traffic is the responsibility of the teacher whose class is exiting from the room." [10]

Leonard describes an all day visit to a classroom, and recommends it as an experience of what the child suffers—constant sitting, no talking, no breaks (for coffee or cigarettes), no moving around. Even the "play" at recess is not real play, but simply the letting off of steam from the repression of the classroom." [11]

Silberman describes the well-known restrictions in movement. "Students in most schools cannot leave the classroom (or the library, or the study hall) without permission, even to get a drink of water or to go to the toilet, and the length of time they can spend there is rigidly prescribed. In high schools and junior highs, the corridors are usually guarded by teachers and students on patrol duty, whose principal function is to check the credentials of any student walking through. In the typical high school, no student may walk down the corridor without a form, signed

---

[10] From the book *Up the Down Staircase*, by Bel Kaufman. © 1964 by Bel Kaufman. Published by Prentice-Hall, Inc., Englewood Cliffs, N.J. Also by permission of McIntosh & Otis, Inc.

[11] George Leonard, *op. cit.*, pp. 106–109.

by a teacher, telling where he is coming from, where he is going and the time, to the minute, during which the pass is valid." [12]

Such controls and restrictions are inhuman. It is unnatural for children—and adults—to be silent and immobile. Learning involves activity. Much of this activity, at the adult level, can be internal, in the form of thinking, but much of it consists of verbal interaction, with the teacher and with other students, and much of it in younger children involves activity with materials. Movement is necessary simply from a physical need.

In the typical classroom there is little if any interaction among students, or between students and teachers. Students speak when called on, or, if they have a question, are given permission to speak only after raising their hands. Education is teacher-controlled, so that there is much teaching, that is, much talking or lecturing by the teacher, but little learning.

The emphasis upon teacher domination, control, and discipline represents a fear that all hell would break loose and terrify the staff if repression did not continue. To some extent the fear is justified, since the repression is so extreme that children are bottled up and ready to blow up. Goodman notes that if a teacher *did* "pursue a proper educational course," there could be "a great outburst of damned up hostility." [13] But the constant preoccupation of teachers with discipline interferes with teaching or the development of a learning atmosphere or relationship anyway.

The system is based upon the assumption that students cannot be trusted, and that freedom of talking and movement would result in chaos. Freedom would, certainly, increase the noise and activity level of the school, and this would certainly disturb many teachers and administrators. Here again is evidence that it is the staff for whom the system is concerned. As for the fear that freedom would lead to chaos and disorder, the evidence is clear—it does not. To be sure, when children who have been unnaturally restrained for a long period are suddenly freed from restraints, temporary chaos does result. But the children soon settle down, and if necessary institute their own controls. This has been demonstrated time and again in experimental schools, and is evident in the English primary schools.

Dependence Versus Independence

Our educational system gives lip service to independence as one of the goals of education, and there is much talk about inculcating self-discipline and responsibility. But there is no opportunity for children to learn these characteristics. In fact, the whole environment of the school

[12] Charles E. Silberman, *op. cit.*, p. 131.
[13] Paul Goodman, *op. cit.*, p. 39.

teaches their opposites—dependence, external discipline, irresponsibility. Administrators and teachers complain about the lack of independence, responsibility and self-discipline, but prevent their development. "Far from helping students to develop into mature, self-reliant, self-motivated individuals, schools seem to do everything they can to keep youngsters in a state of chronic, almost infantile dependency. The pervasive atmosphere of distrust, together with rules covering the most minute aspects of existence, teach students every day that they are not people of worth, and certainly not individuals capable of regulating their own behavior." [14]

Student government is almost invariably a farce, and the students know it. Nevertheless, they have been conditioned to docility, and seldom question rules and controls. That is, they have in the past, up to 1969, seldom done so. But this is changing, and for the past three years high school students have been demanding some input into rules and controls, and are questioning some of the traditional regulations. Nevertheless, the majority of students, under the weight of years of living in the arbitrary authoritarianism of the school, or to survive and get through to graduation, accept the situation. Is it any wonder that they are not prepared to accept the responsibilities of adult life after graduation? Or that, when they encounter the greater freedom and responsibility of college, so many of them fail because they can't discipline themselves to study, plan the use of their time, or prepare for examinations without drill and daily homework assignments?

Conventionality Versus Creativity

Our schools are geared to conformity in thinking as well as in behavior. The creative student is discouraged, so that creative potential, which is present to some degree in everyone, is gradually extinguished in our schools. The schools operate on the assumption that there is one, and only one, right answer, to every question. Curiosity, a basis for creativity, is destroyed.

One of the major things children learn in school is what answer the teacher wants, and to give it back to him. If they can't, or aren't sure, some of them use what Holt calls the "mumble strategy": "A teacher who asks a question is tuned to the right answer, ready to hear it, eager to hear it, since it will tell him that his teaching is good and that he can go on to the next topic. He will assume that anything that sounds close to the right answer is meant to be the right answer. So, for a student who is not sure of the answer, a mumble may be his best bet. If he's

14 Charles E. Silberman, *op. cit.,* p. 134.

not sure whether something is spelled with an *a* or an *o*, he writes a letter that could be either one of them." [15] Some children develop clever strategies to con teachers into "helping them until the teacher actually gives them the right answer."

"Schools give every encouragement to *producers,* the kids whose idea is to get the 'right answers' by any and all means. In a system run on 'right answers,' they can hardly help it. And these schools are often very discouraging places for *thinkers.*" [16]

Holt goes on to discuss the reaction of some children under pressure —they "go stupid." Even some bright children often seem stupid, when, to escape the pressure of right answers they withdraw the most intelligent and creative parts of their minds from school. "The result is that he is not all there during most of his hours in school. Whether he is afraid to be there, or just does not want to be there, the result is the same. Fear, boredom, resistance—they all go to make what we call stupid children. To a very great degree, school is a place where children learn to be stupid." [17]

Students are often reluctant to enter into discussions, for fear of not agreeing with the teacher. Many so-called discussions are not open or free, with the students encouraged to contribute their own personal ideas. Lesson materials instruct the teacher to control the discussion around certain topics and ideas to achieve predetermined outcomes. Kozol gives a simple example from "A Curriculum Guide to Character Education" of the Boston Public Schools: "Guide the children through discussion to recognize the necessity of self-discipline." [18] Holt refers to the method of "answer pulling," in which "the teacher asks a series of pointed questions, aimed at getting students to give an answer that he has decided before hand is right. Teachers' manuals are full of this technique—'Have a discussion, in which you draw out the following points . . .' This kind of fake, directed conversation is worse than none at all. Small wonder that children get bored and disgusted with it." [19]

Teachers are not interested in what the student thinks, but in what some authority has said: "Never mind what you think about that, Jimmy, what does the book say?" [20]

[15] John Holt, *How Children Fail* (New York: Pitman Publishing Corporation, 1964), p. 131.

[16] *Ibid.,* p. 24.

[17] *Ibid.,* p. 157.

[18] Jonathan Kozol, *Death at an Early Age* (Boston: Houghton Mifflin, 1967), (New York: Bantam Books, 1968), p. 182.

[19] John Holt, *How Children Learn, op. cit.,* p. 82.

[20] Arthur W. Combs, Donald L. Avila, & William W. Purkey, *Helping Relationships: Basic Concepts for the Helping Professions* (Boston: Allyn & Bacon, 1971), p. 95.

Leonard describes the education process as "a funnel through which every child is squeezed into an ever narrowing circle; at the end there is room only for a single set of 'right answers'." [21]

The fear of making mistakes inhibits creativity. Creativity must be nurtured, by encouraging students to express their ideas. It is not encouraged by insisting that there is only one right or best answer to every question. It will not manifest itself under a rigid adherence to a text or a lesson plan or a preplanned and controlled discussion. When children are free and unafraid, their creativity becomes manifest. Kohl found evidences of creativeness in the writing of the black children he taught. [22]

But creativeness is disturbing to teachers. The ideas and thoughts expressed in the writing of Kohl's students horrified some of the teachers. Creative activity is disruptive of lesson plans. The behavior of creative children is disruptive in the classroom. [23] Creative children are curious, inquisitive, original, playful (in the sense of "toying with ideas"), nonconforming, imaginative, fanciful. All of these characteristics are out of place in the structured classroom. They are suppressed, so that creativeness declines with age in children.

Creativeness is threatening to society, also, since it leads to questioning of the status quo, and to demands for change. Henry remarks that "contemporary American educators think they want creative children, yet it is an open question as to what they expect these children to create. . . . [T]he function of education is to prevent the truly creative intellect from getting out of hand." [24] The schools, therefore, according to Henry, cannot teach creativity, and even if they recognize it, do not encourage it unless it is shown in the area of mathematics or science, where it is not a threat to the status quo of society. Children who show creativity in the social sciences will be rejected or considered stupid, and will eventually think of themselves as stupid.

Encouragement of creativity would require the encouragement of verbalization, the expression of ideas of all kinds without regard to whether they are "right" or "wrong," impractical, or even irrelevant. New and original ideas are often bizarre, irrelevant, even funny, at first glance, in a traditional context or the standard way of looking at a situation. Thus

[21] George R. Leonard, op. cit., p. 112.

[22] Herbert Kohl, 36 Children (New York: New American Library, 1967).

[23] M. A. Wallach & N. Kagan, "Creativity and Intelligence in Children's Thinking," Transaction, 1967, 4 (3), 38–43.

[24] Jules Henry, "In Suburban Classrooms," in Beatrice Gross & Ronald Gross, (Eds.) Radical School Reform, pp. 77–78. © 1969 by Simon & Schuster, Inc. Reprinted by permission of Simon & Schuster. Condensed from Jules Henry, Culture Against Man. New York: Random House, 1963. Copyright © 1963 by Random House, Inc. Reprinted by permission of the publisher. British Commonwealth Rights by permission of Tavistock Publications, Ltd.

the creative child is often criticized, belittled, even made fun of, by both teachers and, in later grades, by his peers.

Kneller says that "much of the disorder of contemporary youth, we know, is an explosion of potentially creative energy that can find no other outlet. In the schools this energy is frustrated by regulations designed to keep masses of young people in order by making them behave in unison. It is frustrated, too, by tired, overworked teachers, who cannot spare the time to nurture the creativity of the individual student because they struggle amid the impersonal web of administrative detail and mass guidance and counseling procedures to instill into their swollen classes the basic requirements of a stereotyped syllabus." [25]

The preservation of creativity is an obligation of society and the school, and increasing attention is being given to nurturing it in the school. Writers such as Torrance [26] are attempting to help teachers in this task.

Competition Versus Cooperation in the Classroom

Schools, reflecting our existing society, introduce competition among students as a basic motivator for academic achievement. Students are pitted against each other. Another student's success is not a source of pleasure, but of dismay. If other students do very well on examinations, they "raise the curve," so that the rest of the students get lower grades. An eighth grade student expressed it well in a counseling interview:

Student: Oh, and teachers when they start grading on the curve, . . . when we have a teacher that doesn't grade on the curve, or a test that isn't being graded on the curve, if a friend makes an *A* I'm glad for her. "Congratulations, you made an A." If I made an A too, I can go down and congratulate her even more heartily—"You made an A—good." But if it's graded on the curve and she makes an A, I say, I think that that's bad because she made a high A and my grade might be lower because hers, because she did better on the test, you know. On that grading on a curve, you don't respect the kids who make the high grades; you're just mad at them, uh, I don't know.

[25] G. F. Kneller, *The Art and Science of Creativity* (New York: Holt, Rinehart & Winston, 1965).

[26] E. P. Torrance, *Guiding Creative Talent.* (Englewood Cliffs, N.J.: Prentice-Hall, 1962); E. P. Torrance, *Education and the Creative Potential* (Minneapolis: University of Minnesota Press, 1963); E. P. Torrance, *Encouraging Creativity in the Classroom* (Dubuque, Iowa: Wm. C. Brown, 1970); E. P. Torrance & R. E. Myers, *Creative Learning and Teaching* (New York: Dodd, Mead, 1970).

Counselor: I see. That kind of system—you can't help feeling that they're your enemy and yet it isn't their fault.[27]

Jules Henry, in the incident reported in Chapter 1 (page 12) points out that competition leads to the situation where one student's success means another student's failure. He continues: "And since all but the brightest children have the constant experience that others succeed at their expense they cannot but develop an inherent tendency to hate—to hate the success of others, to hate others who are successful, and to be determined to prevent it. Along with this, naturally, goes the hope that others will fail. This hatred masquerades under the euphemistic name of 'envy.' " [28]

Competition breeds fear of failure—a fear which begins in the school and becomes so strongly rooted that it continues throughout life. In school it leads to pathetic submission to the teacher, the willingness to accept and to believe anything that is taught, whether one agrees with it or not. It leads to cruelty to other children—to let the teacher know that they know the right answer, students wave their hands, distracting the student who is trying to think. They laugh at, ridicule, tease, belittle and deride the child who doesn't know the answer.

Competition, it is claimed, is a motivating device, and is necessary to stimulate learning in children. Aside from the fact that motivating devices would not be necessary if the natural motivation for learning in children had not been killed by the school, competition does not motivate children to learn. It motivates them to attempt to avoid failure, which takes many forms but which does not lead to real learning.

Combs, in his analysis of competition as related to challenge or threat, notes three different effects of competition:

1) *Competition has motivating force only for those persons who believe they have a chance of winning.* That is to say it motivates those for whom competition is perceived as a challenge. People do not work for things they feel they cannot achieve. They work only for things that seem within their grasp. . . .

2) *Persons who are forced to compete and who do not believe they have a chance of success, are not motivated by the experience; they are threatened by it.* . . . They ignore the competition whenever they are able. . . . Forcing people to compete can only result in discouragement or rebellion. When the cards are stacked against us we give up playing. . . .

3) *When competition becomes too important, any means become justified to achieve the ends.* The aim of competition is to win, and the temptation is to win at any cost. . . . In the headlong rush to win, competition

27 Julius Seaman, *The Case of Nan* (Record) (Nashville, Tennessee: Counselor Recordings, 1963).
28 Jules Henry, *op. cit.*, p. 84.

too easily loses sight of responsibility. It values aggression, hostility and scorn. "Dog eat dog" becomes its philosophy . . .[29]

Clearly, competition does not lead to the development of humanistic qualities in people. While it presumably represents real life and prepares children for adult competition, its constant use perpetuates a competitive society, in spite of the fact that society is not at all as competitive as is usually assumed. We are actually completely dependent upon the co-operation of others for our lives every day. Competition is becoming less and less appropriate, and, as Leonard points out, may soon be disastrous in the world which is developing.[30] If the schools are to prepare people who can preserve society, and live in the society of the future, they must teach cooperation, not competition.

External Evaluation Versus Internal Evaluation

Education is characterized by evaluation from an external source, the teacher, who is constantly evaluating and expressing these evaluations to students, usually in the form of criticism or often highly artificial praise. Everything is right or wrong, good or bad. At periodic intervals teachers record their evaluations in the form of grades, which follow the children throughout their educational lives.

Dissatisfaction with external evaluation by means of grades is increasing, and modifications are being proposed and tried out. One method is that of self-evaluation, which Carl Rogers has used for many years with graduate students. Students are required to turn in a statement evaluating their work, and a grade. The statement includes the criteria the student used in judging his work, and the ways in which he has met or failed to meet the criteria. If Rogers disagrees with the student's evaluation, he meets with the student to see if they "can arrive at some mutually satisfactory grade which I can in good conscience sign and turn in." [31]

Whether this method could be used at the undergraduate level, in the secondary schools, or the elementary grades may be questioned. In an experiment at Murray Road Annex of the Newton, Massachusetts High School, students evaluate themselves. However, "at the same time, the faculty recognized that high school students may not yet know enough about the subject in question, or may not yet be able to see themselves in a sufficiently objective light, to rely solely on their own evaluation. Hence, Murray Road students' records contain two written evaluations, one by the student and one by the teacher, as well as a brief description of the course content." [32]

[29] Arthur W. Combs, Donald L. Avila, & William W. Purkey, *op. cit.,* pp. 110–111.
[30] George B. Leonard, *op. cit.,* pp. 127–128.
[31] Carl R. Rogers, *Freedom to Learn* (Columbus, Ohio: Merrill, 1969), pp. 61–62.
[32] Charles E. Silberman, *op. cit.,* p. 357.

Silberman reports that Arthur Pearl, who operates a high school equivalency program for high school dropouts in which the student takes an exam when he feels ready and is graded "pass" or "not yet passed," states that "it would be the cruelest of deceptions to suggest to students that they have unlimited decision-making powers." Teachers and administrators retain their authority, but it must be exercised responsibly, and administrators must be willing to defend the purpose of the rules they feel to be necessary.[33]

It is probably true that many if not most students, under present conditions and with their lack of experience in self-evaluation, are not capable of adequately assuming the responsibility for their own grading. The importance of grades in our society, especially for admission to college or graduate school, exerts a tremendous pressure upon students to assign themselves good grades. There is some evidence that poorer students tend to overestimate their achievement and some of the best students, perhaps recognizing, with a sense of humility, the relation of their learning to what is to be learned, tend to underestimate their achievement. But in view of the increasing importance of self-evaluation in our society, and its importance in self-actualization, the schools should begin in a helpful, nonthreatening way to help children develop the ability to evaluate themselves realistically at the elementary level. Scores on tests, which allow the individual to compare himself with others, can be useful in self-evaluation.

The beginning movement toward grading on a pass-fail basis, coupled with the mastery concept in learning, offer some help in evaluating achievement in education. The present grading system is an arbitrary one. It bears no relationship to any standards of what a student should know in any subject area. Obsessive adherence to the normal distribution of letter grades has no rational basis. When applied to different groups of students, the same letter grades may indicate different levels of performance. In some colleges where restriction of admission has resulted in the selection of better students, the distribution of letter grades has remained the same. Teachers who give "too many" high grades or "too many" low grades, on the basis of the normal curve, are criticized as being "too easy" or "too hard."

The mastery concept of learning, proposed by Benjamin Bloom, offers an approach to teaching and learning which can lead to a grading system which uses pass-fail grades. The mastery concept states that "given sufficient time (and appropriate types of help), 95 percent of students . . . can learn a subject matter up to a high level of mastery."[34] This ap-

[33] *Ibid.*, p. 347.
[34] Benjamin Bloom, "Learning for Mastery," in B. Bloom, J. T. Hastings, and G. F. Madaus (Eds.) *Handbook of Evaluation of Student Learning* (New York: McGraw-Hill, 1971).

proach would require that there be agreement on a "high level of mastery," and methods or tests by which the achievement of this level could be determined. This would be no easy task, but not an impossible one. Advanced placement tests in many college subjects provide an example. But the problem is not as great as it may seem if we separate important principles from inconsequential details (see *Facts Versus Principles* on p. 93).

Bloom suggests that the 95 percent of students who achieve the mastery level would be given a grade of A. Presumably the others, who would not achieve this level even after an extended period of time and special tutoring, would fail. In effect, then, this would be a pass-fail system of grading. While this method would probably not be a complete solution to the problem of evaluation, or provide a method of self-evaluation, it would be an advance over the present arbitrary grading system and, in basic subject matter areas, with adequate tests, could provide the student with an objective standard against which he could evaluate himself when he felt he had mastered the subject.

"Beating the System" Versus Personal Integrity

The characteristics of schools which we have discussed lead to learning, but not the kind of learning the schools are supposed to foster. What children learn is how to adapt to and beat the system as it exists. They learn how to survive in the artificial environment of the school. They learn what the teacher considers to be right or wrong, good or bad. They subordinate, suppress, or deny their own values.

The pressure of competition, of the need to please or agree with the teacher to get a good grade, and the resulting fear of failure have an inevitable consequence. In order to achieve the all-important grade, students will resort to any method, including cheating.

The effect of the school system upon character is more pervasive, however, extending beyond those students who cheat. The prevailing authoritarian atmosphere of the school, inculcating obedience through fear, leads to the loss of personal integrity by many students. The Montgomery County Student Alliance, a group of high school students in Montgomery County, Maryland, expressed it well in a statement (principally written by Norman Solomon):

Schools compel students to be dishonest. In order to be "successful" (the school system loses no time in providing the definition), students must learn to suppress and deny feelings, emotions, thoughts that they get the idea will not be acceptable. In the place of these honest feelings, emotions and thoughts, students are taught that to "succeed" other exteriors—dishonest though they be—have to be substituted. The clearly defined rewards and punishments of the school system have an instructional effect on an impressionable child, and the message is clear throughout elementary school, junior high school and senior high school: "unacceptable" honesty will be punished, whether with grades, disciplinary action or a bad "permanent record," "acceptable" responses, however dishonest, are—in the eyes of the school system and therefore according to the values it instills—simply that: "acceptable." [35]

Silberman reports an incident illustrating the cost of expressing an honest opinion. A high school senior was barred from the National Honor Society for "poor character," even though he was a leader or active in many school activities. He had politely asked a question which implied some criticism of the school at a meeting of school board candidates. As Silberman puts it, "criticism of the high school is equivalent to disloyalty, and disloyalty constitutes bad character." [36]

As the Montgomery students point out, the school system stifles self-expression, causing feelings of resentment, alienation, and self-hate, and leading to conforming behavior. Clearly, such effects are inconsistent with self-actualizing behavior or responsible citizenship.

Academic Versus Nonacademic Potentials

Our schools emphasize the development of one kind of potential—the academic or intellectual. This is clearly indicated when one considers the concept of underachievement, which always refers to academic underachievement, never to any other kind. Whether a student is achieving in some other manner is irrelevant—if he is not achieving academically up to his presumed potential he is an underachiever. Little concern or recognition is given to other abilities, with the partial exception of athletics. A student who gives considerable time to athletics may be excused for poor academic achievement. But a student who may be spending a great amount of time in developing a potential other than academic or athletic is not excused. It should be obvious that a student who spends hours a day on music or some other nonacademic ability cannot spend that time on algebra or history or English.

Individuals have multiple potentials, and, for many persons, the development of other potentials than the academic can be more important for self-actualization—and for society. While many schools offer opportunities for activities in music and art, these fields are not highly valued

[35] Montgomery County Student Alliance, "A Student Voice," in Beatrice & Ronald Gross, *op. cit.*, p. 148. Reprinted by permission of Norman Solomon.
[36] Charles E. Silberman, *op. cit.*, p. 154.

nor encouraged, and are not expected to detract from academic study. In fact, in some cases students are not allowed to participate in other activities unless they are performing acceptably academically.

If the schools are concerned with the whole child and his total development, they must recognize other potentials and encourage the development of them. In some cases a child with multiple potentials, including academic, must be allowed to develop them, even at the expense of underachieving academically, if this is his interest and desire.

An Extrinsic Versus an Intrinsic Curriculum

The problem of curriculum is complex, and cannot be adequately explored here. To capture the problem in a phrase, such as the heading used here, is difficult. Other related phrases are external versus internal, irrelevant versus relevant, and logical versus psychological. Perhaps all of these taken together will give an impression of the issue.

In primitive education, what the child learned was obviously relevant to life, since he learned it from observing and living with adults. It was, to the child, intrinsically interesting. Our present system of education is something that is imposed on children by adults, its content abstracted from experience, its relevance in terms of adult thinking and experience. Because what is considered necessary for the child to learn is so vast, it is broken up into segments, courses, or units, by adults, on a logical rather than a psychological basis. As a result, in terms of his direct experience and needs, the curriculum has little meaning to the child. Dennison comments: "Now what is so precious about a curriculum (which no one assimilates anyway), or a schedule of classes (which piles boredom upon failure and failure upon boredom) that these things should supersede the actual needs of the child?" [37] It is paradoxical that, while a basic characteristic of the human organism is its ability and propensity to learn on its own, that in an institution established to promote learning so little learning occurs. Surely this indicates something wrong with the institution rather than with children. One of the things wrong is the dullness and irrelevance of the curriculum, which is extrinsic to the child's life. Because it is dull, it must be drilled into the child with repetition, when, by contrast, materials which are intrinsically relevant are learned quickly and easily, at one exposure or perhaps in one trial.

Holt points out that children see the world as a whole. It is not divided up into separate categories. "It is natural for them," he says, "to jump from one thing to another, and to make the kinds of connections that are

[37] George Dennison, *op. cit.*, p. 17.

rarely made in formal classes and textbooks."[38] The tyranny of the curriculum, with its lesson plans, puts teachers and students in a straitjacket, so that even when an aspect of the subject matter does arouse a student's interest, it is not, or cannot be, pursued.

The curriculum reforms of the 1950's and 1960's did not deal with the problem of relevance. They essentially did no more than repackage contents, by imposing a new logic on old subject matter. The reforms came in response to the criticisms of the essentialists that the schools were academically weak and "soft," and were developed by University scholars, who had little if any concern for the student except as an empty vessel into which knowledge was to be poured. "They knew what they wanted children to learn; they did not think to ask what children wanted to learn."[39] But "the most fatal error of all, however, was the failure to ask. . . . : What is education for? What kind of human beings and what kind of society do we want to produce?"[40]

Curriculum reform is necessary, but on a different basis than that on which it has been undertaken. If we accept a new goal for education, developing self-actualizing persons, then it is clear that this goal must become a criterion for determining the appropriate curriculum. This does not mean that there is no place for the usual content, but that the content must be organized on a psychological rather than logical basis—in terms of its relevance to the life of the child, its relation to his current needs and interests.

In addition to the organizing and sequencing of content in relation to the developmental level of the child, the content can be relevant when it is related to the child as a person. This is an aspect of what Wilhelms calls humanization via the curriculum, or using the curriculum for the purpose of fostering human development.[41] Rather than the emphasis being, as it now is, on "putting across the content," the content should be used as a medium for fostering human growth. The usual method of teaching content has implications for personal development, whether the teacher is aware of them or not. These "side effects," as Wilhelms calls them, remain after the content is forgotten, and thus are almost always more important than the direct effects. "If we want to develop moral strength and ethical values, we can't wait till we get a course on morals and ethics. We have got to learn to *use* the history we need to teach anyway, the literature we need to teach anyway, and all the other resources . . ."[42] The social studies curriculum can be used to stimulate the growth of children into "full sized human beings."

[38] John Holt, *How Children Learn, op. cit.,* p. 167.
[39] Charles E. Silberman, *op. cit.,* p. 180.
[40] *Ibid.,* p. 182.
[41] Fred T. Wilhelms, "Humanization Via the Curriculum," in Robert R. Leeper, *op. cit.,* pp. 19–32.
[42] *Ibid.,* p. 26.

Thus, the standard curriculum can be selected and developed in terms of its potential as a medium for human growth, and explicitly utilized to achieve this objective.

In addition, however, there must be direct concern with the affective development of the child. Affective development must be included as a specific part of the curriculum. (This aspect of the curriculum will be considered in detail in Chapter 10.)

Facts Versus Principles

One of the problems with education, and curriculum, is the concern about how to cover the increasing amount of information and knowledge resulting from the so-called "knowledge explosion." Information is accumulating at an increasing rate. New information makes older information obsolete, and one of the purposes of recent projects in curriculum revision is to eliminate obsolete materials. But facts and information become obsolete more quickly as the rate of accumulation of knowledge increases.

"There is a great deal of chatter, to be sure, about teaching students the structure of each discipline, about teaching them how to learn, about teaching basic concepts, about 'postholing,' i.e., teaching fewer things but in greater depth. But if one looks at what actually goes on in the classroom—the kinds of texts students read and the kind of homework they are assigned, as well as the nature of classroom discussion and the kinds of tests teachers give—he will discover that the great bulk of students' time is still devoted to detail, most of it trivial, much of it factually incorrect, and almost all of it unrelated to any concept, structure, cognitive strategy, or indeed anything other than the lesson plan. It is rare to find anyone— teacher, principal, supervisor or superintendent, who has asked why he is teaching what he is teaching." [43]

A concern with principles would avoid the problem of excessive unrelated and unintegrated factual details. Any scholarly discipline is not simply or mainly a "body of knowledge." It consists more importantly of a system of assumptions, hypotheses, and principles, and a method of obtaining knowledge or information. The basic principles of every branch of knowledge are relatively simple. Combs notes that "In almost any subject there is only a handful of important principles, the rest is all details. A teacher can't lecture very long about principles because there are only a few. But ah, the details, there are a million of them. They can be talked about forever." [44] The emphasis in education should be

---

[43] Charles E. Silberman, *op. cit.,* pp. 172–173.
[44] Arthur W. Combs, "The Person in the Process," in Robert R. Leeper, *op. cit.,* pp. 73–88.

upon the principles (or "laws"), with specific facts or information being used to illustrate or demonstrate the principles.

Learning as Acquisition of Knowledge Versus Learning as Discovery of Meaning

The last two sets of alternatives are related to this one. Knowledge, information, or facts are meaningless if they are not related to organizing principles. But more than this is necessary if learning is to be meaningful. It must also, as we have noted earlier, be relevant to the learner, to his needs and interests. As Dennison puts it, ". . . in the whole of life, there is no occasion within which mere information, divorced from use and the meanings of experience, appears as a motive sufficient in itself." [45] Meaning does not inhere in the subject matter, but in the learner, who discovers it in himself and imposes it upon the subject matter.

In Chapter 5 it was pointed out that change in behavior, i.e., learning, occurs only when there is a new experience—a stimulus, a challenge, or a problem, leading to change in the individual's perception of himself or the world. For anything to become a stimulus, a challenge, or a problem, it must have some meaning to the individual, and a change in one's perception is a change in meaning. The new experience can be presented to the individual from the outside, by the teacher, or through books, but the discovery of meaning occurs within the individual. Presentation of information or facts by the teacher is not teaching, nor does it necessarily result in learning. *Teaching requires that the teacher in some way involve the learner.* Our concern with curriculum revision has been limited to the presentation of information.

The discovery of meaning requires personal involvement, that is, feelings and emotions. Thus all real learning includes affect as well as cognition. It is when students become excited, and emotional—and thus to some extent disturbed and disturbing—that they are ready to learn. But it is just at this point that the teacher pulls back, and rejects the student, and insists on a cold intellectual approach: "I don't care how you feel about it, what are the facts, what does the text say?" If the teacher is to facilitate learning he must do just the opposite, he must enter into a relationship with the student in which he puts himself in the place of the student so he can understand what the student is experiencing and participate with him in the discovery of meaning. Teaching machines cannot do this, and thus they can never replace the teacher. They can only present information; they cannot assist the student in the discovery of

45 George Dennison, *op. cit.,* p. 256.

meaning. But if all the teacher does is to present information, he can easily be replaced by the machine.

"It is truly incredible how successfully we have eliminated meaning from our public schools. We could hardly have done better if we had set out with that goal in mind. It should not really surprise us that dropouts believe that 'school is a place where you learn about things that don't matter.' " [46] The emphasis upon information, knowledge, and facts as objective is a major reason for the elimination of meaning from education. We must recognize that knowledge and facts are not objective, that in fact they have no existence outside of people's minds. The most objective scientist is far from being actually objective. He is deeply involved. The basic reason for the scientific method is to attempt to prevent his results from being determined by his own personal meanings. Yet his results have significance only if they have meaning to other scientists, and often the personal involvements of other scientists delay the recognition of scientific discoveries. Affect and cognition cannot be separated; they do not exist apart from each other.

Education must change from its obsession with facts and information to concern with personal meanings. The memorization and reporting back of information to the teacher or on tests is clearly not learning.

Teaching Subject Matter Versus Teaching Children

Concern with personal meaning is the basis for the statement that teachers should teach children, not subject matter. This dictum is hardly more than a cliché; there is little evidence that it is widely practiced, for the current system makes it difficult if not impossible to practice it.

But in a sense it can be said that teachers are always teaching children, not only subject matter. As Combs points out, "we are affecting people's concepts of themselves positively or negatively or not at all in every contact we have with them. What's more, this happens whether we know it or not." [47] The tragedy of education is that so much of the contact of teachers with children has negative effects on children, and that most teachers are blissfully unaware of this.

Educators must recognize that whether they realize it or not, whether they intend it or not, teachers are teaching more than subject matter. Then it becomes necessary to consider the nature of this something more, and to teach in such a way that it is positive rather than negative in its influence on the personal development of children.

[46] Arthur W. Combs, *op. cit.*
[47] *Ibid.*

SUMMARY

We have considered a number of practices in education which are inconsistent with a humanistic approach to education. Some of these practices indicate that the schools assume that students are bad and not to be trusted or respected, that they are not capable of assuming any responsibility for their own education. Other practices create a situation which is inimical to real learning or the development of self-actualizing persons. We have indicated that these practices must be changed if the schools are to become humanistic. The schools must encourage active rather than passive learning, independence rather than dependence, creativity rather than conventionality, cooperation rather than competition, internal evaluation rather than external evaluation, nonacademic as well as academic potentials, an intrinsic rather than an extrinsic curriculum, principles rather than facts, the discovery of meaning rather than the acquisition of information, and the teaching of children rather than the teaching of subject matter.

None of these changes would mean that the school would not be a place concerned with academic learning and achievement, though it would not be only that. In fact these changes would lead to more and better learning of subject matter. Many academicians contend that we don't know enough about learning to attempt to change our educational practices. This view is stated by one writer as follows:

> What we would propose . . . is that we should learn still more about how children learn, and how different children learn differently, before any solutions are proposed. When we have enough data, we think it may be possible to construct a better fit beween the objectives of the currriculum and the pupil's perceptions; and certainly a better fit between those objectives, the evaluative system, and the pupils' evaluative map.[48]

Granted that we do not know as much as we would like to know, it also appears that such writers do not know what we do know. And we are not applying what we do know, particularly in the area of the personal conditions of learning, outlined in the last chapter. We do know the basic conditions under which children learn, but the schools are not providing these conditions. In fact, the prevailing practices in the school are the opposite of those which we know are conducive to learning.

The basic condition for learning is a facilitative personal relationship, as described in the last chapter. In the next chapter we shall consider the kind of teacher required to provide this relationship.

[48] Mary Alice White, "The View From the Pupil's Desk," *The Urban Review,* 1968, 2 (No. 5, April). Quoted in George Dennison, *op. cit.,* pp. 250–251.

7 The Humanistic Teacher

I want to be a teacher when I grow up
Then I can write on the marking board
And I can pull kids' ears
Put them in the closet
Punch and shake them till they cry
And I can smack them.

—In THE VISTA VOLUNTEER, April, 1968

Be virtuous and good yourselves, and the examples
you set will impress themselves on your pupils'
memories, and in due season will enter their hearts.

—Rousseau, EMILE

Good teaching is not a matter of techniques or methods, for, as curriculum is not education, so method is not teaching. Research indicates that good teachers and poor teachers cannot be differentiated on the basis of teaching "methods." [1] The method is inseparable from the person of the teacher; in fact, the person of the teacher is more important than the method.

It has been said that the success of good teachers, such as Pestalozzi

---

[1] Ellena, W. J., Stevenson, M., & Webb, H. V., *Who's a Good Teacher?* (Washington, D. C.: National Education Association, 1961).

and Neill, is due to what they were rather than to their methods or systems, implying that it would be desirable to separate the two, or that the system wasn't viable by itself. The latter is perhaps the case. No system is viable by itself. Teaching is not the application of a system or methods, but a personal relationship, and it is more important what kind of person the teacher is than what his system or method is. "What educators must realize is that how they teach and how they act may be more important than what they teach," says Silberman.[2] He should have said "is," not "may be."

In this chapter we shall consider the personal characteristics of the humanistic teacher. These characteristics are the core or basic conditions of a facilitative personal relationship, and it is only in such a relationship that learning takes place, that self-actualization is made possible and fostered. The good teacher is not an instructor, who simply provides information, facts, and knowledge, but a facilitator of learning for the student. Good teachers are not those who are simply experts in subject matter, or experts in teaching methods, or curriculum experts, or who utilize the most resources, such as audiovisual aids. The best teacher is one who, through establishing a personal relationship, frees the student to learn. Learning can only take place in the student, and the teacher can only create the conditions for learning. The atmosphere created by a good interpersonal relationship is the major condition for learning.

THE AUTHENTIC TEACHER

Too many teachers are playing a role which they assume when they enter teaching, because their education has not prepared them for the teaching relationship. They are afraid of the students they face, and so they retreat behind a facade, or their concept of the teacher role. Their fear is reinforced in their early teaching experience by what they are told by other teachers, and by their supervisors, and by the expectations of their administrators. The fears of losing control, of a noisy classroom, and of having "disciplinary problems" (a major basis for non-renewal of a teaching contract) lead the teacher to develop a routine and a class structure whose major purpose is to maintain control. To be personal, open, and warm is to risk being taken advantage of, and to lose control. As a result, many teachers develop into the teacher stereotype—authoritarian, immobile, unfeeling, cold and impersonal—hardly a human being.

This view of the teacher is supported by many of the concepts or at-

---

[2] Charles E. Silberman, *Crisis in the Classroom* (New York: Random House, 1970), p. 9.

tributes associated with the teacher. Greenberg refers to them as myths.[3] In trying to live up to these myths, teachers lose their humanity and become role players. Let us consider briefly the nature of these myths.

THE MYTH OF CALMNESS. The teacher is expected to face any situation calmly and coolly. No matter what the teacher's condition is, he is expected to retain control of all feelings. The teacher never displays anger or irritation, nor elation or joy. But it is obviously impossible for any real person to do this.

THE MYTH OF MODERATION. Not only do teachers not express their feelings, but they are not supposed to experience extreme feelings. They must remain neutral about events. Their attitudes must be impartial—they cannot express an opinion or take sides on any social issue or problem. Clearly this is a demand that teachers cannot meet.

CHILDREN'S FEELINGS ARE MORE IMPORTANT THAN THE TEACHER'S FEELINGS. The importance of the teacher's behavior on the children is clear. Therefore, the teacher must carefully control his behavior for fear of having a harmful influence on the child. The harmful effects of child behavior on the teacher is unimportant—the repression of feelings aroused by the children's behavior is expected. But in any interaction people influence each other, and the teacher cannot avoid being influenced by, and reacting to, the behavior of children.

THE "I LOVE ALL CHILDREN" MYTH. Teachers are supposed to like all children equally, to have no dislikes. They are expected to love all children, with no mixed feelings, or without any feelings of anger, hate, or rejection. But love is often mixed with negative feelings when those we love hurt us or fail us or do not live up to expectations. Greenberg also says that "to be able to love all children is a basic denial of one's special uniqueness and of the true complexity of love. . . . To feel love for all children in the classroom is blatantly unrealistic." [4]

THE "I TREAT ALL CHILDREN ALIKE" MYTH. Teachers are expected to treat each child the same, but this clearly ignores individual differences among children, and the special needs of each child. A related myth is the *"I have no Favorites"* myth, which insists that teachers feel the same toward all children, regardless of their differences in personality or behavior.

[3] Herbert M. Greenberg, *Teaching with Feeling: Compassion and Self-awareness in the Classroom Today* (New York: Macmillan, 1969), Chapter 1.
[4] *Ibid.,* p. 27.

THE PERMISSIVE MYTH. This myth promulgates the idea that any behavior of children should be permitted, because it is good for them to express themselves. Greenberg relates this to the permissiveness of the psychotherapist. However, this is a misunderstanding of psychotherapy. Since there are limits to the behavior which the psychotherapists will permit, and there are limits to the behavior which society will permit, there should also be limits to the behavior which parents and teachers will accept. This concept of limits will be considered later.

THE "CHILDREN NEED TO BE PROTECTED FROM THE TEACHER'S FEELINGS" MYTH. This myth perpetuates the idea that children are delicate, weak and vulnerable, and thus must be shielded and protected from any expression of negative feelings by teachers. Teachers must be all sweetness and light, and protect children from all failure, disappointment, frustration, and criticism. But children have experienced reality before they come to school, and are aware of the existence of frustration and failure. They differ in sensitivity to failure and criticism, and the teacher must be aware of these differences, as indicated above. But life is not all sweetness and light; there is a real world that the child must live in. And the teacher who pretends to be always positive, warm and affectionate is recognized as pretending.

THE "I CAN HIDE MY TRUE FEELINGS FROM CHILDREN" MYTH. This is similar to the myth of calmness and the "I love all children" myth. It says that even if the teacher is upset and has disturbing or negative feelings, he can hide his real feelings. But children can't be fooled. It is impossible to hide one's real feelings completely or indefinitely, and to try to do so leads to rigidity and tenseness rather than ease and spontaneity in relationships with children.

THE "I HAVE NO PREJUDICES" MYTH. The ideal teacher is supposed to hold no prejudices, to have no biases. Yet we are realizing that everyone has biases and prejudices, even though unrecognized. The existence of prejudice even when it is denied is clearly illustrated in the books by Kozol and Herndon.[5] All of us are biased, and prejudge people in terms of these biases. The important thing is to realize that we are prejudiced, and to be aware of the operation of prejudice so that we can deal with it in ourselves.

THE "I HAVE TO KNOW ALL THE ANSWERS" MYTH. Teachers are expected to know or be experts on everything, at least in their subject matter field.

[5] Jonathan Kozol, *Death at an Early Age* (Boston: Houghton Mifflin, 1967), (New York: Bantam Books, 1968); James Herndon, *The Way It Spozed To Be* (New York: Simon & Schuster, 1965).

This myth is powerful because it appeals to the need for feeling adequate and being respected or looked up to. As a result, many if not most teachers are unable to admit they were wrong, or to say "I don't know." The extent of this is indicated by an experience of mine in a class of beginning graduate students. When, in response to a question, I discussed the issue and suggested sources of information, I was pressed for a direct answer, to which I responded "I don't know." The student was shocked and said that no teacher in his experience had ever said that.

Sharon Scott, a student of mine, writes of this as follows:

> If I am real, my students will be able to relate to me as I am—a human being with feelings and ideas, not an authority figure who issues mandates from above. They will realize that I am being my whole "self," and that I can and do make mistakes; furthermore, when I make mistakes, I will be able to admit them. It is only human to make mistakes, but very few teachers are accustomed to letting their students know that they are less than infallible. In my opinion, students would feel more at ease with a teacher who is able to admit errors, and who relinquishes his role of all-knowing authority. The teacher would also become a learner in the eyes of the student if he were able to admit that his ideas are not always absolutely correct.

THE "LEARNING CAN TAKE PLACE WITHOUT CONFUSION AND UNCERTAINTY" MYTH. The learning process is too often misconceived as a simple, clear, orderly process in which material is passed from the teacher to the student with no change. But learning is not clear and orderly. The learner does not grasp things immediately—there is a process of confusion with new concepts and ideas, followed by increasing clarity and understanding.

THE MYTH THAT THE "MATURE" TEACHER (OR CHILD) SHOULD COPE WITH LIFE WITHOUT STRESS, ANXIETY AND CONFLICT. This myth says that normal growth is smooth and pleasant with no disturbances—no conflicts, fears, frustrations, failures. But actually "normality" is the constant recurrence of problems accompanied by anxiety, stress, and tension. The solution of one problem only leads to the individual being presented with another. To have no problems, and thus have constant quiet, peace and inactivity would be dull and monotonous.

These myths present teachers with an idealized unattainable goal—which in fact is not an ideal and should not be attained. But these myths are widespread, to some degree at least, and the failure of teachers to attain them leads to feelings of guilt and inadequacy. The attempt to teach according to them leads to teachers becoming unreal, to their playing a role.

Role-playing is appropriate in the theatre, but not in the school. The teacher is a human being, a real person, and should not try to be something he is not. The humanistic teacher is genuine and real. He is not presenting a facade, trying to play the role of the mythical teacher, and is thus free from the preoccupation of trying to be something which he is not, free from the tension and anxiety which this creates. Furthermore, it is not possible to "get away" with role-playing for very long. People detect phoniness, and children particularly seem to be sensitive to lack of genuineness in others, though they may conceal this recognition from adults. But their behavior evidences their recognition. A teacher who is pretending to be something he is not creates feelings of uneasiness and tension in students who see beneath his pretensions to what he really is. They even begin to "test" the teacher, through deliberate misbehavior. If one is to establish a workable relationship with another person, one must know what to expect from the other. If a teacher is not himself, but is attempting to play a role, he is unsure of himself, inconsistent, and changing from one approach or method to another. Students, unable to know what to expect, behave erratically.

Genuine, open, honest behavior on the part of the teacher does not lead to, but *reduces* discipline problems. The students know who the teacher is and where he stands. To be sure, if students have been held down by an impersonal, controlled, authoritarian discipline, there will be a period, sometimes a relatively long period, in which, following a change in the classroom atmosphere, they will become active, noisy and undisciplined in a nonconstructive way. A sixth grade teacher, who changed from the traditional teacher-dominated to a student-centered method of teaching found that some students were discipline problems, and did little or no work. But these were students who were failing under the teacher controlled system.[6]

Now it often happens that a teacher who assumes the role of a controlling, dominating classroom autocrat really becomes such a person. Such a method of teaching appears to be successful, for the class is quiet, the students appear to be working and learning, and there are no discipline problems. The teacher is considered to be a good teacher, by other teachers and administrators, and in fact, is presented as a model for beginning teachers. But is he a good teacher? Is an authoritarian teacher good because he is genuine? No, he is not. An authoritarian environment is not conducive to learning, or to self-initiated behavior change, which will continue when controls are removed. The classic study of Lewin, Lippitt and White compared groups of children exposed to autocratic and democratic methods. The autocratic groups were either more hostile or more submissive, and showed less initiative and spontaneity while the demo-

[6] Carl R. Rogers, *Freedom to Learn* (Columbus, Ohio: Merrill, 1969), p. 14.

cratic groups were more friendly, open and cooperative.[7] Many other studies have corroborated these results. An authoritarian atmosphere is not conducive to the development of self-actualizing persons. It appears that a genuine autocrat is not a good teacher. This means that when we speak of genuineness we must think of it as facilitative (or therapeutic) genuineness.

The genuine teacher is, then, not using a method or a technique as something outside himself, for his methods or techniques are an integral part of himself. He is not preoccupied with whether he is following a method or technique. "Authenticity frees the helper to devote his full attention to the problems at hand. His behavior can be smoothly congruent and *en rapport* with students."[8] The behavior of authentic teachers is not a highly self-conscious attempt to apply techniques, or to reason through the "right thing to do," but is spontaneous, intuitive, based on the feeling that it is the best thing to do. The teacher trusts himself, his feelings. Dennison puts it another way. "The so-called 'methods' of education taught in our colleges cannot in fact be used. They are mere potentialities, are often impediments, and are worth nothing until they vanish and reappear again as technique. And technique cannot be taught, though indeed it can be learned. The reason is simple: each appearance of technique, each application, each solution, is unique. The work of the teacher is like that of the artist, it is a shaping of something that is given, and no serious artist knows in advance what will be given."[9] The person of the teacher, not his knowledge of teaching methods, is what is important.

It is thus apparent that it is important, as noted earlier, what kind of person the teacher is, what his beliefs, attitudes, and values are. This has implications for the selection of those who are to become teachers and for their preparation.

The authentic teacher is not all sweetness and light—not never impatient, angry, irritated. Events in the classroom, as in the rest of life, provoke these feelings, and the authentic teacher recognizes them and doesn't attempt to hide them. He doesn't feel one thing and say another.

---

[7] K. Lewin, R. Lippitt, & R. K. White, "Patterns of Aggressive Behavior in Experimentally Created Social Climates," *Journal of Social Psychology,* 1939, 10, 271–294; Ronald Lippitt, "An Experimental Study of the Effect of Democratic and Authoritarian Group Atmospheres," *University of Iowa Studies in Child Welfare,* 1940, 16, 43–195. See also H. H. Anderson, J. E. Brewer, & M. F. Reed, *Studies of Teachers' Classroom Personalities: Part III.* Follow-up Studies of the Effects of Dominative and Integrative Contacts on Children's Behavior. *Applied Psychology Monographs,* 1946, No. 11.

[8] Arthur W. Combs, Donald L. Avila, & William W. Purkey, *Helping Relationships: Basic Concepts for the Helping Professions* (Boston: Allyn & Bacon, 1971), p. 292.

[9] George Dennison, *The Lives of Children* (New York: Vintage Books, 1969). p. 257.

He isn't likely to be able to conceal his real feelings completely or consistently, but in his expression of his feelings he recognizes and accepts them as *his* feelings. He does not project blame for his feelings and reactions onto the students. He accepts responsibility for his own behavior. He says "I'm irritated," "I'm angry," "I'm disturbed," not "you irritate me," "you make me angry," "you disturb me." He can be bored as well as enthusiastic. "He can like or dislike a student product without implying that it is objectively good or bad or that the student is good or bad. He is simply expressing a feeling for the product, a feeling which exists within himself. Thus he is a person to his students, not a faceless embodiment of a curricular requirement nor a sterile tube through which knowledge is passed from one generation to the next." [10] He may judge products, or behavior, but not the person.

The damaging effects of anger directed at children are clear.[11] Children become confused, hurt, frightened, guilty, tense, and angry. They may in response disobey, fight with each other, and do less studying. Therefore, one cannot encourage teachers to express every feeling of anger, and certainly a teacher who was extremely irritable and quick to become angry would be an undesirable teacher. Realness or genuineness is important, but is not an excuse for cruelty, nor for continuing to employ a cruel, disturbed teacher.

But anger is a human reaction and inevitable at times. It is necessary that teachers know how to express their anger with the least damage to children—or even, at times, so that it is beneficial to children. The expression of anger or other negative feelings by the teacher is not damaging to students and their learning when it is clearly an expression of the teacher's feelings without blaming, condemning, evaluating negatively, or threatening. As indicated above, he recognizes it as *his* feeling and accepts responsibility for his behavior. If a child's behavior angers him, he makes it clear that it is the behavior, not the child which does so. And the perceptive teacher, aware of his own feelings and the beginning of a situation leading up to an outburst of anger can often avoid this outcome by expressing his incipient anger: "All right, kids, cool it before I blow my stack." [12] But this cannot be used as a technique to control children without destroying the genuineness of the relationship.

A student of mine recognized the desirability of the teacher becoming aware of her feelings and doing something about them before they reach the explosive stage. She reports her experience in student teaching:

"Last semester I went through a traumatic and distressing time, in connection with my student teaching. I had been given advice by teachers in

10 Carl R. Rogers, *op. cit.,* p. 106.
11 Herbert M. Greenberg, *op. cit.,* p. 61 ff.
12 *Ibid.,* p. 65.

how to conduct a good classroom. I was told not to smile too much, to establish my authority at the outset, and never to show my emotions, because the students would then know they could 'get my goat.' For six weeks I labored to follow this advice, because it came from supposed experts. One day I became so angry at the noise in the classroom that I burst out in an emotional attack upon the students, screaming at them for their terrible behavior. The students were startled; they felt that I had been unfair. If I had been more real in this situation I would have been able to tell the students that I got annoyed at this noise much earlier, and we could have worked out some sort of compromise on the noise level. This realness could have avoided my personal attack on them as bad persons. It could also have helped me to avoid my tremendous feelings of guilt; for, even though my cooperating teacher felt that the students got what they deserved, I knew that I had been most unfair. In the future, when in the teaching situation, I will try my personal best to be real, to express my feelings as they occur truly in my awareness."

The sixth grade teacher referred to above didn't like the mess which the students made during the art period, though it didn't bother the students. She expressed her feelings: "One day I told the children . . . that I am a neat and orderly person by nature and that the mess was driving me to distraction. Did they have a solution? It was suggested there were some volunteers who could clean up. . . . I said it didn't seem fair to me to have the same people clean up all the time for others—but it would solve it for me. 'Well, some people like to clean,' they replied. So that's the way it is." [13]

Dennison describes an incident with a nine-year-old girl who was monopolizing some magnets and was asked to give them back to the children from whom she had taken them. "She refused and fought with me and kicked me in the shins. I got angry and took them from her and shook her by the shoulders. She cursed me and fought back, and so I took her into the next room, where we wouldn't be observed (for I didn't want to embarrass her), and for the first time turned her over my knee and spanked her. . . . She sulked and yelled at me for a while . . . Then very quickly she grew peaceful." Later, while he was working with her at the art table, she said "Are you still mad at me?" Dennison replied: "No, I'm not mad at you anymore." She responded with "Help me make a star for my crown . . ." [14]

A simple expression of humanness in the teacher is the incident in Kozol's *Death at an Early Age* when a rotting window caved in and fell into the classroom, endangering several children. Kozol writes: "The ones who had been under the glass were terrified but the thing that I noticed with most wonder was that they tried very hard to hide their

[13] Carl R. Rogers, *op. cit.,* p. 108.
[14] George Dennison, *op. cit.,* p. 69.

fear in order to help me get over my own sense of embarrassment and guilt. . . . I asked one of the children in the front row to run down and fetch the janitor. When he asked me what he should tell him, I said: 'Tell him the house is falling in.' The children laughed. It was the first time I had ever come out and said anything like that when the children could hear me." [15]

In Chapter 4, Neill was quoted as saying: *"It doesn't matter what you do to a child if your attitude toward that child is right."* [16] This clearly does not mean that the teacher can take an "anything goes" attitude and take out all his negative feelings on children. We are talking about feelings which are a result of the behavior of the children themselves, and not projections of feelings originating from other sources. There is no place for the emotionally disturbed teacher in the classroom with children.

Being real is a difficult thing for many if not most people in our society, being as it is so impersonal, competitive, and evaluative. Teachers particularly find difficulty because of the fears engendered by the expectations represented in the myths of the good teacher. As a student put it, "I cannot become real just by verbalizing this wish; it is not an easy thing to become, because so much of my experience has conditioned me to put up appropriate fronts for the different roles I should play in society, according to normative standards." Rogers notes that:

"Only slowly can we learn to be truly real. For, first of all, one must be close to one's feelings, capable of being aware of them. Then one must be willing to take the risk of sharing them as they are, inside, not disguising them as judgments, or attributing them to other people." [17]

The attitude which the teacher has toward children is basic. This attitude constitutes the second major condition for learning and the development of self-actualizing behavior.

RESPECT FOR THE CHILD AS A PERSON

A second basic characteristic or attitude of the humanistic teacher is a profound respect for each child as a unique human being, a person of worth in his own right. Respect involves an acceptance of each child as he is, for what he is. It makes no demands that he must be different—it is unconditional. It is not an impersonal respect, but includes a liking for, and what Rogers calls a prizing of, another—his feelings, his opinions, his person.[18] It is also a caring for another, a feeling of warmth toward

---

[15] Jonathan Kozol, *op. cit.,* p. 32.
[16] A. S. Neill, *Summerhill* (New York: Hart, 1960), p. 144.
[17] Carl R. Rogers, *op. cit.,* p. 114.
[18] *Ibid.,* p. 109.

him—but a nonpossessive caring and warmth, recognizing his integrity as an individual. It is a trust, a recognition of the other as trustworthy. The totality of this attitude is inconsistent with exerting control over another, guiding or directing him in the way you think he should go, manipulating him by subtle means.

This does not require that another be perfect, or that he agree with us, or that all his behavior must be acceptable to us, or "good" or "right" in our opinion. There is an acceptance of imperfections, mistakes and errors, changes in mood and motivation, etc., as aspects of being human. There is a confidence in the basic goodness of each individual, of the capacity of the individual to grow and to develop, to actualize his potentials in an appropriate environment.

It will be remembered that one of the myths of the good teacher is that he likes all children. It was indicated that this is an unreasonable expectation. Yet we are saying now that the humanistic teacher not only accepts but likes all children. This appears to present a contradiction and a dilemma, and to some extent this is a real dilemma. But we must note two things which may help to resolve the apparent contradiction. First, when one accepts or likes another as a person, it does not mean that one must accept or like all his characteristics or behaviors. This is implied in the discussion above about perfection in others. This appears to be the source of some confusion and misunderstanding. Greenberg, for example, appears to equate disliking of behaviors and characteristics with dislike of the child as a person.[19] The teacher must make this distinction. Second, when one is able really to understand another, in the manner to be discussed later, then one almost always finds some basis for liking and respect for him as a person.

It appears that one cannot help—through teaching or in any other way —someone whom one does not like, at least to some extent. This suggests that as in all myths, there is some truth in the myth that the teacher must like all children. Yet there are instances where one just cannot like another. All teachers cannot like all children. It appears, therefore, that if a teacher cannot develop a minimal liking for a particular child, it would be better that the child be placed with a teacher who could feel some liking for the child.

Respect for students engenders self-respect in the students. Confidence in them breeds self-confidence in them. Moustakas presents an incident illustrating the influence of lack of respect upon a student's behavior:

> Recently I visited a second-grade classroom during a reading lesson. When the children saw the principal and me enter the room, they were eager to read to us. The teacher asked for volunteers. A child, with a smiling face and shining eyes, sitting next to me, is called to read. She sighs with joy

[19] Herbert M. Greenberg, *op. cit.,* Chapter 3.

as she begins, "Casey Joins the Circus." Apparently, she has learned that a good reader varies her tone of voice, reads loud enough for others to hear and reads fluently. Wanting to make an impression, wanting to get the praise of her teacher and classmates, she hurries through the paragraph assigned to her. But something is wrong. Mrs. Bell interrupts the child. She pushes the book away from the child's face and says in a slow, deliberate voice, hovering over the child, "You are reading carelessly. That's not showing respect for what's on the printed page. It's not showing respect for our visitors or the other boys and girls. You are making sense but you simply are not reading the words in the book. I've told you about this before, Betsy. Now you go back and read what's printed there so we can all follow you." The child returns to the beginning of the paragraph but something has happened. She has no direct, open way of responding. The staring, judging faces of the other children frighten her. She reads in a reluctant manner, pronounces words haltingly. There is a weak, muffled quality in her voice. She has been hurt. She is no longer certain. She completes the reading and slumps wearily into her chair.[20]

Contrast this with the following incident:

Dolores, age nine, and Elena, age ten, both Puerto Rican, began talking to each other during the lesson in arithmetic, paying no attention to Susan, their teacher. To make matters worse, several of the children began listening to them. Instead of calling the class to order, however, Susan also cocks an ear. Elena is talking about her older sister, who is eighteen. Their mother had bought a voodoo charm, and the charm had been stolen. Dodie, a Negro girl of nine, enters the conversation, saying in a low voice, "Voodoo. It don't mean nuthin'!" "What kind of charm?" says Susan. "A charm against *men*" says Elena. And now the whole class begins to discuss it. . . . Susan agrees with Dodie that voodoo probably doesn't work, "though maybe it has a psychological effect." "Yeah," says Elena, "it makes you afraid." The discussion lasts ten or twelve minutes and they all return to arithmetic.[21]

EMPATHIC UNDERSTANDING

The third characteristic of the effective teacher, and the third condition for real learning, is empathic understanding. As indicated in Chapter 5, this is a particular kind of understanding. It is not the understanding obtained from the content of a file on the child or the cumulative record, nor that usually conveyed by one teacher to another as the child moves

---

[20] Clark Moustakas, *The Authentic Teacher: Sensitivity and Awareness in the Classroom* (Cambridge, Mass.: Howard A. Doyle, 1966), p. 3.
[21] George Dennison, *op. cit.,* pp. 22–23.

from grade to grade, nor the kind of understanding one gets from the usual reports of psychologists, social workers or psychiatrists. It is not evaluative or diagnostic understanding.

Empathic understanding requires that the teacher put himself in the student's place and become sensitive to his perceptions and feelings about what is happening. "It is the completely unbiased attitude of seeing what an experience means to the child, not how it fits into or relates to other experiences, not what causes it, why it exists, or for what purpose. It is an attempt to know attitudes and concepts, beliefs and values of the child as they are perceived by him alone." [22]

Information or "facts" from outside sources may interfere with empathic understanding. Comments and observations of other people are not "facts," but represent their perceptions, and are usually judgmental or evaluative.

This kind of understanding is rare in our society, with its evaluative orientation. It is also rare in teachers. Rogers' states that it is "almost unheard of in the classroom. One could listen to thousands of ordinary classroom interactions without coming across one instance of clearly communicated, sensitively accurate, empathic understanding." He continues: "If any teacher set himself the task of endeavoring to make one non-evaluative, acceptant, empathic response per day to a student's demonstrated or verbalized feeling, I believe he would discover the potency of this currently almost non-existent kind of understanding." [23]

The example from Moustakas above illustrates lack of understanding as well as lack of respect. Silberman presents another:

A boy, being put on detention, protests his innocence, politely but insistently presenting his version of what happened. (The incident in question had involved another teacher.) The teacher giving the punishment responds each time by telling the boy how important it is to respect his elders, insisting that he should go on detention first and then tell the teacher involved why he thought the punishment was unfair. "You have to prove you're a man and can take orders." The boy finally agrees to go to detention, "but under protest." The scene ends with the teacher smirking as the boy walks away.[24]

Dennison provides an illustration of understanding in discussing one of his individual sessions with José, a thirteen year old boy who couldn't read:

[22] Clark Moustakas, *op. cit.*, p. 30.
[23] Carl R. Rogers, *op. cit.*, p. 112.
[24] From the film *High School*, produced by Frederick Wiseman, cited in Charles E. Silberman, *op. cit.*, pp. 153–154.

Sometimes he would become angry—at himself, at me, at the task; it was hard to tell, because he would clamp his jaw and glower, convinced that he had no right whatsoever to be angry. Once I said, "You're pissed off, aren't you?" He scowled still deeper and said, "Yeah." "So why don't you yell, or something?" When he saw that I meant it, he opened up his mouth and roared, "Shit!" Then he giggled. Then he became angry again and said, "I hate those fuckin' words!"—smacking the word list with his hand. I suggested that he smack it good and hard, and he doubled up his fist and pounded the words. Then he picked up his pencil and obliterated the words with fierce black lines, and gouged the paper with the pencil. His face was flushed, but his anger had changed into an excitement that was not unpleasurable. He did not tear out the page or throw the notebook on the floor. He seemed to have reached the end of that impulse. He looked at me with a very animated face. I said, "I'll write one new word for you, and then we'll go to gym," and I wrote "pissed off" in his notebook. He laughed exuberantly and jumped up and shouted, "Pissed off!" and then, "Let's go to gym." [25]

THE ESSENCE: LOVE

These three characteristics or conditions—authenticity or genuineness, respect, and empathic understanding—together make the humanistic teacher. They are demanding, yet not unrealistic to attain, as are the extreme requirements of the myths of the good teacher considered earlier. Myths, as suggested, have some basis, but are unrealistic and extreme. These three basic conditions incorporate the truths in the myths. A teacher who met all the requirements of the myths would be hardly human, since the teacher is a human being in the sense of being imperfect, fallible and possessing human weaknesses. But he must also be human in the highest sense of the word, or humane; to be an effective teacher he must possess these three characteristics, or offer these conditions, to students, at least to a minimal degree. The minimal level necessary will be considered later in Chapter 8.

These conditions are necessary for the development of self-actualizing persons. They are necessary for self-initiated, meaningful, experiential learning. They permit the child to actualize his potentialities.

The totality of the conditions can be summarized in two ways: First, they are nonthreatening. The humanistic teacher reduces the tension, fear, and anxiety which are so prevalent in classrooms and which we know inhibit learning. Second, as noted in Chapter 5, the essence of these conditions is love. It is the love which has been recognized by the humanistic teachers described in Chapters 3 and 4 as the basic requirement of

[25] George Dennison, op. cit., p. 175.

the good teacher. Real love respects the child, wants him to grow in his own way, and is confident that he will do so if he is allowed to. "In humane affairs—and education is *par excellence* a humane pursuit—there is no such thing as competence without love." [26]

Love must be real if children are to learn and grow. Too many teachers feign a syrupy sweetness with children, especially when being observed. As Ackerman notes:

> In many classrooms today, a teacher pats a child's head, addresses the child in endearing terms, "darling," or "honey." One is reminded of the Hollywood style where people indiscriminately address strangers as *darling* and *honey*. How far is this true loving? How far is it rather a pose, a gesture, a gimmick with a concealed motive of controlling or obligating the child, a tactic for bribing the child to good behavior? How far does it reflect the teacher's need to seduce and bind the child against a show of rebellion and hostility? How far does it signify the teacher's need to aggrandize the self or to show up the inadequacy of the child's parents. To the extent that this is a true expression of warmth and affection, both teacher and child are enriched thereby, and the child may likely respond with greater receptivity to learning. To the extent that the offering is a false, hypocritical gesture, it will complicate the relationship, stir resentment and bring a further block to learning. [27]

It is clear that the teacher, while being an imperfect human being, must be a self-actualizing person, for only self-actualizing persons can foster self-actualization in others. The teacher cannot facilitate learning or self-actualization in others if he is continuously preoccupied with his own problems and frustrations, is unable to respect and trust children, or is afraid to be himself and function as a humanistic teacher because of the threat from the school administration and even from other teachers. Too many potentially humanistic teachers are prevented from becoming humanistic teachers because of the school administration. Some leave teaching; others, like Jonathan Kozol and James Herndon, are fired. Teaching is a demanding occupation, and a crucial one for the future of society. Thus it must become possible for teachers to function humanistically in our schools, and only teachers who can so function must be permitted to teach. Teaching is in one respect more difficult than psychotherapy: though it demands the same characteristics in its practitioners, it is more difficult to provide the conditions for personal growth and development to thirty unique and often disturbed children for 5 or 6 hours

[26] *Ibid.,* p. 276.
[27] Nathan W. Ackerman, in *Summerhill: For and Against,* p. 270. Copyright 1970. Hart Publishing Company, Inc., New York.

a day than to provide the conditions to 4 or 5 patients in individual interviews.

The teacher, however, is not a therapist in the conventional sense of the term, but the humanistic teacher is therapeutic. Indeed, if children were exposed to humanistic teachers (and, prior to entering school, to humanistic parents), few children would need formal psychotherapy. The humanistic teacher will have fewer "problem children." Contrary to the fears of administrators, parents and others, understanding, acceptance, respect, and genuineness do not lead to increased behavior problems in children. The teacher performs her mental hygiene function simply by being a humanistic teacher. It is interesting and important also to note that the teacher who functions or begins to function humanistically grows and develops him- or herself. This is because of the fact that the characteristics of the humanistic teacher produce, through what has been called the principle of reciprocal affect, the development of the same characteristics in the children. (It will be remembered that in Chapter 5 it was noted that the conditions and the outcomes are similar.) Thus the teacher experiences these conditions in the behavior of the students and benefits as a person.

EVIDENCE OF EFFECTIVENESS

We have referred (Chapter 2 and Chapter 5) to the fact that knowledge and understanding of the conditions for self-actualizing behavior have accumulated in the practice and study of counseling or psychotherapy. There is now considerable research providing evidence for the effectiveness of these conditions, though it is not possible, or relevant, to review this research here.[28]

There is also some evidence for the effectiveness of these conditions in teaching and learning. In an early study by Robert Bills of play therapy combined with standard teaching, it was found that retarded readers who participated in play therapy characterized by the humanistic conditions improved their reading significantly during the therapy period as compared to control periods prior to and following the experimental period.[29] In a later study of teachers Bills found that teachers rated as adequate and effective by their superiors and oriented toward releasing student's potentials were rated higher by their students on a scale to measure the

---

[28] See, e.g., Charles B. Truax & Robert R. Carkhuff, *Toward Effective Counseling and Psychotherapy* (Chicago: Aldine, 1967); Robert R. Carkhuff & Bernard G. Berenson, *Beyond Counseling and Psychotherapy* (New York: Holt, Rinehart & Winston, 1967); and Robert R. Carkhuff, *Helping and Human Relations,* vols. I & II. (New York: Holt, Rinehart & Winston, 1969).

[29] Robert E. Bills, "Nondirective Play Therapy with Retarded Readers," *Journal of Consulting Psychology,* 1950, 14, 140–149.

conditions (the Barrett-Lennard Relationship Inventory, reproduced in Chapter 8) than teachers judged as less effective and who had a negative orientation toward students.[30] Rogers also reports an unpublished study by J. B. Macdonald and Esther Zaret, in which an analysis of teacher-student behavior of nine teachers and their students showed that "when teacher behaviors tended to be 'open'—clarifying, stimulating, accepting, facilitating—the student responses tended to be 'productive'—discovering, exploring, experimenting, synthesizing, deriving implications. When teacher behaviors tended to be 'closed'—judging, directing, reproving, ignoring, probing, or priming—the student responses tended to be '*re*productive'—parroting, guessing, acquiescing, reproducing facts, reasoning from given or remembered data." [31]

Lewis, Lovell and Jessee compared the gains on the Iowa Test of Basic Skills (sixth grade students) and on the Iowa Test of Educational Development (ninth grade students) of students whose teachers were rated high on a Teacher-Pupil Relationship Inventory (see Chapter 8 for a description of this) measuring the students' perception of the humanistic conditions, and of students whose teachers were rated low. For the sixth grade students there was a significant difference in gains favoring the students of the high rated teachers. The difference for the ninth grade students was in the same direction but was not quite great enough to be statistically significant, but this failure to reach significance might be related to the fact that only English teachers, rather than all teachers, were studied at the ninth grade level; at the sixth grade the students had the same teacher for all classes.[32]

Aspy studied 8 teachers and 120 students in third-grade classes. The students of the teachers who were rated high in genuineness, respect and empathic understanding showed a significantly greater gain on the Stanford Reading Achievement Test than the students of teachers rated low on these conditions.[33] In a further study Aspy and Hadlock found that third to fifth grade students taught by teachers high in genuineness, respect and empathy showed a reading gain of 2.5 years during a five month period, compared to a gain of only 0.7 years by students of teachers low in the conditions. The truancy rate was twice as high among the latter students.[34]

Thus it is clear that the humanistic teacher facilitates intellectual or

[30] Robert E. Bills, unpublished study cited in Carl R. Rogers, *op. cit.,* p. 117.
[31] *Ibid.,* p. 118.
[32] William A. Lewis, John T. Lovell, & B. E. Jessee, "Interpersonal Relationship and Pupil Progress," *Personnel and Guidance Journal,* 1964, 44, 396–401.
[33] D. N. Aspy, "A Study of Three Facilitative Conditions and Their Relationships to the Achievement of Third-grade Students," Unpublished Doctoral Dissertation, University of Kentucky, 1965.
[34] D. N. Aspy & W. Hadlock, "The Effects of High and Low Functioning Teachers upon Students' Academic Performance and Truancy," unpublished study, referred to in Robert R. Carkhuff, *op. cit.,* II, 258.

academic achievement. But of more significance is the fact that the characteristics manifested by humanistic teachers lead to significant personal learnings and personal development. Rogers presents statements from college students whose teachers have made an effort to function as humanistic teachers. They report that they enjoyed the courses more than others, that they have done more work, learned more—both in the subject matter field and about themselves and about personal relationships.[35] Similar comments have been made by students in my own classes at the graduate level:

> The professor was open, honest, and accepted our criticisms. He listened and modified his views when conditions warranted it. This was great! And very unusual. Hope I can find some more courses like this.

> We've just come to know each other and the semester has ended. It seems like a waste—all the discussions we've had and now we seem able to communicate, but the course is at an end.

> . . . this course has entirely changed my outlook on education, and has meant so much to me in a personal way. . . . People must evolve in their own way. . . . The way the course was run allowed me to make a very positive evolution as a human being. . . . I gained the insights I so badly needed right now in my life, and found the answers to many questions. . . . Now that I have gone through this semester of learning what I *needed*, I have the strength and hope to face life with a smile again. Now I feel there is some hope for humanity, and I feel that I, as a teacher, will be able to do something about making this hope a reality. This course has been the most real and genuine thing that has happened to me in a long time. I feel like my life has taken some sort of direction, that my life finally has some meaning.

> . . . this paper is a representation of some of the most meaningful and deep thoughts which I have experienced in life. It indicates some of the most significant learning which I have undergone in my education. . . .

Rogers presents some statements made by the sixth graders in the class referred to earlier:

> I feel that I am learning self abilty [sic]. I am learning not only school work but I am learning that you can learn on your own as well as someone can teach you.

> I like this plan because there is a lot of freedom. I also learn more this way than the other way you don't have to wate [sic] for others you can go at your own speed rate it takes a lot of responsibility.[36]

---

[35] Carl R. Rogers, *op. cit.*, pp. 120–123.
[36] *Ibid.*, p. 122.

Carkhuff summarizes the evidence for the effectiveness of the conditions:

> . . . there is extensive evidence to relate the offering of facilitative and action-oriented conditions by parents, teachers, counselors, and therapists to constructive change or gain on the part of their children, students, and clients on both emotional and intellective indexes. Similarly, the initiation of low levels of facilitative and action-oriented dimensions has been related to the deterioration of children, students and clients on emotional and intellective indices.[37]

Carkhuff and Berenson state it as follows:

> When we look at the data, we find that high-level functioning teachers elicit as much as two and one-half years intellectual or achievement growth in the course of a school year, while teachers functioning at low levels of facilitative conditions may allow only six months of intellectual growth over the course of a year: *students may be facilitated or they may be retarded in their intellectual as well as emotional growth, and these changes can be accounted for by the level of the teacher's functioning on the facilitative dimensions and independent of his knowledgeability.*[38]

SUMMARY

While many writers have criticized teachers for not being humanistic, none have described the characteristics of the humanistic teacher. In this chapter, drawing upon experience and research in counseling or psychotherapy, we have discussed the three basic characteristics of the humanistic teacher: genuineness or authenticity, respect or warmth, and empathic understanding.

The evidence is that when the teacher is more than an expert in subject matter and method—a real human being—and the student is not under pressure to learn at a time and rate determined by the teacher, learning and change in the intellective and emotional realms occur to a significantly greater extent and at a significantly greater rate than when the teacher is less humanistic.

"The existential teacher, the humanistic teacher, is an authentic human being interacting with other human beings, all of them with the goal of facilitating human development and personal autonomy." [39]

---

[37] Robert R. Carkhuff, *op. cit.,* I, 22.

[38] Robert R. Carkhuff & Bernard G. Berenson, *op. cit.,* p. 14.

[39] David C. L. Davis, *Model for Humanistic Education: The Danish Folk High-school.* (Columbus, Ohio: Merrill, 1971), p. 100.

Some writers have become overly concerned about making teaching psychotherapy, or about "bringing psychotherapy into the classroom," but the conditions for psychotherapy and for good teaching are the same. And if, when they are applied in the classroom, they reduce the need for psychotherapy, teaching is therefore therapeutic. We must overcome our unreasonable fear of mixing teaching and psychotherapy. Psychotherapy —or the application of the facilitative conditions for personal development—cannot be relegated to the hospital and the clinic. It must be brought into the school—and into the home. We can't, and won't, improve education without making it therapeutic.

We turn now to a consideration of the ways in which the humanistic teacher implements the conditions for learning and personal development.

8 Implementing And Evaluating The Conditions For Learning And Self-Actualization

*Many a liberal educational reform has foundered on
lack of specific tools for accomplishing its purposes—
even if a tool may be something as simple as
knowing precisely when to leave the learner entirely
alone.*

—George Leonard, EDUCATION AND ECSTASY *

It may seem to be peculiar that we must consider how one functions as
a human being, and it is. But it is necessary in a society which is becoming more impersonal and less human in many respects. It is not
enough to tell teachers to be more authentic or genuine, more respecting
and warm, more empathic—more loving. They ask: "But how do I act,
just what do I do?" While it is not sufficient that teachers simply behave
in certain ways ("what you are speaks so loudly I cannot hear what you
are saying"), it is helpful for teachers to know some of the ways in which
they can implement or practice the conditions for facilitating students
learning and personal development. In a sense, then, this is the methods
chapter for humanistic education.

If it seems to be a paradox to raise the question about how one functions as a human being, it perhaps may seem inhuman to attempt to
measure the extent to which a person—or a teacher—is humanistic in

* (New York: Dell, 1968), p. 18. British Commonwealth Rights by permission
of John Murray (Publishers) Ltd.

his behavior. Yet this is necessary if we are concerned about evaluating teacher candidates and teachers. Therefore, the second part of this chapter will deal with the evaluation of the capacity of teachers to offer a facilitative human relationship to their students.

IMPLEMENTATION

Listening

Few people really listen to each other. Most of what is called listening is simply waiting for one's turn to talk. Rather than really listening to the other, one is thinking about what one is going to say. One of the frequent complaints of students is that teachers don't listen to them. The teacher meting out punishment to the student in the incident reported in the last chapter clearly was not listening to the student. Studies have found that teachers in the classroom talk approximately seventy-five percent of the time. Not only is much of this talk trivial, boring and repetitious, but when one is talking one is unable to listen.

Real listening is not a passive thing, but an active following of what the other is saying. It is giving one's attention completely to the other, without interference by one's own personal reactions or associations. It requires that one put oneself in the place of the other—in other words, to be empathic. It requires that the listener divest himself of the external frame of reference and assume the internal frame of reference of the speaker. This kind of listening leads to the empathic understanding discussed in the last chapter.

Such listening is not easy. It requires concentration on the other. The person who is concerned and preoccupied with himself and his own problems is unable to listen, for such listening requires that one be really interested in and concerned about the other. Listening is a simple but basic manifestation of respect for another.

The experience of really being listened to is helpful, even therapeutic, to the student. This is especially so when his expression of his feelings and emotions are listened to. Contrary to the idea of many teachers that emotions, particularly negative emotions, should be repressed, such repression is harmful, and intensifies the feelings. The freedom to verbally express emotions, even hostility and anger, does not result in the increase of such emotions but rather allows them to be drained off, thus allowing more positive and constructive feelings to be expressed.

If the child is to express his real feelings, he must feel that he is free to do so, that he won't be evaluated, criticized, or condemned for having negative feelings. If he is to express any ideas or thoughts, he must feel that they will be accepted as worthwhile. The teacher must therefore convey genuine interest, concern, and respect for the child by his willingness to listen and his ability to listen empathically.

Responding

While listening alone is often helpful, and can give another the feeling of being understood, it is often necessary or desirable that the listener communicate his understanding. To effectively communicate empathic understanding, the listener's responses must remain in the internal frame of reference, rather than being judgmental or evaluative.

Understanding responses may be nonverbal, such as a nod of the head. Simple verbal responses may be "Yes," and "I see," "I understand," "Uh huh," "Mm mmm." A simple restatement of what another has said indicates that one has heard and understands.

Responses may also represent *attempts* to understand, or to understand better where there are doubts. A puzzled or quizzical expression indicates that you are having difficulty understanding. Saying "I don't understand", or asking a question such as "Can you say that again?" can be helpful. Or "I'm not sure I know what you mean," or "Are you saying . . . ?" can help the other to clarify what he is saying. Sometimes his feelings may be confused, and it helps him to try to get another to understand what he is trying to say. It is important that the listener does not pretend to understand when in fact he does not.

No one can completely understand another, and complete understanding is obviously not necessary. If one is sincerely trying to understand another, the other person appreciates this and feels better or is helped.

Mutual listening and responding with understanding is more than simple interaction. It is an *encounter*. An encounter is a highly personal, genuine relationship. Such a relationship is rewarding and enhancing for both individuals, or, in a group, for all those who participate in it.

Some encounters involve conflicts or controversies, which are resolved in a *confrontation* where there is mutual respect and genuineness. The resolution may not eliminate differences in beliefs or attitudes, but does lead to a working relationship or an agreement to disagree. In a teacher-student confrontation, the student must be free to disagree and to maintain his own identity. Moustakas writes:

> Paradoxical as this seems, only when persons can openly disagree, if this is the reality of their experience, is it possible for them to establish genuine

bonds. When the teacher forces the child, through repetitious phrases and commands, through conditioning, belittling, and group pressures, when the teacher uses subtle, brainwashing devices, and cuts the child off or beats him down, the child soon realizes that the only acceptable way is the path of conformity, taking on the words and ways of the one in authority. Increasingly, the child becomes insensitive to his own self and unresponsive to his own experience. He becomes numb to criticism and rebuke, develops a suspicious and mechanical approach against further attacks, and comes to be unfeeling in his associations with others.[1]

The avoidance of confrontation with a student by a teacher can lead to the accumulation of feelings until an explosion occurs. It is better to face the conflict early, both for the teacher and for the student. This is particularly true for those conflicts which revolve around the limits of acceptable behavior.

Setting Limits

In all social situations, there are, and must be, limits for acceptable behavior. Progressive education was misunderstood as advocating no limits on behavior. In counseling or psychotherapy there are no limits on verbalization, but there are limits on behavior. In the classroom, also, they must exist; hopefully, the limits on verbalization are much wider than those on behavior. The problem of limits, which is essentially the problem of discipline, is one of the most difficult problems a teacher faces, for if limits are too restrictive and unreasonable, they generate tension and interfere with learning. Limits are necessary in a negative sense to protect individuals from unfair imposition of others, but from a more positive standpoint they provide structure for the development of relationships. The absence of limits or vaguely defined limits leads students to seek to determine what the limits are, behavior known, though not ironically, as "testing the limits."

The teacher must determine reasonable limits and then enforce them consistently, though the fewer the restrictions, it should be emphasized, the fewer the disciplinary problems. One of the most frequent complaints of students about teachers concerns the inconsistency with which limits are enforced. An articulate eighth grade boy who was being counseled by one of my students expressed it as follows:

Student: "It just seems to me that since the teachers and the principal are the people who are in authority, well, they kind of have to take

[1] Clark Moustakas, *The Authentic Teacher: Sensitivity and Awareness in the Classroom* (Cambridge, Mass.: Howard A. Doyle, 1966), p 23.

care of everybody else, it seems like they ought to be a little more careful about what they say and things like that."

Counselor: "You feel that the teachers and principals are not very careful about the way they use their power?" (Student: "mmh mmh") "And that they seem to sort of . . ."

Student: "A lot of times they'll—well, just for a little thing—if they're in a bad mood they'll take and—well not many times—I know it has happened to some people—take and send somebody out into the hall, when they didn't do anything—and sometimes, you know, it's what they're leading up to—they maybe hadn't done anything all day, and then just for a little thing they'll fly off the handle and get real mad and—it just doesn't seem fair that they should take it out on this one person. They should call each person down as he does something instead of waiting until . . ."

Counselor: "uh hu."

Student: "finally taking it out on one person."

Counselor: "It's sort of cornering one person in the class?"

Student: "uh hu."

Counselor: "That usually causes most of the problems."

Student: "I think that the schools ought to give the kids so much leeway and then enforce it strictly instead of saying you don't have any leeway and then when they go ahead and do something they don't enforce it very strictly and . . . sort of like you give them an inch and they'll take a mile. I think they ought to stop you as soon as you get as far as you should go and after a while the kids would learn, but the way it is they let them go on and on until they decide they don't like it then they take it out on one person and . . ."

Counselor: "You feel then that the rules are not defined . . . Is this what you're saying, that if you go beyond a certain point . . ."

Student: "They should, well, say they give you so much room . . . things you can do in the room—each teacher usually sets that up herself—and I think as soon as you've gone that far . . . if you're doing anything you're not supposed to I think they should call you down for it . . . maybe give you a warning—you know— one time—and then the next time you do it they send you out in the hall or down to the principal's office if you do it again. But the way it is they just let certain people go on past that and then after a while somebody else saw them do it and they didn't get into any trouble so they do the same thing and they'll get called down for it. And I think they should call everybody down for the same things. Because quite often one person does— maybe the teacher likes this person just a little bit more than another person . . . and this other person does something and gets sent out in the hall but this person does it and she just says 'now don't do that' . . ."

Different teachers set different limits, and to see what they are students test out a new teacher or a substitute. The opening pages of the books by Herndon and Kohl portray the difficulties a new teacher faces.[2] Kozol also describes his early days in two classrooms.[3] Though these are extreme examples because of the nature of the schools they worked in, every teacher faces the problem of structuring limits with every class. To some extent limits are determined by what the teacher can be comfortable with, but if a teacher is comfortable only with narrow limits which are not conducive to learning, which are unreasonable to impose on active, living children, then the teacher will need, probably with help from a psychologist or counselor, to learn to become comfortable with more reasonable limits. Too often strict limits represent fear of loss of control.

As noted earlier, though, some limits are necessary. In addition, as Combs and Snygg point out, "Limits have important growth-producing values for people, and the lack of limits makes adjustment to new situations more difficult. A stable structure has important positive values in providing expectancies against which to judge one's behavior. Clear and reasonable limits provide important security values."[4]

It has long been maintained that the goal of discipline is the development of self-discipline in students. Seldom, however, has the system made it possible for self-discipline to develop, for fear and lack of trust have stood in the way. But where students have been involved in or permitted to determine limits, as in Summerhill and some of the open or free schools, there have been no discipline problems. Where students are interested in learning as a group, they will set the limits which are necessary for learning to take place.

The Power of Expectations

We have mentioned in Chapter 5 the importance of the teacher's concepts or beliefs about the nature of man. Teachers also have beliefs and atttudes towards particular groups of children, as well as individual children, which influence the behavior of the children through influencing what teachers expect of them. Teachers' expectations, in other words, are a powerful factor in the actual performance of children in school. The importance of expectations in behavior has long been recognized in

---

[2] James Herndon, *The Way it Spozed to Be* (New York: Simon & Schuster, 1965); Herbert Kohl, *36 Children* (New York: New American Library, 1967).

[3] Jonathan Kozol, *Death at an Early Age* (Boston: Houghton Mifflin, 1967), (New York: Bantam Books, 1968), pp. 46–47, 161–162.

[4] Arthur W. Combs & Donald Snygg, *Individual Behavior: a Perceptual Approach to Behavior* (New York: Harper & Row, 1959), p. 391.

the saying, "Give a dog a bad name and he will live up to it." This is the theme of Shaw's *Pygmalion,* in which the flower girl becomes a lady when she is expected to be a lady and is treated like one. Robert Merton, the sociologist, called this phenomenon the self-fulfilling prophecy, a term which has become standard in the literature.[5]

Robert Rosenthal and Lenore Jacobson conducted a study of the expectations of classroom teachers. They administered a test of general ability to all the students in grades K through six of a school in the spring, and the teachers were told that the test was able to predict which of the children would be expected to show a spurt in academic achievement. The following September each teacher was given a list purporting to contain the names of these children—in fact, the names on the list were selected at random. The children were retested the next January and May. The authors concluded that those children whose names appeared on the lists gained more, on the average, than the other children.[6] Unfortunately, the results are poorly reported and have been questioned statistically. But there has also been a mass of literature supporting the effects of expectations, including research with animals. In one study two groups of psychology students were given rats to be tested for performance in running mazes. One group was told that their rats were maze-bright, while the others was told that theirs were maze-dull, while in fact the rats were from the same litters. The results reported by the students, however, were in the expected direction—the students who thought that their rats were brighter reported better performance.

The way in which expectations alter behavior is not clear, though. A student of mine, in one of the most detailed studies of expectations, was able to identify few observable behaviors related to the expectancy effect. It appears that the behaviors may vary with the sex of the experimenter and of the subject, with the nature of the task and the situation, as well as characteristics of the subjects, and are very complex. Awareness of the phenomenon of the expectancy effect may lead to an attempt to counteract an unfavorable effect, resulting in a "reverse effect." [7] The modes of influence are subtle yet effective, particularly over a period of time.

It is well known that expectations are transferred from teacher to teacher by communication of stereotypes. A seventh grade boy who was a client of a counseling student of mine expressed it as follows:

[5] Robert K. Merton, "The Self-Fulfilling Prophecy," *The Antioch Review,* 1948, Summer. Reprinted in Robert K. Merton, *Social Theory and Social Structure* Rev. Ed. (New York: Free Press, 1957).

[6] Robert Rosenthal & Lenore Jacobson, *Pygmalion in the Classroom* (New York: Holt, Rinehart & Winston, 1968).

[7] Nitza Yarom, "Temporal Localization and Communication of Experimenter Expectancy Effect with 10-11 Year Old Children," unpublished doctoral dissertation, University of Illinois, Urbana-Champaign, 1971.

Student: "It wouldn't have been so bad if it was like in the lower grades, you know, primary grades, where we had only one teacher. Now you've got four teachers, and Mrs. Thompson, she just about can't stand me, and then they go down and sit together at the lunch table and she tells all about the things I do, and I have a funny feeling she exaggerates just a little bit. And then the other teachers hear about it and they're on edge and everytime I breathe too deeply they get down on me too and its like having the whole school down on you."

Counselor: "Things you do aren't quite as bad as what the teachers seem to . . ."

Student: "uh uh."

Teachers pass on expectations from year to year. The student above went on later to say:

Student: "You walk into a new class, you know, the teacher has never had you and she doesn't know all your names yet. You look up and she's all big smiles and everything, you know, and goes down the line asking everybody their names, and you say Ronald James—and she falls through the floor or something."

Counselor: "It gets that bad."

Silberman states it clearly and simply: "The teacher who assumes that her students cannot learn is likely to discover that she has a class of children who are indeed unable to learn; yet another teacher, working with the same class but without the same expectation, may discover that she has a class of interested learners. The same obtains with respect to behavior: the teacher who assumes that her students will be disruptive is likely to have a disruptive class on her hands." [8]

Perhaps one of the major problems in the education of the "disadvantaged"—poor whites, blacks, Puerto Ricans, Chicanos, American Indians —lies in this matter of expectations. Teachers expect little, demand or require little, and get little. An unusual aspect of this problem is referred to by Silberman. He says that expectations can be lowered by empathy. That is, the efforts to help teachers of the disadvantaged by impressing on them that they fail through no fault of their own leads teachers to accept— and expect failure.[9] It could be questioned, of course, whether this is really empathy. Yet the fact remains that whole classes of children are condemned to a poor education because it is assumed that they are not capable of learning. This is a basic theme of Kozol's book depicting the

[8] Charles E. Silberman, *Crisis in the Classroom* (New York: Random House, 1970), p. 83.
[9] *Ibid.*, p. 86.

education of blacks in the Boston schools, of Herndon's book about the education of blacks in California, and of Kohl's book.[10] In these schools the communication of negative attitudes and expectations becomes clear and obvious. *The concepts which the teacher has of the children become the concepts which the children come to have of themselves.*
Silberman reports an example of negative attitudes:

> A fourth-grade math teacher writes a half-dozen problems on the board for the class to do. "I think I can pick at least four children who can't do them," she tells the class, and proceeds to demonstrate, for all to see, how correct the teacher's judgment is. Needless to say, the children fulfill the prophecy.[11]

That this situation can be changed, or reversed, has been shown in a number of experimental and demonstration projects. The essential element in these projects has been an attitude and expectation that the children could and would learn, and it is this factor, rather than special methods or techniques, to which success can be attributed, even though some would emphasize the methods and techniques.

The humanistic teacher, who respects each student as a unique human being, who believes that each one has more potential than is evident, conveys this in his treatment of the student. High expectations can be expressed in the maintenance of high standards. However, one must be careful that the standards are not too high or unrealistic, and standards must be adapted to the individual student.

What students *can* do is often surprising. Borton notes the performance of children in art and drama, surpassing their own expectations. One self-conscious girl of seventeen, after participating in a creative experience, became almost ecstatic. "Over and over, bouncing on the grass, she said, 'I did it. I did it!' " [12] In another instance, Borton was surprised by the creation of "Fred, the one kid in the class whom I considered a dolt." His poorly written paper, which, "graded as a conventional essay . . . was a disaster", when respaced on the page and with the spelling corrected became striking blank verse. Borton writes: "I still cannot explain how Fred did it. He never came close to repeating that high performance though he often tried." [13] The atmosphere created by Borton, combined with the interest of the student, ignited a brief spark or flame of expression.

Although it is not possible to identify just how expectations are com-

[10] Jonathan Kozol, *op. cit.;* James Herndon, *op. cit.;* Herbert Kohl, *op. cit.*
[11] *Op. cit.,* p. 139.
[12] From Terry Borton, *Reach, Touch, and Teach* (New York: McGraw-Hill, 1970), p. 33. Copyright 1970 by Terry Borton. Used with permission of McGraw-Hill Book Company.
[13] *Ibid.,* pp. 18–19.

municated (except in extreme situations), it is possible for the teacher to become aware of his expectations and thus to anticipate the direction of his influence on students.

The teacher who is concerned about his students, who respects them, who recognizes the great unused potentials which they possess, expects much—even "demands" much. Love expects the best. The expectations others have of us act as a challenge to us to do our best, to be our best.

Dennison discusses his desire to teach José to read:

> And so I did not wait for José to decide for himself. When I thought the time was ripe, I insisted that we begin his lessons. . . . My own demands, then, were an important part of José's experience. They were not simply the demands of a teacher, nor of an adult, but belonged to my own way of caring about José. And he sensed this. There was something he prized in the fact that I made demands on him. This became all the more evident once he realized that I wasn't simply processing him, that is grading, measuring, etc. And when he learned he *could* refuse—could refuse altogether, could terminate the lesson, could change its direction, could insist on something else—our mutual interest in his development was taken quite for granted. We became collaborators in the business of life.
>
> Obviously, if I had tried to compel him, none of this would have been possible. And if I had made no demand—had simply waited for him to come to class—I would in some sense have been false to my own motives. . . .
>
> It boils down to this: that two strong motives exist side by side and are innately, not antagonistic, but incongruous. The one is that we adults are entitled to demand much of our children, and in fact lose immediacy as persons when we cease to do so. The other is that children are entitled to demand that they be treated as individuals, since that is what they are. The rub is this: that we press our demands, inevitably, in a far more generalized way than is quite fitting for any particular child.[14]

The fact is that one cannot care deeply for another without expecting, even demanding, that he do and be the best of which he is capable.

The Self as Instrument

Interpersonal relations are not a matter of techniques. Humanistic teaching, therefore, cannot be reduced to a bag of tricks or techniques. This is the error of those writers whose educational backgrounds have imprinted on them the importance of methods. In the effort to be objective, concrete, specific, and practical they have focused on developing

[14] George Dennison, *The Lives of Children* (New York: Vintage, 1969), pp. 112–113, 115.

lists of activities, procedures, projects, devices, etc. for the teacher to use. These are often not much more than tricks or gimmicks to initiate and give content to an interaction. To some extent, perhaps, this is necessary for teachers who have been so content oriented, so lesson-plan dependent, that they are unable to enter a relationship spontaneously, without an agenda, but to the extent that they are and continue to be dependent on such crutches they will be prevented from becoming free to enter and establish a spontaneous relationship.

It is true that some writers (e.g. Brown [15]) present evidence to support the effectiveness of such an approach. But they fail to realize that the success is probably more dependent upon the effectiveness of the teachers as persons—their interest, concern, enthusiasm—than upon the methods or techniques per se.

One cannot really tell another how to express his caring or his love. Each of us must find his own way of doing it—his own style of implementing his attitudes and beliefs, his own way of giving himself. In a basic sense one's self is the instrument of teaching, as of all human relationships, and one must learn to use one's self as an instrument for facilitating the development of others. The individual can be assisted in doing this (we shall consider ways in the last chapter) but he must do it himself.

Receptiveness of the Student

There is an important aspect of any human relationship that must be noted. Failure to recognize and be aware of this has caused many teachers to suffer feelings of guilt and inadequacy, to feel that they have failed a student.

In addition to the offering of understanding, respect or warmth, and genuineness by the teacher these must be received—or perceived and accepted—by the student. Young children are usually open and receptive. But some young children, and perhaps many older children, are not. Their experiences have closed them up, sometimes so tight that they are unaware of, or insensitive to, warmth and genuineness. In other cases, their experiences have led to distrust and suspicion. In still others, resentment and resistance prevent them from recognizing or accepting the genuine interest and concern of the teacher. These children have been mistreated—deceived, mistrusted, let down, treated as inadequate, etc.

The teacher can only offer himself, and try repeatedly to break through walls of suspicion, distrust, resistance, hostility and insensitivity. The

[15] George T. Brown, *Human Teaching for Human Learning: an Introduction to Confluent Education* (New York: Viking Press, 1971).

theme of many of the books concerned with humanistic teaching—Dennison, Herndon, Kohl, and Kozol—is the attempt to break through to such students. When the attempt is successful the results sometimes appear as miraculous. But sometimes—too often—the attempt is not successful. When it is not, it is not always the fault of the teacher. It takes two to establish a good relationship, and mutual trust is necessary.

The books by Dennison, Herndon, Kohl, and Kozol contain illustrations of students who were difficult, and sometimes impossible to reach. Borton presents an instance from his experience:

> Bob—a senior in my slow section. On my first day of teaching he took the seat directly in front of my desk and interrupted my introductory remarks by asking, "You new?" When I nodded my head, he grinned, "we got your number." From then on he made my life miserable, always quitting just before I got to the breaking point. A month later he was suspended by some other teacher, a month after that he was jailed. At about the same time I learned that he had started out as a freshman in the best academic class, and had been moved down one track each year as various teachers retaliated for his wisecracks.[16]

Such children might have been reached by humanistic teaching in the early grades. Later may be too late. Though often psychotherapy is recommended and even attempted, these students usually do not accept therapy and if it is attempted it is not often successful.

EVALUATION

It was noted in Chapter 1, and again in Chapter 5, that knowledge of the conditions for a good human relationship has been derived from studies in the field of counseling or psychotherapy. Following the identification of the major aspects of this relationship, attempts have been made to develop instruments to evaluate or measure the extent to which an individual in counseling or psychotherapy is able to offer these conditions to his clients. Several instruments have been developed.

It has been emphasized in this book that the essence of good teaching is that it is a good human relationship. As such, it would be expected to share the conditions identified as essential for a facilitative counseling or psychotherapeutic relationship. And as has also been emphasized in this book, the three basic or core conditions which are shared are empathic understanding, respect and warmth, and genuineness. It might be expected that these conditions would be implemented somewhat differently

[16] Terry Borton, *op. cit.*, p. 153.

in the teaching than in the counseling or psychotherapy relationship. Their implementation in teaching has been considered in a general way in the first part of this chapter.

The somewhat different way in which the conditions are implemented in teaching requires that instruments developed for use in counseling or psychotherapy be modified or adapted to the teaching situation. We shall consider here the adaptations of some of these.

In addition to their use as evaluative instruments both in teacher education and with experienced teachers, these instruments can also be considered, and used, as a source for ideas and illustrations of some of the more specific ways in which the teacher can implement the basic conditions of a humanistic teaching relationship. They can thus be used for self-evaluation by teacher education students and teachers.

Before discussing recent instruments which have been derived from those used in counseling or psychotherapy, mention should be made of an earlier measure developed independently. This is the Minnesota Teacher Attitude Inventory.[17] It consists of 150 statements relating to teacher attitudes in a teaching situation. The Inventory is to be completed by students, who indicate their degree of agreement or disagreement with the statements. The Inventory has high reliability, and scores have correlated significantly with ratings of teachers by students, principals and teaching specialists. It measures the teacher's affective attitudes rather than cognitive teaching methods. Since the Inventory is not available to teachers, items cannot be presented, and it cannot be used by teachers for self-study. Therefore, no further consideration will be given to it.

The Teacher-Pupil Relationship Inventory (TPRI)

In 1950 Heine collected statements from 24 clients describing their therapists. The ten statements which clients considered to be most conducive to treatment and the ten they considered to be most deleterious were selected.[18]

---

[17] C. H. Leeds, "The Construction and Differential Value of a Scale for Determining Teacher-Pupil Attitude," Unpublished Doctoral Dissertation, University of Minnesota, 1946; W. W. Cook, C. H. Leeds, & R. Callis, *Minnesota Teacher Attitude Inventory* (New York: The Psychological Corporation, 1951). (Sale is restricted; teachers may not buy it.)

[18] R. W. Heine, "An Investigation of the Relationship Between Change in Personality from Psychotherapy as Reported by Patients and the Factors Seen by Patients as Producing Change," Unpublished Doctoral Dissertation, University of Chicago, 1950, reported in Fred E. Fiedler, "Quantitative Studies on the Role of Therapist's Feelings Toward their Patients," in O. Hobart Mowrer (Ed.) *Psychotherapy Theory and Research* (New York: Ronald, 1953), pp. 296–315.

Lewis, Lovell and Jessee adapted these statements so that they would be applicable to teachers rather than to therapists, and so that the vocabulary level would be appropriate for fifth-grade students. The resulting instrument was called the Teacher-Pupil Relationship Inventory, and it was found to be a reliable instrument.[19]

The twenty statements comprising the instrument are:

1. The teacher always let me feel that I was to take responsibility for what I learned.
2. It seemed to me that the teacher didn't take his work very seriously.
3. The teacher got across the feeling that we were really working together to help me learn.
4. I felt sure that I could trust the teacher and he seemed to feel that he could trust me.
5. The teacher seemed not to want me to show it when I was very happy or sad.
6. I had the feeling that the teacher was so sympathetic that he couldn't really be helpful.
7. The teacher was very natural. He did not try to be like someone else.
8. Without thinking about anything else, the teacher was a likable person.
9. I somehow caught the feeling that the teacher couldn't think of me as an equal.
10. It seemed as if the teacher always started wordy explanations when he might have let me finish.
11. I had the feeling that here was one person I could really trust.
12. I never had the feeling that the teacher really understood what I was trying to get across.
13. The teacher always seemed to know what I was trying to get across to him.
14. The teacher often seemed to be lost in his own thoughts rather than thinking about what I said.
15. I had the feeling that the teacher knew what he was doing in trying to teach me.
16. It was easy to talk to the teacher. He seemed interested.
17. I always had the feeling that I was just another student as far as the teacher was concerned.
18. I often felt, "I'd better not tell the teacher that."
19. The teacher seemed to be in pretty good control of himself at all times.
20. I was a little afraid really to tell the teacher what I thought about myself and the class.

[19] William A. Lewis, John T. Lovell, & B. J. Jessee, "Interpersonal Relationship and Pupil Progress," *Personnel and Guidance Journal,* 1965, 44, 396–401.

Knoblock and Goldstein have further simplified the items for use with disturbed third- and fourth-grade students.[20]

In the last chapter it was reported that teachers' scores on this inventory were found to be related to the academic progress of sixth-grade students. A study of teachers by Knoblock and Goldstein is of interest here as well as for teacher preparation (Chapter 12). The six teachers of disturbed children participated in seventeen semi-structured group sessions. Following both the fifth and fifteenth sessions they completed the TPRI (adapted for teachers to respond to) under four different instructions: *Self*: responded to in terms of her typical classroom behavior; *Ideal*: responded to in terms of her view of the ideal teacher's classroom behavior; *Other*: responded to in terms of how she felt each of the other teachers typically behaved in the classroom; and *Pupil*: responded to in terms of how she felt her pupils would rate her behavior. In addition, the modified pupil version was completed after the fifth group session by all the students in each teacher's class.

The comparisons, by means of correlation coefficients, of the various scores yielded some very interesting results. At the fifth session self and ideal scores correlated .75, but the correlation at the fifteenth session was .04 (not significant). The scores indicated that the teachers were fairly well satisfied with themselves at the first testing, but that this self-satisfaction decreased as they apparently learned to see themselves more as they really were. Their relatively high perceptions of themselves at the fifth session were apparently unrealistic, since these perceptions did not agree very closely with how the other teachers perceived them (the correlation was .47). Their perceptions of themselves did not agree with their pupils' perceptions of them either (the correlation was .14). The other teachers and the pupils agreed quite closely in their ratings (the correlation was .72). At the fifteenth session their self-perceptions apparently became more realistic (as well as less close to their ideal), correlating .96 with the perceptions of them by the other teachers, and .73 with the perceptions of their pupils. The evidence seems clear that teachers are not generally realistic in their perceptions of their teacher-pupil relationships, and that they overestimate the favorableness (or closeness to the ideal) of their relationships. Group sessions in which teacher-pupil relationships are discussed lead to more realistic self-evaluation.

The Barrett-Lennard Relationship Inventory

In 1959 Barrett-Lennard developed a Relationship Inventory to measure emphatic understanding, level of positive regard (or respect), uncondition-

---

[20] Peter Knoblock & Arnold P. Goldstein, *The Lonely Teacher* (Boston: Allyn & Bacon, 1971), pp. 144–146.

ality of regard, genuineness, and openness or willingness-to-be-known of the therapist. One form was for use by the therapist and another for use by the client.[21] Barrett-Lennard found that clients who improved, as measured by various instruments, perceived their therapists as more emphatic, more genuine and showing more positive regard (respect) than clients who improved less perceived their therapists.

Barrett-Lennard suggested that the instrument tapped "broad attitudinal qualities that could be measured in *any* form of significant interpersonal relationships." [22] Emmerling found that teachers who were concerned about helping students think for themselves, be independent, and express individual needs were rated by their students on the Relationship Inventory as more empathic, respecting and genuine than teachers who saw students in negative terms were rated by their students.[23]

There are sixty-four items in the revised Relationship Inventory. Each item is responded to on a 6-point scale from "yes, I strongly feel it is true," to "no, I strongly feel it is false." For scoring purposes the responses are rated from +3 to −3 according to the degree of favorableness of the response. Scores are obtained for four variables: Level of Regard, Empathic Understanding, Congruence, and Unconditionality of Regard, as well as a total score. The items are as follows (the pronoun "he" is substituted for "she" when male teachers are rated):

1. She respects me as a person.
2. She wants to understand how I see things.
3. Her interest in me depends on the things I say or do.
4. She is comfortable and at ease in our relationship.
5. She feels a true liking for me.
6. She may understand my words but she does not see the way I feel.
7. Whether I am feeling happy or unhappy with myself makes no real difference to the way she feels about me.
8. I feel that she puts on a role or front with me.
9. She is impatient with me.
10. She nearly always knows exactly what I mean.
11. Depending on my behaviour, she has a better opinion of me sometimes than she has at other times.

21 G. T. Barrett-Lennard, "Dimensions of the Client's Experience of His Therapist Associated with Personality Change," Unpublished Doctoral Dissertation, University of Chicago, 1959; G. T. Barrett-Lennard, "Dimensions of Therapist Response as Causal Factors in Therapeutic Change," *Psychological Monographs,* 1962, 76 (3), Whole No. 562.

22 G. T. Barrett-Lennard, 1962, *op. cit.,* p. 29.

23 F. C. Emmerling, "A Study of the Relationship Between Personality Characteristics of Classroom Teachers and Pupil Perception of These Teachers," Unpublished Doctoral Dissertation, Auburn University, 1961.

12. I feel that she is real and genuine with me.
13. I feel appreciated by her.
14. She looks at what I do from her own point of view.
15. Her feeling toward me doesn't depend on how I feel toward her.
16. It makes her uneasy when I ask or talk about certain things.
17. She is indifferent to me.
18. She usually senses or realises what I am feeling.
19. She wants me to be a particular kind of person.
20. I nearly always feel that what she says expresses exactly what she is feeling and thinking as she says it.
21. She finds me rather dull and uninteresting.
22. Her own attitudes toward some of the things I do or say prevent her from understanding me.
23. I can (or could) be openly critical or appreciative of her without really making her feel any differently about me.
24. She wants me to think that she likes me or understands me more than she really does.
25. She cares for me.
26. Sometimes she thinks that *I* feel a certain way, because that's the way *she* feels.
27. She likes certain things about me, and there are other things she does not like.
28. She does not avoid anything that is important for our relationship.
29. I feel that she disapproves of me.
30. She realizes what I mean even when I have difficulty in saying it.
31. Her attitude toward me stays the same: she is not pleased with me sometimes and critical or disappointed at other times.
32. Sometimes she is not at all comfortable but we go on, outwardly ignoring it.
33. She just tolerates me.
34. She usually understands the whole of what I mean.
35. If I show that I am angry with her she becomes hurt or angry with me, too.
36. She expresses her true impressions and feelings with me.
37. She is friendly and warm with me.
38. She just takes no notice of some things that I think or feel.
39. How much she likes or dislikes me is not altered by anything that I tell her about myself.
40. At times I sense that she is not aware of what she is really feeling with me.
41. I feel that she really values me.
42. She appreciates exactly how the things I experience feel to me.

43. She approves of some things I do, and plainly disapproves of others.
44. She is willing to express whatever is actually in her mind with me, including any feelings about herself or about me.
45. She doesn't like me for myself.
46. At times she thinks that I feel a lot more strongly about a particular thing than I really do.
47. Whether I am in good spirits or feeling upset does not make her feel any more or less appreciative of me.
48. She is openly herself in our relationship.
49. I seem to irritate and bother her.
50. She does not realize how sensitive I am about some of the things we discuss.
51. Whether the ideas and feelings I express are "good" or "bad" seems to make no difference to her feeling toward me.
52. There are times when I feel that her outward response to me is quite different from the way she feels underneath.
53. At times she feels contempt for me.
54. She understands me.
55. Sometimes I am more worthwhile in her eyes than I am at other times.
56. I have not felt she tries to hide anything from herself that she feels with me.
57. She is truly interested in *me*.
58. Her response to me is usually so fixed and automatic that I don't really get through to her.
59. I don't think that anything I say or do really changes the way she feels toward me.
60. What she says to me often gives a wrong impression of her whole thought or feeling at the time.
61. She feels deep affection for me.
62. When I am hurt or upset she can recognize my feelings exactly, without becoming upset herself.
63. What other people think of me does (or would, if she knew) affect the way she feels toward me.
64. I believe that she has feelings she does not tell me about that are causing difficulty in our relationship.[24]

Rating Scales of Empathy, Respect, and Genuineness

Perhaps the most widely used instruments for the measurement of the conditions of a facilitative interpersonal relationship are the rating scales

[24] Reproduced with the permission of G. T. Barrett-Lennard.

developed by Charles Truax and Robert Carkhuff. The early forms were 9-point scales.[25] The current forms of the scales consist of 5 levels.[26] In addition to the empathy, respect, and genuineness scales, other scales have been developed, but these three are of interest to us here.

The literature on the use of these scales in counseling or psychotherapy and related fields is voluminous. The evidence is clear that the scales are reliable measures of qualities that are related to positive outcomes in human relationships. Some of the studies using the scales with teachers were referred to in Chapter 7.

In a study by a doctoral student at the University of Illinois, the three scales were adapted to make them more applicable to the classroom situation.[27]

The scales as adapted follow. A C rating (level 3) is considered to be minimal for a facilitative teaching relationship.

Empathy

GENERAL. Do I feel he is likely to *understand me,* enter into my frame of reference?

A. I feel that the teacher senses where I am, what is going on inside me, something of what I am trying to say even *through* my poor expression of it. I feel he is here with me. He may not understand all that I am trying to say, but he is *with* me and understands *me.*

B. Somehow he seems to understand something of *why* I feel the way I do about things. I feel I don't have to explain or defend myself or my position to him.

C. (Voice quality and/or content or remarks may have indicated some acknowledgement of feelings expressed by the students, and some indication that he understood or was trying to understand.)

He picks up the fact that I have strong feelings about this, and that helps, but he doesn't go anywhere with this. I'm not turned off, but I'm not helped very much, either. He understands me a little, I feel, but I still feel some need to justify or explain myself, or my position to him.

---

[25] Charles B. Truax & Robert R. Carkhuff, *Toward Effective Counseling and Psychotherapy* (Chicago: Aldine, 1967).

[26] Robert R. Carkhuff, *Helping and Human Relations,* Vol. II. (New York: Holt, Rinehart & Winston, 1969).

[27] Robert R. Waggener, "The Effects of a Structured Group Experience on Teachers' Empathy, Regard, and Genuineness in the Classroom," Unpublished Doctoral Dissertation, University of Illinois, Urbana-Champaign, 1971.

D. (The teacher's own feelings, or his desire to be understood, keep him from listening to the *student*, although he may pick up *a little* of what the viewpoint or position or frame of reference is.)

He seems to be somewhat aware (at least not unaware) that I have feelings about this. I feel he is off track when he tries to tune in on them, though. He acts as though he might want to understand me, enter into my frame of reference, but if he tries he shows mostly that he doesn't know how, or that he has missed my point.

E. The teacher is not interested in hearing my position or my side of things. He doesn't understand and wouldn't understand. I've got to search for *his* frame of reference, explore *his* ideas. I feel he doesn't care whether this means anything to me or not. I would hate to go to him with a personal problem. I just don't think he would understand at all.

Respect

GENERAL. To what extent does the teacher see students as persons, respecting them for what they are rather than for their accomplishments or response to him? To what extent do you think a student would feel safe and respected in asking the teacher a question? In differing with him?

A. The teacher communicates such respect and acceptance for his students as persons that they feel safe in disagreeing with him or rejecting his position, or even him as a person without lowering their standing with him in any way. Even the timid would feel safe in asking questions.

B. Not only does the teacher see students as *persons*—not just as students—but he communicates the impression that they are *important* as persons. Their viewpoints are worthy of consideration even if the teacher doesn't understand them fully (he tries). He tends to show acceptance of the student even when the student disagrees. He doesn't, by his attempts to persuade the student, convey the impression that the student doesn't understand, or hasn't grasped what has been said, or that his remarks or questions may be off target *and therefore* that the student is wasting class time, etc. There is, however, some indication that the teacher responds a little more favorably to those students who show progress, who accept the teacher's viewpoint, or who respond favorably to the teacher as a person.

C. There is some indication that the teacher sees the students as persons, not just as students. There is some communication of respect and concern for the students, but there is also communicated the notion that the teacher feels some definite responsibility for the student ending up with the "right" position. There may be some impatience, for example, if the student persistently is unable to acknowledge or accept the teacher's viewpoint. When it comes to asking a question, the attitude of the student might well be, "I would just as soon not bother. I'm not sure it would be worth the trouble."

D. The teacher sees the students more in terms of information transaction than as persons, and therefore prizes the student who shows signs of accepting the teacher's position and/or the teacher as a person. There is an occasional glimmer (totally lacking in E) that the teacher sees the students as persons as well as students, but he tends to shy away from this, placing emphasis on the teacher-student relationship, on the task situation with these roles defined within it. When it comes to asking a question, the attitude of the student might well be, "I'd rather not. I don't think my question would be very welcome or accepted by the teacher. I would probably end up feeling foolish or uncomfortable after asking a question."

E. A total concentration on conveying information—or rather *dispensing* it and having it received in its unadulterated form—although the burden of receiving it properly may be placed entirely on the student. The students are important to the teacher only as objects of his effort to convey his material. When it comes to asking a question, the attitude of the student might well be, "No way!"

Genuineness

GENERAL. Being oneself, in this context, means being oneself in an intentional, open, sharing way. There is no attempt to misrepresent one's feelings or position. There is an awareness of where one is, of who one is, of what is going on inside, and of acceptance of these. The posture might be described as follows: "This is where I'm at. This is who I am. I may look foolish or proud to you or to me or to both, but this is the way it is with me now. I am not going to tell you something just because you send out cues that you need to hear it, and I am not necessarily going to tell you *all* that I feel now. But I am not going to dissimulate or play games or court pleasant responses. When we interact you will sense that you are in contact with the real me."

Do you feel comfortable with this teacher—that he is not trying to "con" you in any way (that he may not even recognize)? Is he *on the level?*

This does not necessarily entail going into one's history, talking *about* oneself.

A. The teacher is fully himself. His responses are very much "him"—spontaneous rather than "programmed," calculated, or carefully weighed. He is very comfortable with being himself and could accept pleasant or unpleasant responses from the students without embarrassment or defensiveness. He is willing to share his feelings and positions openly with the students if the occasion arises.

B. The teacher shares something of himself, his personal feelings and positions, with the students in a non-demanding way. There is no doubt that he means what he says. Not quite as much at ease with being himself, or as fully in touch with himself and his feelings, or as spontaneous as A.

C. Not the *suspicion* of role playing of D, but a hesitancy to reveal or commit or entrust himself *as a person* to these students. He does not *hide* within a professional role (D), but simply does not show much of himself.

D. The teacher does not necessarily seem insincere. The main point is that the teacher does not "lay himself on the line" to any extent. He dispenses information, fields questions, may be provocative, but there is that quality which arouses suspicion that he is living the *teacher* role, that he may not personally espouse what he is saying, even though academically he may submit or ascribe to it as something to be taught.

E. From the teacher's words and voice quality it seemed that he had inner feelings about his students that he was not acknowledging or expressing. He reacted as though he felt personally attacked in the face of questioning or disagreement. A teacher who was obviously insincere, or who was "playing up" to the student, would be operating at this level, also.

SUMMARY

In the last chapter we defined the nature of the conditions for learning and self-actualization—empathic understanding, respect or warmth, and genuineness. In this chapter we have attempted to indicate how the teacher can implement these conditions in relationships with students.

A basic requirement of any good relationship is that one listen to another. And, having listened, one responds in a way to indicate that one has listened and understood what the other is saying, or trying to say—what he is thinking and, especially, feeling. An interaction in which each listens and responds in this way is an encounter. Sometimes interactions are confrontations. In this case there is a conflict, and this must be worked through if a good relationship is to be established.

In any relationship, limits must be established. The problem of discipline is essentially the problem of establishing and enforcing limits. Some principles regarding the establishment of limits were discussed.

Expectations are powerful influences on behavior, which operate sometimes in subtle and unknown ways. It is important that teachers examine their expectations, which are related to their basic beliefs and attitudes. The humanistic teacher, who respects each person as an individual and recognizes the existence of unused potential in each student, expects the best. He avoids being influenced by stereotypes and the negative opinions of other teachers.

It is not possible to reduce human relationships to simple techniques which are to be automatically applied. A total relationship is a unique, individual thing, and each of us has his own style of relating to others. Yet it is possible to be objective about determining the degree to which the basic conditions of a good human relationship are present in an interaction, and a number of instruments have been developed for this purpose. Several of these are presented so that teachers and student teachers can examine themselves in terms of the specific items which comprise these instruments.

9 The Learner In The Process

For him [Holt] everyday teaching is what it should be: a process of mutual discovery, interaction, and exploration of the self as well as of another person and a subject matter.

—Allan Fromme, in Introduction to John Holt,
HOW CHILDREN FAIL *

In Chapter 1 we saw that a number of writers have noted that there is a change in many, if not most, children as they progress from the 1st to the 4th, 5th or 6th grade. We are now in a position to suggest an answer as to why this change occurs.

THE CHILD: A NATURAL LEARNER

In Chapter 3 we noted that early humanistic educators emphasized the natural desire of children to learn. Anyone who observes an infant or child will see that he is constantly active, engaged in exploration of himself and his environment. During most of his waking moments, the infant is exercising his physical capacities, and developing his potentials

* (New York: Pitman Publishing Corporation, 1964).

as he matures. Children learn to sit up, crawl, and walk, even without any formal teaching or instruction. They learn to walk, whether or not parents make any attempt to teach them.

The normal child is curious and interested in his environment. He needs no encouragement to explore it. He is responsive and persistent—there is no problem of motivation. As Skinner says, "No one asks how to motivate a baby. A baby naturally explores everything it can get at, unless restraining forces have been at work, and this tendency doesn't die out . . ." [1]

The child is by nature a learner, and is motivated to learn. This is a characteristic of life, of all living organisms except the very lowest species. In terms of the theory of behavior upon which this book is based, we can say, as in Chapter 2, that every human being strives for self-actualization or to develop his potentials. The process of doing so is called learning.

The humanistic view of man sees the child as an active, growing, creating, changing individual engaged in the search for adequacy or self-actualization. Since learning is the normal state of the organism, we do not need to teach in the sense of imposing or putting something on or into the child; the function of the teacher can be to offer the conditions and provide the resources for learning. In an appropriate environment, again, children learn by themselves. What we call play is in fact the principal means of learning before school age. Even the most significant learning of many older children occurs in play outside of school.

Infants and young children are constantly active, exploring their environment, attempting to organize, make sense out of, control and master it. They are open, receptive, and perceptive. They experiment. They are not afraid, discouraged, or hurt by mistakes. They are patient and persistent. They can tolerate uncertainty, confusion, ignorance, suspense, and failure because these are not felt to be bad but are simply stages in discovering their environments. Infants and young children are not yet, or not greatly, dependent on adult approval; they are not simply trying to please or appease adults. The rewards of their behavior are its natural consequences—the sense of achievement, the satisfaction of curiosity.

Holt observes:

> Nobody starts off stupid. You have only to watch babies and infants, and think seriously about what all of them learn and do, to see that, except for the most grossly retarded, they show a style of life, and a desire and ability to learn that in an older person we might well call genius. Hardly an adult in a thousand, or ten thousand, could in any three years of his life learn as much, grow as much in his understanding of the world around him, as every

[1] Reprinted with permission of the Macmillan Company from *Walden Two*, by B. F. Skinner. Copyright, B. F. Skinner, 1948.

infant learns and grows in his first three years. But what happens, as we get older, to this extraordinary capacity for learning and intellectual growth? [2]

WHY CHILDREN FAIL

Something does happen, something described in the quotation from George Leonard in Chapter 1. What it is, many writers have noted, must be related to the school environment.

In the first few years of school the curiosity, interest, enthusiasm and persistence in learning of many children are destroyed, and they become passive, silent, bored, and resistant. One need not detail the classroom behavior of children which indicates resistance to learning—every teacher is familiar with it, and the many recent books criticizing the schools portray it clearly. It is clear that for many children the major activities in school are getting through the day, "getting by," finding out what the teacher wants and giving it to him, getting the "right" answers by hook or by crook, and avoiding failure as much as possible. After a few years of doing this, these children can hardly remain normal or able to learn naturally.

There are of course many reasons entering into this failure of children in school, some of which do involve the particular characteristics of individual children, or others which are related to the practices considered in Chapter 6. But one general characteristic of the school pervades the whole—the atmosphere of threat; which is created and perpetuated by the practices followed in the school. The behavior of children in the classroom is the kind of behavior which results from threat and stress.

The general reaction to threat and stress is fear, and it is fear which permeates the behavior of many if not most children in our schools. Fear of failure, of being wrong, leads to the undesirable behaviors which interfere with and prevent *real* learning, which differs from what Holt calls *apparent* learning.[3] Apparent learning is rote learning, memorization, giving the right answers, giving back facts and information on tests. Children develop (what Holt calls) strategies to deal with the threatening requirement of giving the right answers. Both the "mumble strategy" and "going stupid," which were referred to in Chapter 6, are protective strategies. Holt describes why, "for some children, the strategy of weakness, of incompetence, of impotence, may be a good one. For, after all, if they (meaning we [the teachers]), know that you can't do anything, *they* won't expect you to do anything, and they won't blame you or punish

[2] John Holt, *How Children Fail* (New York: Pitman Publishing Corporation, 1964), p. 167.

[3] *Ibid.*, p. 104.

you for not being able to do what you have been told to do." [4] It is analogous to an animal "playing dead" in extreme fear or danger. Some students simply "turn off" and "tune out" when things get too difficult or boring, while others show the "panic" reaction, being literally unable to think, as we saw in the case of Boris as cited by Henry in Chapter 1. The behavior of most children in school is defensive or protective, and avoids trouble, embarrassment, punishment, disapproval, being wrong, or failure.

When children react in this way, what do teachers do? Failing to recognize their fear, or ignorant of the effects of threat and fear on behavior and learning, they increase the threat, and the result is greater fear. Holt, discussing how to deal with failing students, says, among other things, "Keep a steady and resolute pressure on them." [5] Yet, later, he writes: "After all I have said and written about the need for keeping children under pressure, I find myself coming to realize that what hampers their thinking, what drives them into their narrow and defensive strategies, is a feeling that they must please the grownups at all costs." [6] Borton also reports that the staff of a special summer program which pushed the students "sometimes had exactly the opposite effect from what we hoped for—we sometimes made kids more suspicious, dependent, and uneasy—rather than more open, independent, and confident." [7] It appears that even the best teachers, such as Holt and Borton, have been at times, if not frequently, threatening. This may be because students, on the basis of their experiences, are extremely sensitive to threat, and continually fearful. Holt notes that even in a special room period, where he did all he could to make the work nonthreatening, he was amazed that the children were hesitant to take a stand, constantly hedging, fence-straddling, afraid to commit themselves. [8] Noting the extent of fear in the school, he wonders why so little is said about it, or why it is not recognized, since the disastrous effects destroy learning and the desire to learn.

We must discuss two questions here before we turn to how children learn. First, "Aren't high expectations threatening, and therefore shouldn't we expect little of children to avoid threatening them?"

Herndon reports the advice he was given by an experienced teacher:

"Well, now, the first thing is, you don't ever push 'em, and you don't expect too much. If you do, they'll blow sky-high and you'll have one hell of a time getting them down again. May never do it. Now, its not their fault, we

---

[4] *Ibid.*, pp. 58–59.
[5] *Ibid.*, p. 6.
[6] *Ibid.*, pp. 17–18.
[7] From *Reach, Touch, and Teach* by Terry Borton. Copyright 1970 by McGraw-Hill, Inc., p. 69.
[8] *Op. cit.*, p. 48.

all know that. But you have to take them as they are, not as you and me would like them to be. That means, you find out what they can do, and you give it to them to do." [9]

Kozol was given the same advice again and again.[10]

But remember here the self-fulfilling prophecy from Chapter 8—if you expect little or nothing you get it.

Holt's statement in the quotation on pages 142–143 was stimulated by a girl whose surprisingly good performance on a spelling test left her anxious rather than pleased. He says that he "could almost hear the girl saying plaintively to herself, 'I suppose he's going to expect me to spell right all the time now and he'll probably give me heck when I don't.' "[11] Reactions like both the teacher's in Herndon and this student's occur in a general atmosphere of threat, punishment, emphasis on being right, and competition, rather than of acceptance and respect; where self-worth is tied almost exclusively to academic achievement, expectations are unreasonable, and perfection or near perfection is required. It occurs where adult approval, and external evaluation, rather than self-approval or self-evaluation, are emphasized. As Holt goes on to say, "Children who depend heavily on adult approval may decide that, if they can't have total success, their next best bet is to have total failure," and continues: "Perhaps, in using the giving or withholding of approval as a way of making children do what we want, we are helping to make these children deliberate failures."[12] Incompetence, however, not only reduces what others expect or demand of you, but also what you expect of yourself. It leads to a self-concept of failure.

Expecting much of children can be threatening and lead to problems when acceptance, respect, liking, or approval depend upon consistently high performance. If there is no leeway or allowance for mistakes without loss of the teacher's respect and liking, acceptance and respect are *conditional*, that is, they depend on the child's behavior, rather than *unconditional*, given to him as a person to be respected regardless of behavior. This is the problem of rewards and reinforcements, of the behavioristic approach, where behavior is controlled by external influences rather than by creating the conditions for internal control. More will be said about this approach later.

Much of the misbehavior of children is as well a testing of the teacher's liking and respect for them. They ask, "Does he really like *me*, regardless of what I do or how I perform?" This simply shows the need every-

[9] James Herndon, *The Way It Spozed to Be* © 1965, 1968 by James Herndon. Reprinted by permission of Simon and Schuster, p. 22.

[10] Jonathan Kozol, *Death at an Early Age* (Boston: Houghton Mifflin, 1967), (New York: Bantam Books, 1968).

[11] John Holt, *op. cit.,* p. 59.

[12] *Ibid.*

one has to feel liked and accepted for who one is, rather than for what one does. Love is unconditional, though it expects much. Though we may be disappointed when those we love fail to live up to our expectations, we continue to love them nevertheless. It is the essence of love that it is challenging without being threatening. Goethe stated it well: "If we take people as they are, we make them worse. If we treat them as if they were what they ought to be, we help them become what they are capable of becoming."

The second question is this: If the fear of failure is so devastating to learning, then shouldn't we create a situation where no child experiences failure? This question represents a confusion between fear of failure and actual failure. Failure could not be completely eliminated or avoided if we tried to, for life outside as well as inside the school is not devoid of failure. It is not the fact but the meaning of failure which is the problem. Failure is threatening because it means not simply that the student has made a mistake, or is unable to do a particular problem or task, but that *he is a total, complete, personal failure*. But failure is simply the inability to do something at a particular time and place, and need not have a negative connotation, or be something to which fault is attached. The infant and preschool child fails often and sometimes miserably, but his failures do not prevent him from learning, because they are not accompanied by derision, punishment, disgrace, shame, or loss of love and respect. We learn, it is often said, from our mistakes, but only if because of them we are not made to feel that we are no good, hopeless, unable to learn—in short, *a* failure.

When expectations, or demands, lead the child to feel inadequate, they threaten. When they lead to a feeling of adequacy, when the child feels he can meet the expectations, they challenge—provided also that a failure does not lead to loss or withdrawal of love and respect or the labelling of the child as a failure.

HOW CHILDREN LEARN

The question of why children learn has already been answered. Children learn because every individual has a natural propensity for it. Indeed, learning is the normal activity of life; failure to learn shows something has gone wrong. Paradoxically, the school, which is supposed to facilitate learning, in many instances destroys the child's natural learning tendency. What has gone wrong is that, rather than being exposed to conditions which facilitate learning, as described in Chapters 7 and 8, children have been exposed to threat and fear, conditions which destroy the ability to learn.

The solution might seem obvious—to substitute a humanistic approach to education for the current approach. If applied early and persistently enough, many children could be rescued from the condition created in them after just a few years of school. It will be difficult, as the experience of Herndon, Kozol, and Dennison indicates, and it may not be successful with every child, but before learning can occur, the natural propensity for learning must be restored where it is dead or dying. The humanistic approach to education offers the remedy for most of what is wrong with education today, by restoring the natural desire to learn where it has been dulled, and preserving it where it is still present.

This digression has been necessary as a prelude to considering how children learn, since so many children do not and cannot learn through no fault of their own. For learning to take place, we must presuppose and count on the presence of the normal drive to learn. Given this, we can then look at the process of learning.

First, learning or thinking takes place only, as Dewey says, in the presence of a relevant problem, that is, there must be a need to learn. In another sense, the normal external stimulus for learning is being faced with a problem which has some relevance to an individual, for we really learn only when we need to learn, or need to know something, to be able to do something. "Significant learning takes place when the subject matter is perceived by the student as having relevance for his own purposes." [13]

The basic problem of education in the school is that school is unreal and insulated from life, and presents children with problems which may be important and relevant to adults but which are unimportant and irrelevant to most children. Thus it is necessary to develop a curriculum which has relevance, and this is what some of the new and experimental schools have been experimenting with, with some success. The successful teacher is one who can make the curriculum meaningful to children, so that it faces them with real problems which can engage their interest and intelligence.

When real problems are involved, students are interested, even excited. Usually, though, such problems are not part of the lesson plan, or of the course of study, and teachers, regarding them as interruptions or digressions, cut off discussion, to "get back to the subject." Kozol reports his experiences in introducing poetry and art to which the children responded:

> The children are offered something new and something lively. They respond to it energetically and they are attentive and their attention does not waver. For the first time in a long while perhaps there is actually some real excitement and some growing and some thinking going on within that one small room. In each case, however, you are advised sooner or later that you

[13] Carl R. Rogers, *Freedom to Learn* (Columbus, Ohio: Merrill, 1969), p. 158.

are making a mistake. Your mistake, in fact, is to have impinged upon the standardized condescension on which the administration of the school is based.[14]

Kozol's mistake was that he had used a poem which was not "a Fourth Grade poem" but was scheduled for the sixth grade. Another mistake he made was to introduce the children to the "Ballad of the Landlord" by Langston Hughes, which they liked and learned and recited. A father of a white boy objected to the poem and Kozol was reprimanded by the principal because it was not in the official Course of Study. Immediately afterwards he was fired. It was denied that it was because of the poem, although it is mentioned in the legal opinion on his dismissal.

The problem of education is not to obtain and organize information and knowledge, that is, the curriculum, but to select materials which are meaningful to students in terms of their life experiences, or to help them to recognize the relevance and personal meaning in materials which are not, or do not appear to be, immediately relevant.

Second, it was emphasized in Chapter 6 that learning is the discovery of personal meaning; this, in a sense, makes teaching impossible, for only the student can discover personal meaning. This is why Rogers says: "Teaching, in my estimation, is a vastly over-rated function." [15] Emphasis on teaching nevertheless focuses on the teacher rather than the learner, on content, rather than process. Thus, "anything that can be taught to another is relatively inconsequential and has little or no significant influence on behavior. . . . The only learning which significantly influences behavior is self-discovered, self-appropriated learning. Such self-discovered learning, truth that has been personally appropriated and assimilated in experience, cannot be directly communicated to another." [16]

Exploration is the process by which meaning is discovered. This is the way the infant and young child learn about their environments. The learner must be and feel free, unrestricted, and unpressured. The common practices of the school, seen in Chapter 6, are not conducive to this. An atmosphere of threat and fear does not allow the student to explore freely, but a relevant problem plus the presence of the conditions for learning in the environment, including a humanistic teacher, do.

Bruner states that learning and problem solving depend upon the exploration of alternatives. He distinguishes three aspects of exploration. The first, *activation,* he considers a major condition. This involves the presence of some optimal level of uncertainty, which stimulates curiosity. "A cut-and-dried routine task provokes little exploration; one that is too

---

[14] *Op. cit.,* pp. 192–193.
[15] *Op. cit.,* p. 103.
[16] *Ibid.,* pp. 152–153.

uncertain may arouse confusion and anxiety [or threat], with the effect of reducing exploration." [17] Essentially, this is what we have described above as a relevant problem.

The second aspect, the *maintenance* of the process, "requires that the benefits from exploring alternatives exceed the risks involved. Learning something with the aid of an instructor should, if instruction is effective, be less dangerous or risky or painful than learning on one's own." (p. 44) Unfortunately, this is too often not the case in the school. Here the humanistic teacher can make a major contribution, by making it safe for the student to engage freely in a wide-ranging process of exploration, without restrictions, without criticism.

The third aspect, *direction,* according to Bruner, is two-fold: first, at least an approximate sense of the goal of the task, so that alternatives can be tested against it; and second, knowledge of the results or feedback from the testing of alternatives to the goal. Bruner feels that instruction should be better than spontaneous learning in providing such knowledge. Again, this may be questioned if learning is the development of personalized meanings. However, the instructor who is able to enter, through empathy, into the process of exploration with the student can be helpful here, and Holt's discussion of his work with children in mathematics illustrates this process very well.[18,19]

Is the exploration process the same as the inquiry or discovery method of teaching? This is a difficult question, because there are differences among methods which go by the name of inquiry or discovery. The application of the discovery method in mathematics has appeared to be useful. The student is lead through the steps necessary to develop mathematical principles. Some of Holt's illustrations of his work with students appear to use this method. Yet he writes:

> We must not fool ourselves, as for years I fooled myself, into thinking that guiding children to answers by carefully chosen leading questions is in any important respect different from just telling them the answers in the first place. Children who have been led up to answers by teacher's questions are later helpless unless they can remember the questions, or ask themselves the questions, and this is exactly what they cannot do. The only answer that

[17] Jerome S. Bruner, *Toward a Theory of Instruction* (New York: Norton, 1966), p. 43.

[18] John Holt, *op. cit.,* pp. 73–76; 83–85; 95–98; 103–107.

[19] *Ibid.,* pp. 73–129. One might question whether the process of exploration would be appropriate or necessary in arithmetic. Isn't it efficient simply to memorize the multiplication tables and the rules of addition, subtraction, multiplication and division? Holt clearly demonstrates that this is not sufficient, and that it does not lead to understanding the meaning of numbers and operations upon them which are necessary if arithmetical processes are to be used intelligently. Every teacher should read this account.

really sticks in a child's mind is the answer to a question that he asked or might ask of himself.[20]

Discovery methods may range from free, unguided search by the student for solutions to problems, to the guided approach that most teachers use, to highly guided approaches. Such highly guided approaches may appear faster and more efficient but they do not lead to real understanding and thus to retained knowledge, for the student is simply led to "discover" standard "right" answers. Students who know this, and are intent on getting the right answer, may feel considerable pressure and threat, so that their thinking may become disorganized or even paralyzed. This is especially true when the teacher is pushing and pulling for the right answer rather than going at the student's rate.

Skinner also points out another problem in using the discovery method in class. He asks:

> How are a few good students to be prevented from making all the discoveries? When that happens, other members of the class not only miss the excitement of discovery but are left to learn material presented in a slow and particularly confusing way.[21]

Even in free and unguided discovery, "the teacher arranges the environment in which discovery is to take place, he suggests lines of inquiry, he keeps the student within bounds. The important thing is that he should tell him nothing." [22] Skinner recognizes that since people learn without being taught, it would be desirable that more be learned this way, since what the student learns on his own is more likely to be remembered. The surprise and accomplishment of personal discovery is in itself reinforcing or rewarding.

> But discovery is no solution to the problems of education. A culture is no stronger than its capacity to transmit itself. It must impart an accumulation of skills, knowledge, and social and ethical practices to its new members. The institution of education is designed to serve this purpose. It is quite impossible for the student to discover for himself any substantial part of the wisdom of his culture, and no philosophy of education really proposes that he should. Great thinkers build upon the past. It is dangerous to suggest to the student that it is beneath his dignity to learn what others already know, that there is something ignoble (and even destructive of "rational powers") in memorizing facts, codes, formulae, or passages from literary works, and that to be admired he must think in original ways. It is equally dangerous to

[20] *Ibid.,* p. 119.
[21] B. F. Skinner, *The Technology of Teaching* (New York: Appleton-Century-Crofts, 1968), p. 111.
[22] *Ibid.,* p. 109.

forego teaching important facts and principles in order to give the student a chance to discover them for himself.[23]

Obviously, no person can by himself discover all the knowledge that exists, even following a highly guided discovery method in a class situation. Yet if this is the most effective method of learning there appears to be a dilemma. But the problem is not as great a one as it might appear. First, much of what is known is not important or relevant and does not have to be learned by everyone. Second, much learning occurs informally, without the learner being taught, as Skinner recognizes. Third, the use of discovery methods does not, as Skinner implies, mean that the student would ignore past thinkers and writers and never read. In fact, when students become interested and involved in a problem, often on their own, they use the discovery method without guidance and without realizing it, and do a tremendous amount of research and reading on their own.

The discovery method can be used to stimulate students to discover their own meanings. At the very least such methods involve students more actively than the lecture method, and at their best, when pressure and threat are absent, they can arouse curiosity, create a relevant problem, and encourage exploration by the student.

For Skinner, the most efficient method of teaching is through the application of the methods of operant conditioning. "Teaching," he says, "may be defined as an arrangement of contingencies of reinforcement under which behavior changes." [24] It is necessary at least briefly to examine this contention, which involves the use of computer assisted instruction, but the problem is a complex one, and cannot be dealt with adequately here. In Chapter 1 we considered the use of computer assisted instruction and indicated some of its implications for education, and we concluded that essentially its applications are limited and that its excessive use could lead to dehumanizing education.

There is no question about the effectiveness of the methods of conditioning and reinforcement in changing behavior, but questions arise about their usefulness in achieving the kinds of changes represented by the goal of humanistic education, as well as the possible consequences of their use in addition to achieving the specific objectives for which they are used.

There is no doubt that much of behavior is controlled by outside stimuli, which the success of the behavioristic approach to education shows. But the use of external rewards and reinforcements leads to continued and increasing dependence upon externals. It can be argued that it is desirable that the individual become less dependent on externals, and more self-

[23] *Ibid.,* p. 110.
[24] *Ibid.,* p. 113.

determining in his behavior. Skinner, as noted in Chapter 1, recognizes the desirability of the student moving toward these intrinsic rewards. Just how this transition is to occur is not clear.

Computer-assisted instruction, at least as it now exists, has predetermined goals, and predetermined "right" answers. It requires that experts choose these goals and answers, and so far the experts are the behaviorists themselves. As Resnick states it, "Programmed instruction is not interested in the teacher as stimulator of interest, role model, or evaluator of progress. It is interested in him as instructor, or controller of behavior. This means that programmed instruction is applicable only where we do in fact want to change behavior in a given direction." [25] Goodman questions who is "we", and what is the limitation to "want"? He says that "compulsory schooling, so far as it is programmed, is identical with compulsory training to the goals of the controllers of behavior," and asks for the constitutional justifications for such control by the behaviorists.[26] For there is no place for self-determined learning or free exploration, and instruction is prescribed:

> What the individual does must be prescribed in terms so narrow as to leave no room whatsoever for the exercise of individuality. The system simply cannot accommodate a student who wants to strike out on his own. If any number of students attempted to do so—if, for example, they decided to satisfy their curiosity about American history by reading everything they could find in their school or home or local public library instead of limiting themselves to the prepared programs, the whole system would break down! [27]

Again, computer-assisted instruction can efficiently teach arithmetical computation, and other content which can be memorized or learned by rote. But as Holt clearly demonstrates, ability to recite multiplication tables and to do computations may be present without any understanding of the processes involved.[28]

Goodman feels, with some justification, that operant conditioning is over-rated both as a method of controlling human behavior and of teaching. He says "It is extremely dubious that by controlled conditioning one *can* teach organically meaningful behavior. Rather, the attempt to control *prevents* learning." [29]

The behaviorists may reply that understanding could be taught by

[25] Lauren Resnick, "Programmed Instruction of Complex Skills," *Harvard Educational Review,* Fall, 1963. Quoted in Paul Goodman *Compulsory Mis-education and the Community of Scholars* (New York: Vintage Books, 1962), p. 81.

[26] *Ibid.,* pp. 84–85.

[27] Charles E. Silberman, *Crisis in the Classroom* (New York: Random House, 1970), p. 200.

[28] John Holt, *op. cit.*

[29] *Op. cit.,* p. 89.

teaching machines, and if exploratory behavior is desired, this can also be done. Possibly they are right, but it will be necessary to compare the results, on a long term basis, with the results obtained from the personal, humanistic approach to education. There is some evidence that programmed instruction is more effective than the lecture method, probably because the student is more active, and is required to make more responses than if he were a passive listener.

A major limitation of the behavioral approach is its refusal to be concerned with anything that can't be reduced to simple, objective, measurable variables. Its reduction of complex variables to simple, measurable, variables can leave out much of the significance of the complex behavior, and cannot be substituted for it. Silberman comments that "The weakness . . . of computer-assisted instruction is inherent in the behaviorist approach to education itself, with its insistence that the goals of education not only can, but should, be defined in precise behavioral terms. This insistence on behavioral definition of objectives, as Professor Lee J. Cronbach of Stanford points out, is a prescription for training and not for education. . . . 'The person who wants us to specify the acts the learner is to perform as a result of instruction is deluding himself when he talks of history, science, or other nonskill subjects,' Cronbach writes." [30]

Man is, as was noted in Chapter 5, a reactive being, and can be treated as such. To treat him *only* as a reactive being, as behavioristic approaches do, is to limit him to this level. A behavioristic approach leads to the dependence of behavior on external sources—the approval of others, or extrinsic rewards. We need to go beyond this stage of development to the stage of maturity where we are capable of determining our own behavior and of course assuming responsibility for it, in a word, to become fully human. It is probably necessary to go through a stage of being influenced by others so that we can learn to recognize and accept to a reasonable degree the demands of others, and of society, upon us. But the self-actualizing person, it will be remembered from Chapter 2, is to a degree autonomous, independent of culture and environment. He trusts his organism, as Rogers puts it, to arrive at the most satisfying, satisfactory course of behavior.[31]

Behavioristic methods may appear to be useful where intrinsic motivation for learning has been lost or destroyed. External reinforcers appear to be effective in stimulating learning in children who have no desire or "motivation" to learn. Goodman is impressed by the use of programming for remedial instruction of "academically retarded" children who

[30] Charles E. Silberman, *op. cit.*, pp. 201, 202.
[31] Carl R. Rogers, *On Becoming a Person* (Boston: Houghton Mifflin, 1961), p. 189.

have developed severe blocks to learning. "For youngsters who have lost all confidence in themselves, there is security in being able to take small steps entirely at their own pace and entirely by their own control of the machine." [32] But then it would appear that programmed instruction, or the behavioristic method in general, is useful in situations where we have destroyed the ability to learn in a free environment, and we must use contrived, controlled rewards to substitute for the natural desire to learn. It is only where we have made learning unpleasant that children must be bribed to learn, only where intrinsic motivation is lacking that extrinsic motivation must be created, and only where the material is irrelevant that repetition with rewards must be used. Free learning of relevant material requires few if any repetitions—much if not most of learning is one trial—or "insight"—learning.

Perhaps this rehabilitation could be an important use of programmed instruction, but only if, after he developed some feelings of confidence and adequacy, we were to provide a humanistic environment which would allow the child to continue to learn on his own. Certainly some provision should be made for absorbing the child in the regular curriculum, and to avoid an "addiction" or dependency on programmed instruction. Certainly if, as appears to be the case in many instances, the lack of humanistic teachers and a humanistic environment is an important factor in academic retardation, programmed instruction by itself is not the answer. The child must be given confidence in good humans.

Programmed instruction also has a place in a humanistically oriented education, in the way suggested by Rogers. The student who is engaged in self-initiated learning may discover that he needs certain skills, knowledge, or information. Programmed instruction can be an efficient way for him to obtain these. If he needs to know a language, algebra, or statistics, he can turn to programs which provide instruction when he needs them, and proceed at his own rate independently.

Behavioristic approaches can also be used to remedy discipline problems in the classroom so that a more favorable learning environment is created. Borton reports an illustration. A student described a classroom as follows:

"I entered a classroom in which eighteen children seemed to be devoting all their energies to massacring one another, destroying school equipment and breaking the sound barrier. They were not only oblivious to observers but did not acknowledge the existence of their teacher. The teacher could not prevent the children from disassembling desks, tearing up classmates' papers, hurling books across the room, and running around the halls at will.

[32] *Op. cit.,* p. 90.

I saw no evidence of friendship among the children. In fact, during one half-hour's observation each of the eighteen children was hit or kicked at least once, ten of the children being aggressors." [33]

With the help of Professors Michael Orme and Richard Purnell of Harvard, the teacher, Mrs. Gollub, "designed a more appealing curriculum and classroom setting and then set up a system of 'positive reinforcement' in which all undesirable behaviors of the students were ignored and desired ones were reinforced." Points were awarded which could be used for "buying" candy, puzzles, games, and trips to the zoo. The students were involved in determining the behaviors to be rewarded. The teacher was also liberal in praise and physical hugging. The behavior of the children changed markedly and quickly, so that the teacher was able to teach.

As in most such experiments, this one did not continue long enough to determine what would happen when the rewards were discontinued. Presumably other rewards for their behavior, such as better relationships among the students, with the teacher, and satisfaction in learning, would become effective in continuing the desired behavior. It should also be pointed out that the teacher provided praise and physical evidence of affection, which presumably showed her interest, concern, respect, and liking for the children. There is a real question about the effectiveness of impersonal rewards given in an impersonal manner.

There is no question about the desirability of maintaining an atmosphere conducive for learning in the classroom. The reports of Herndon, Kohl and Kozol indicate that, although they were to some extent successful in creating such an environment, it was a long, slow process and even then it was not ideal. Probably they would have been more successful if they had systematically attempted to apply the principles of reinforcement, a process which may here be viewed as nothing more than applying the principles of good discipline, or of common sense— the principles of consistency and persistence. The behaviorists have simply done what most teachers have been told they should do, in a more consistent and persistent manner than teachers usually do.

From the standpoint of the students, such a procedure creates a stable, consistent, trustworthy, or predictable environment. Such an environment leads to more stable, consistent and trustworthy behavior.

Finally, the relationship of the human conditions for learning and self-actualization to behavioristic principles deserves some mention. In a broad sense, the conditions may be considered as reinforcers. That is, empathic understanding, respect and warmth, and genuineness are the most powerful reinforcers of desirable human behavior. These conditions "reinforce"

[33] Terry Borton, *op. cit.,* p. 137.

exploration. They reinforce similar behavior in others. They thus "reinforce" self-initiated learning of the kind we are concerned with here, and self-actualizing behavior. But they are only effective, in the long run, when they are real, and sincere, and not contrived or applied as technique. The myths of the teacher described in Chapter 7 lead to teachers' attempts to use acceptance, liking, interest, and praise as techniques on the mistaken assumption that they must be manifested at all times.

Viewing the conditions as reinforcers, however, poses a problem. Though reinforcers are conditional upon the behavior of the student, yet we have said that love (the epitome of the conditions) is unconditional. Perhaps there must be a minimal level of unconditional love and acceptance, beyond which students evoke higher levels when they function at higher levels themselves. One may perhaps also look at it in reverse. The level of love and respect must in general be high, but can fall when the loved one disappoints us or fails to live up to our expectations. This is an undesirable situation, analogous to punishment. If the teacher manifests the conditions for facilitating learning, he becomes a significant person in the student's life, and the student is concerned about how he affects the teacher. He wants to deserve and retain his respect, understanding, and liking. Finally, as indicated in Chapter 7, there is a distinction between accepting and liking a *person* and approving and liking his *behavior*. Thus the level of the conditions offered does not vary, greatly at least, with the student's behavior, but the teacher can make clear his attitudes toward the student's behavior. Thus the principles of reinforcement may not be as applicable to the basic conditions or attitude of the teacher to the student as a person, as to attitudes toward specific behaviors. Nevertheless, the student's behavior may to some extent affect the basic attitudes—the teacher may be puzzled, disappointed, or shocked at some student's behavior, and may say, and feel, "I don't understand you." In addition, persistent behavior unacceptable or ununderstandable to the teacher can lead to a lowering of empathic understanding, liking, and respect.

In short, the principles of reinforcement apply to human relations, but in a complex manner which is not yet completely understood. Any influence of the behavior of one person on another cannot be divorced from the relationship the persons have with each other.

LEARNING AND THE SELF-CONCEPT

Personally relevant material involves the self, and has implications for the self-concept. The self-concept may be defined as the way in which a person views or perceives himself—his attitudes, beliefs and feelings, and expectations about himself. The perceptions one has of oneself are not neutral or valueless: the self, and its various aspects, are viewed as good or bad, adequate or inadequate.

In Chapter 5 it was stated that the self is the center or focus about which the individual organizes his perceptions, the center of his world. The relationship of subject matter to the self determines its relevance, and it is the source of personal meaning. The self-concept determines how a person perceives things, what meaning they have, and thus how they influence his behavior. The self-concept is the major determiner of behavior. Although individuals react to stimuli in their environment, they react to *their perceptions* of the objective stimulus, and the same objective stimulus can lead to different behaviors in different people and in the same person at different times. What will challenge one is a threat to another. The person who feels inadequate is easily threatened, in fact his world is a threatening place to live in. The Coleman report indicated that certain characteristics of children are more important than school facilities for academic achievement. A core factor is the extent to which an individual feels he has some control over his own destiny, which is an aspect of the self-concept.[34]

Since the self-concept operates selectively, people tend to see what is consistent with their existing self-concept. Thus there is a circular effect: people who believe they are failures believe they can't, and then don't, succeed, or even if they do, since they can't believe it, they deny that they have succeeded. Success breeds success; failure breeds failure.

Thus the self-concept is resistant to change, and tends to perpetuate itself. We have considered the conditions for changing the self-concept in Chapter 5. These are the conditions necessary for learning—*real learning involves a change in the self*. One of them is an experience which is relevant to, or involves the self. Subject matter which is relevant, for example, does involve the self. Things consistent with the self-concept are easily absorbed, but they do not lead to change, for there is no problem, or challenge. When the individual is open to learning, when his natural curiosity and exploration has not been killed, however, the individual is searching for new experiences, for ways to enhance himself, to satisfy the need for using his potential, or actualizing himself. Thus he is open to new stimuli, ready to explore them, and to incorporate new experiences into a constantly changing self. Learning is pleasurable, enjoyable. Rogers compares two students taking a course in statistics. One is not interested, and is taking it only because it is required. The other is doing research for which statistics is necessary. He learns more

---

[34] James S. Coleman, et al., *Equality of Educational Opportunity* (Washington, D.C.: U.S. Government Printing Office, 1966).

easily and rapidly than the first student.[35] And his learning is pleasurable, for all learning is not necessarily painful. Change can be either challenging or threatening. The new can be either exciting or fearful. Learning, which is new, and change, can be either pleasant or painful. Which it is depends both upon the state of the learner and the nature of his environment, including the teacher.

Thus learning may be painful, for there is a resistance to change, which in itself is often painful. Learning which involves a basic change in one's self-concept is especially difficult and painful, and experiences and perceptions which are inconsistent with the self-concept are threatening. It is here that the humanistic teacher can be an important, even an essential, factor in facilitating learning. Where the student is threatened by the implications of perceptions and experience for the self-concept, further threat from the teacher can prevent any learning from occurring. But if threat from the environment, from the teacher, is minimal or reduced, the student's learning is facilitated. The humanistic conditions are not in themselves threatening, nor do they add to the threat the student perceives in the materials or experiences. Where the student does not feel that the respect, interest, and liking of the teacher are dependent on his performance, he is free from the threat of their loss. The learner must have some security before he can risk change.

The self is, then, involved in all meaningful learning. Perhaps the most important thing a teacher can do for a child is to so change his self-concept that he feels he is somebody, a respected person, of worth, who is adequate rather than inadequate, and not a failure as a person. A positive self-concept, and a positive change in the self-concept, makes learning more likely to occur, since the student isn't so easily threatened, and is better able to risk the changes required by learning. A study in New South Wales found that teachers varied in their sensitivities to children's self-concepts, and that children of those teachers who were more sensitive showed evidence of greater growth. This was true whether or not the teacher was consciously concerned about their self-concepts. Thus, whether he is aware of it or not, the teacher affects the self-concepts of children.[36]

Combs, Avila and Purkey write:

> When everything in a child's life outside of school is teaching him that he is unliked, unwanted, and unable, a loving teacher, skilled in providing ex-

[35] Carl R. Rogers, *Freedom to Learn, op. cit.,* p. 158.

[36] J. W. Staines, "The Self-Picture as a Factor in the Classroom," *British Journal of Educational Psychology,* 1958, 28, 97–111. Cited in Arthur W. Combs, Donald L. Avila & William W. Purkey, *Helping Relationships: Basic Concepts for the Helping Professions* (Boston: Allyn & Bacon, 1970), pp. 55–56.

periences of success, may make a world of difference. She may not be able to turn the tide of events completely. If she does no more than help such a child keep his head above water, however, the effort expended is surely not wasted. Teachers rarely get credit for this kind of help, but it probably occurs with far more frequency than any of us realize.[37]

SUMMARY

This chapter has been concerned with the child as learner and with the learning process. The evidence is that the infant and young child are natural learners, yet too many children no longer show this natural tendency after a few years of school. A consideration of why children fail indicates that a major reason is fear, fear of failure.

We next turned to an examination of how children learn. Learning begins with a relevant problem. The learning process is essentially a process of exploration leading to discovery of personal meaning. The function of the teacher is to facilitate this process, not to direct or control it toward predetermined ends or answers.

Since learning is a matter of discovering personal meanings, the self is involved in any real learning. The self-concept is central to learning since it determines what is perceived as relevant, it determines the learner's openness to learning in terms of feelings of being adequate or inadequate, a success or a failure, since real learning leads to changes in the self and self-concept.

The involvement of the self in learning makes clear the importance of the environment of the classroom, and of the teacher as a person, for learning. Exploration and changes in the self are only possible when the student feels secure, accepted, respected, and not under threat or fearful. The importance of the characteristics of the humanistic teacher for learning is thus clearly apparent.

[37] *Ibid.*, p. 59.

10 Learning To Feel: Affective Education

*In most schools today, curriculum is based more
on the requirement of the various subject disciplines
than on other needs. Rarely is curriculum designed
to help the student deal in personal terms with the
problems of human conduct.*

—Gerald Weinstein and Mario D. Fantini, TOWARD
HUMANISTIC EDUCATION: A CURRICULUM OF AFFECT*

In Chapter 2 we contended that the ultimate goal of education is the production of self-actualizing persons. Such persons can not only think, but feel; they not only have the knowledge necessary to function in today's world, but are able to relate to and live with other persons. They are concerned not only with scientific or technological problems, but with the problems of human relationships.

As Rome divided Gaul into three parts, so did early psychology divide all human experience into cognition, emotion, and conation (striving). We now realize that experience cannot be divided, for every experience, and all behavior, partakes of all three aspects. Yet we assume we can educate and develop the intellect apart from feelings and emotions! While we recognize attitudes, values and feelings as important in behavior and in being a good citizen and member of society, we value intellectual and

* (New York: Praeger, 1970), p. 17. Reprinted by permission.

cognitive development more in providing only for it in our school system. We assume that affective development can proceed with no formal education, or with the family and the church responsible for fostering its development. Our educational system, as our society, has had reason enshrined as our God.

Nevertheless we are feeling as well as thinking beings, and reason is often—perhaps usually—the servant of feeling and emotion. We are rationalizing rather than rational beings, then. And it is not undesirable that reason serve emotion. Reason must be directed by values and feelings, or otherwise it can be inhuman, as it often is. The effort to eliminate emotion from our lives, or relegate it to a back seat, is responsible for many of our human problems today.

The limitation of a one-sided intellectual or rational approach to man has been recognized by psychologists who are called, and call themselves, humanistic. (This approach is also sometimes called the Third Force psychology, the first being psychoanalytic psychology, the second behaviorism.) The writings of these psychologists have provided a basis for a humanistic approach to education.

During the past twenty years, however, the major concern in education has been curriculum reform, with the curriculum limited to the cognitive area. Some of the best minds in mathematics, and the physical and social sciences have been recruited for this endeavor. This difficult task has not led to entirely acceptable results, for curriculum reform, as noted in Chapter 6, has not faced the problems of the acceptance of the curriculum by teachers nor its relevance or appropriateness to the children for whom it is intended. Both of these problems involve feelings and attitudes. But tremendous resources of money and time have been poured into curriculum revision.

Little if any attention has been given or money spent on the major problem, for though we face difficult scientific and technical problems in society, our greatest problem is that of living together in peace, of creating a society which produces self-actualizing persons. Yet we have made no concerted effort to educate people in how to live together, how to understand, respect, and love each other. While some lip service has been given to this as an education objective, almost nothing has been done to implement it. There has been a lot of talk about educating for citizenship and for democratic living, but the goal of developing better humans and better citizens is a distant one for the schools—the curriculum stops at subject matter achievement. It is vaguely hoped that this will lead to the ultimate goal. But the result, as judged by the adults who are the products of our schools, is a dismal failure. The purely cognitive approach to the development of democratic attitudes and human values is not effective.

THE GENERAL NATURE AND PURPOSES
OF AFFECTIVE EDUCATION

Feelings must be integrated with cognitive learning. This has been the burden of this book so far. But we must go beyond this and directly foster the affective and emotional development of the student, and his ability, which involves feelings, to function adequately in interpersonal relationships. "The fact is, the intellect divorced from feelings is empty and meaningless. An education that is to be effective in preparing a child for life must take into account emotional as well as mental development." [1] Otherwise, we will continue to produce what Lyon calls "the intellectual half man."

Man is a sensing, feeling, thinking, and acting being. Our present society and its system of education lead not only to fragmention of the individual, but to neglect and underdevelopment of sensing and feeling. It is the purpose of affective education to redress this imbalance, so that we can produce whole, integrated, self-actualizing persons.

In the early 1950's a group of psychologists and educators became interested in developing a classification system of educational objectives. They divided objectives into three broad areas or realms: the cognitive, the affective and the psychomotor. In 1956 the results of work in the first area were published.[2]

In 1964 the second volume on affective goals was published.[3] An outline of the taxonomy of affective objectives follows.

1.0 *Receiving (Attending)*. This level is concerned with sensitization to the existence of phenomena or stimuli.

1.1 Awareness. This is the first level of receiving—the consciousness of something.

1.2 Willingness to Receive. This level is the willingness to tolerate a stimulus rather than to avoid it. It is a listening, tolerance of differences, sensitivity to social problems.

1.3 Controlled or Selected Attention. At this level there is a focusing, with differentiation into figure and ground.

2.0 *Responding*. This level goes beyond passive acceptance, to an involvement with or interest in a subject, phenomenon or activity.

[1] Harold C. Lyon, *Learning to Feel—Feeling to Learn* (Columbus, Ohio: Merrill, 1971), p. 18.

[2] Benjamin S. Bloom, Max D. Englehart, Edward J. Furst, Walker H. Hill, & David R. Krathwohl, *Taxonomy of Educational Objectives, Handbook I: Cognitive Domain* (New York: David McKay, 1956).

[3] David R. Krathwohl, Benjamin S. Bloom, & B. B. Musia, *Taxonomy of Educational Objectives, Handbook II: Affective Domain* (New York: David McKay, 1964).

2.1 Acquiescence in Responding. At this level the individual complies with rather than initiates a response.

2.2 Willingness to Respond. Here there is a voluntary response.

2.3 Satisfaction in Response. At this level responding behavior is accompanied by feelings of pleasure, satisfaction or enjoyment.

3.0 *Valuing.* At this level behavior takes on the characteristics of a belief or an attitude.

3.1 Acceptance of a Value. This is the level of tentative acceptance of a value or belief.

3.2 Preference for a Value. Here the individual desires or seeks out a value.

3.3 Commitment. At this level there is a conviction or certainty about one's values or beliefs.

4.0 *Organization.* This consists of the development of a value system.

4.1 Conceptualization of a Value. At this level a quality of abstraction or conceptualization is added.

4.2 Organization of a Value System. At this level values are integrated into an ordered relationship, ideally internally consistent and harmonious, in effect a philosophy of life.

5.0 *Characterization by a Value or Value Complex.* Here the individual acts consistently and without emotional disturbance in terms of his value system.

5.1 Generalized Set. At this stage there is a basic orientation which enables the individual to reduce and order the complex world and to act consistently and effectively.

5.2 Characterization. The final level in the hierarchy is the characterization of the individual by a consistent, internalized philosophy of life.[4]

We see that this taxonomy is concerned with the stages in the development, or internalization, of values, attitudes, or beliefs. Perhaps because it is concerned with only a limited part of personal or emotional development, it has not been utilized by writers in the field or at least mentioned or referred to in the literature of affective education.

Affective education is broader than this. The development of the self is its concern, though attitudes and values are indeed an important part. The work of Krathwohl and his associates, while ostensibly concerned with the affective domain, neglects the development of the self and the role of feelings and emotion in the development of values and a philosophy of life, and intellectualizes the process.

Affective education is concerned with the development of self-awareness. This development requires first that the individual be permitted and be able to express and disclose himself, so that he can see or perceive himself as he is. This requires that he feel free to be himself, to be open and honest, in his expression of himself. Second, the individual must be able to explore, look at, and evaluate himself. Part of this process includes

---

[4] *Ibid.,* pp. 176–185.

feedback from others on how he is perceived by them. These two processes lead to self-awareness, to the development of a self-concept realistic because the individual's perceptions of himself are not greatly inconsistent with the perceptions of others. Finally, if or where the self-concept is inconsistent with what one wants to be, with one's self-ideal, the individual can attempt to change himself, to become more what he wants to be or is capable of being, to develop a positive self-concept.

Affective education is also concerned with developing the awareness of others, exploration in interpersonal relationships and the fostering of good interpersonal relationships characterized by empathic understanding, respect and warmth, and genuineness.

These two areas of concern represent the affective component of an education whose objective is the development of self-actualizing persons.

There are three major approaches to affective education, which will be considered in turn: (1) modeling; (2) didactic instruction, (a) indirect and (b) direct; and (3) experiential learning. The first two will be treated in the remainder of this chapter, and the third will be dealt with in the next chapter.

MODELING

So far we have emphasized the importance of empathic understanding, respect, and genuineness in facilitating subject matter or cognitive exploration and learning. They also lead to the learning of empathy, respect, and genuineness in those who are exposed to these conditions. We have mentioned this incidentally as occurring through the principle of reciprocal affect, which operates through the process of modeling.

Currently modeling is claimed as a behavioristic method, and though it is true that, for use in changing or modifying behavior, behavioristically oriented psychologists have developed or made adaptations of it, the behaviorists did not develop or discover modeling. Conscious and unconscious modeling and imitation were the earliest ways of teaching and learning; indeed they constituted education in primitive societies. Bandura and Walters quote the anthropologist Reichard who says that in many languages "the word for 'teach' is the same as the word for 'show'." [5] Even in our society today a great deal of learning, particularly at the preschool level, takes place through imitation of models. The importance of this kind of learning has been underestimated.

Learning through a model is usually acquired as a whole or total pat-

[5] Gladys A. Reichard, "Social Life," in Franz Boas (Ed.) *General Anthropology* (Boston: Heath, 1938), pp. 409–486. Quoted in Albert Bandura & Richard H. Walters, *Social Learning and Personality Development* (New York: Holt, Rinehart & Winston, 1963), p. 47.

tern, rather than on a piece-by-piece process as in the case in reinforcement (or rewarded) learning, and is thus more efficient than part learning through reinforcement. In addition, it is not explainable through reinforcement since learning occurs often in one trial and the response can be a new or novel one not previously in the learner's repertoire. It is true, however, that the consequences that may occur to the model as a result of the behavior he exhibits influence the behavior's acquisition by an observer. Thus children who see a teacher punished or criticized (e.g., by an administrator) for humanistic behavior toward others may be inhibited from expressing such behavior. "In addition, models who are rewarding, prestigeful, or competent, who possess high status, and who have control over rewarding resources are more readily imitated than models who lack these qualities." [6] Teachers, as well as parents, meet these standards or criteria.

Since modeling allows for learning of complex patterns of behavior as wholes, and is particularly effective in the learning of social behaviors, it is a preferred method for the kind of learning we are here concerned with. Some behaviorists have attempted to break such behaviors down into their elements or components, and to teach these separate elements, often by means of reinforcement. This can result in a long, laborious process, and creates the problem of putting the elements together again, which may be similar to putting Humpty-Dumpty together again after his fall. But, as Bandura notes:

> Fortunately, for reasons of survival and efficiency most social learning does not proceed in the manner described above [gradual shaping through reinforcement]. In laboratory investigations of learning processes experimenters usually arrange comparatively benign environments in which errors will not produce fatal consequences for the organism. In contrast, natural settings are loaded with potentially lethal consequences that unmercifully befall anyone who makes hazardous errors. For this reason it would be exceedingly injudicious to rely primarily on trial-and-error and successive approximation methods in teaching children to swim, adolescents to drive automobiles, or adults to master complex occupational and social tasks. . . . Apart from the question of survival, it is doubtful if many classes of responses would ever be acquired if social training proceeded solely by the method of approximations through differential reinforcement of emitted responses. . . . In cases involving intricate patterns of behavior, modeling is an indispensable aspect of learning.[7]

Modeling is thus a widespread and powerful method of teaching and learning. Its effectiveness is recognized in numerous clichés, folk sayings,

---

[6] Albert Bandura & Richard H. Walters, *ibid.*, p. 107.
[7] Albert Bandura. *Principles of Behavior Modification* (New York: Holt, Rinehart & Winston, 1969), pp. 143–144.

and in common sense observations. It influences the myths of the good teacher discussed in Chapter 8, and the high social standards demanded of teachers, for we want our teachers to be "good examples" for children. It is particularly useful for teaching the complex aspects of social behavior represented by empathy, respect, and genuineness, since it is difficult if not impossible to teach these in the usual sense, or entirely didactically, although, as we shall see, efforts are being made to do so. The most effective way in which a teacher can teach understanding, respect and warmth, and genuineness is to be empathic, respecting, warm, and real.

Michael, discussing the teaching of styles of life, actualization, the enlargement of the self, and the avoidance of alienation, writes:

> The only way a teacher can teach these things is to *be* these things. You cannot exhort the student to do it; *you have to be it.* You have to be a model. . . . the only way to "teach actualization" is to be people who are courageous enough, trusting enough, compassionate enough, sympathetic enough, to be vigorously and openly involved in the whole world and to carry that involvement into the teaching environment.[8]

Modeling may not be the only way, but it is probably the most effective way, especially if combined with some explanation. If a teacher is not the kind of person he is trying to teach students to be, no matter what he does, he cannot teach this. But he will teach whatever he is, whether he is aware of it or intends to or not.

This is the problem of much of the education in attitudes and values. The principles of democracy are taught in a classroom and a school which are anything but democratic. No wonder students don't learn democracy and respect for others. Borton reports that, at the end of a summer teaching in a special program,

> It became evident that neither I nor the other members of the staff were using the principles we were trying to instill in our students. . . . It is as though we teachers have become so accustomed to teaching irrelevant curricula that we can hardly believe it is possible to teach material which actually could make a difference—not only to our students' lives, but to our own. Once that realization comes, once a teacher is growing because of his own efforts, . . . he . . . will serve as the same example for his students that the math teacher's expert knowledge provides for his young mathematicians.[9]

[8] Donald Michael, "Tomorrow's Sources of Actualization and Alienation," In Robert R. Leeper (Ed.) *Humanizing Education: the Person in the Process.* (Washington, D. C.: Association for Supervision and Curriculum and Development, National Education Association, 1967), p. 40.

[9] Terry Borton, *Reach, Touch, and Teach* (New York: McGraw-Hill, 1970), p. 175.

In short, the teacher will have become a self-actualizing person, and, being such, will by example help his students develop as self-actualizing persons.

INDIRECT AND DIRECT TEACHING OF
FEELING AND HUMAN RELATIONS

Humanization Through the Curriculum

Humanizing education doesn't require that we throw the present curriculum out entirely and replace it with one completely different devoted to affect and human relations. However, we can't take the opposite view that we can *only* operate with the current curriculum, and limit ourselves to working with students through it. I do not, therefore, agree with Wilhelms, who says: "if we cannot help them with their human becoming in every one of the subjects they are taking, each in its appropriate way, we are not going to help them very much. . . . Most of what we call humanization has to be the long accretion of subtle influences built right into the curriculum." [10] It is true, of course, as Wilhelms goes on to say, that "wholesome human qualities . . . are not going to emerge somewhere else from some extraordinary miracle." That is why we have to include them directly in the curriculum as well as use the existing curriculum to teach them indirectly. And Wilhelms is right in emphasizing that the curriculum must be used to humanize students, and, regarding a subject that contains (it might be argued) no such possibilities, he asks: "What is it doing in the curriculum in the first place?" [11]

To the objection that it is difficult to find subject matter which produces knowledge, skill, and also can be used to teach humanization, Wilhelms contends that it is abundant. The problem is to select out of the vast materials of the sciences, the humanities, mathematics, etc., those elements which have the greatest potential to promote human development. But the teacher must also actually exploit the materials. Wilhelms talks about an English teacher who looks at themes not simply in terms of grammatical exercises, but at what they say, and uses them to understand students, and to encourage creative expression and honest communication. Thus the English curriculum can be used "to teach each young person to be sensitive to his own ideas and feelings, to listen to them, and to honor them. It has become part of the curriculum to teach that all com-

---

[10] Fred T. Wilhelms, *Humanization via the Curriculum* In Robert R. Leeper, *op. cit.*, pp. 21, 24.
[11] *Ibid.*, p. 21.

munication rests on honesty and sensitivity and the courage to be one's self, out in the open." [12]

As Wilhelms notes, this is essentially what liberal education, the approach of the classical humanists we saw in Chapter 2, was designed to do. Subject matter was conceived of as a medium for personal development. But it now has become an end in itself, important only for its content.

The recent new curriculums in the physical and social sciences and in mathematics did not use Wilhelms' criterion of potential to promote human development in the selection of content. Whether because of this lack, or for other reasons, no one appears to have attempted to exploit the social studies curriculum for the education of feelings and emotions.

There have been a number of attempts to introduce affect into education through the curriculum. Lyon describes in summary form some of these,[13] but most of them have been limited, providing illustrations rather than full scale programs of affective education. Three attempts which are rather extensive deserve consideration.

In the first attempt, Richard Jones, taking Bruner, the developer of the first course, to task for his highly cognitive orientation in the course,[14] illustrates how the emotions aroused by a fifth-grade social studies course entitled "Man: A Course of Study" can be utilized educationally, or for the emotional development of the students.

The course does deal with human development:

> The content of the course is man: his nature as a species, the forces that shaped and continue to shape his humanity. Three questions recur throughout:
> What is human about human beings?
> How did they get that way?
> How can they be made more so? [15]

The potential for relating the social studies to human development is greater than, say for mathematics. Any and all subject matter has such potential, and it is clear in the materials in "Man: A Course of Study." But this potential must be exploited, and the teacher should be helped in doing this. Moreover, the potential is for more than a cognitive, intellectual understanding of the development of man. The feelings and emotions the materials arouse in children should not and cannot be ignored, but many teachers will not be aware of them unless they are prepared for

[12] *Ibid.,* p. 24.
[13] *Op. cit.*
[14] Richard M. Jones, *Fantasy and Feeling in Education* (New York: New York University Press, 1968), (Also Harper & Row Torchbooks).
[15] *Ibid.,* p. 12.

and sensitized to their occurrence. The feelings—human feelings about the behavior and experiences of other human beings—are a source for affective learning and development.

Jones first shows the potential and the failure to use it. Twenty-five fifth grade children were studying the unit on the Netsilik Eskimo. After three weeks they have begun to show signs of empathizing with the Netsilik, the unique problems they faced, and the unique solutions they found. They are then shown a color film of Netsilik men hunting the ringed seal, while the women and children wait in their igloos. The children are told that they are to observe the film with these questions in mind: What must the Netsilik (1) know (2) do and (3) use, in order to (1) find (2) kill and (3) retrieve a seal?

Jones, who was observing the lesson, made the following notes:

1) *Re* nakedness of male baby playing in igloo with mother and grand-mother: children are agape; not sure they are supposed to see this.

2) *Re* breast feeding scene: girls whisper inaudible secrets to each other.

3) *Re* mother giving fish eye to baby (who eagerly swallows it): children moan, groan, squirm.

4) *Re* baby pushing grandmother off balance, grandmother laughingly hitting head against wall of ice: children delighted.

5) *Re* blood-filled breathing hole after spearing of seal and matter-of-fact skuring of the nostrils, and labored pulling of dead seal out of red hole in white ice: children audibly distressed, look to teacher as if to say: do you really mean for us to see this? Child: "Does it have to be so bloody?" Teacher: "That's part of hunting. Pay attention." (Child reassured, screws up courage, and looks—proudly.)

6) *Re* men cutting and eating raw meat: "Ugh!" [16]

Jones then reports some of the comments of the master teacher (Mr. Koeller), assistant teacher, subject matter specialist, psychologist (Jones) and a psychometrist:

Master Teacher: "It was a ball! They didn't want to, but they used their heads. What I liked was the din of learning in the room, not only about Netsilik technology but about how to think."

Assistant Teacher: "And at the end they were loving it!"

Assistant Teacher: "They resisted seeing the film a second time ('Oh, all that blood again') but they seemed disappointed when you stopped it in the middle. Is it that they're repulsed or fascinated by the gory parts?"

Master Teacher: "The gory parts didn't get in the way. I wanted them to think—not feel."

[16] *Ibid.,* p. 16.

Assistant Teacher: "God, that bloody hole!"

Unit Coordinator: "Well, what do we say to ESI? The film serves the purpose at this point, I think, and it can be shown again when we get into the family. They seemed to want to talk about the baby and they finally got to see a live grandmother."

Assistant Teacher: "That's all very well, but I was thinking during the film that I'd lose them. Their stomachs were really turning during the gory parts. Mr. Koeller was so involved in the hunting techniques, and he got the kids so involved, that they got over their revulsions, but I'm not sure I could ever do it. I'd have had mayhem on my hands and been thinking more of classroom management problems than of cognitive skills and how to use the chart."

Subject Matter Specialist: "No doubt they learned a lot about tool use and that's what we set out to teach them, but I too find myself thinking about all that emotional hubbub during the film. They were visibly disturbed at many points. You got them over it and back to the lesson nicely, but wasn't there an awful lot being bypassed? Was that good or bad? What does the psychologist say?"

Psychologist: "They learned a lot about technology. On that we're agreed. And they had a good exercise of the cognitive skills involved in concept attainment: focused observation, identification, categorization, classification, generalization, analytical thought, objectivity, and the rest. Good. They also had a healthy exercise in the emotional skills necessary to support such cognitive activities: control, containment, postponement."

Master Teacher: "That's right. The kids aren't so finicky that they can't look at the world as it really is if you give them a good reason and hold them to it."

Psychologist: "From which I gather we are about to heave a sigh of relief that 'the gory parts' and the attendant images didn't obtrude on the lesson, and let it go at that?"

Assistant Teacher: "Isn't that enough?"

Psychologist: "Is it enough to put your money in the bank? Don't you want to remember which bank, so you can collect the interest? Tomorrow, or next week, or next month we're going to want these children to exercise another kind of cognitive skill, to think not only analytically and objectively, with an eye to solving the problems we pose for them, but to think intuitively and subjectively with an eye to posing problems for themselves. And for that we are going to want them to indulge their imaginations, their off-beat thoughts, a different order of cognitive skill presuming different orders of emotional skill: expression, sharing, use. We've prepared them for that by teaching them control. So far so good. People can't express, share, or use emotions that they can't control. But we're only halfway there, and if we forget where we helped them to leave their emotions we shouldn't be surprised if later they can't find the images that went with those emotions."

Psychometrist: "Are you suggesting we take time out to conduct a group therapy session?"

Psychologist: "I'm suggesting we remember where Mr. Koeller directed these children to stow their imaginations this morning: in their well-contained emotional reactions to the sight of a baby's penis, a bloody hole, and the swallowing of an eye. When we want them to think sensitively and with feeling, whether in respect to mythology or child rearing practices or what have you, we needn't devise any special new hardware. We need only provide relevant ways for them to share what they obviously put away for safe keeping this morning." [17]

It is obvious that the deep potential of the lesson, and of the film, for affective education was entirely and deliberately sacrificed to cognitive learning. Indeed, the emotional reactions of the children were considered to be not only irrelevant but an *interference* and thus ignored and suppressed. Jones predicts that this film, and others like it, will not even be used at all by many teachers because of "lack of confidence in their ability to control the emotions it stirs—their own as well as the children's." [18]

It is difficult for teachers to utilize the potential for personal human development in materials such as the film on the Netsilik Eskimo, especially without help. But Jones goes on to show how two young teachers were able to do so. Only the briefest discussion is possible here.

The children had been told about the Netsilik practice of female infanticide and senilicide. They had seen a film of a Netsilik family traveling, in which an old woman was barely able to keep up. The children were concerned, but the discussion had been directed away from their concern. One of the teachers developed a lesson plan in which the conditions of an Arctic winter were summarized, the film was reviewed, and the class read the tale of Kigtaq. The tale concerned treatment of the old who could not keep up with the necessary travel, and indicated the conflict of feelings the Eskimo had, to struggle for survival in a difficult environment. The tale stated that "Our custom up here is that all old people who can do no more, and whom death will not take, help death take them. They do this not only to be rid of a life that is no longer a pleasure, but also to relieve their nearest relatives of the trouble they give them."

The children showed some feelings, but they were not developed, and teacher and children hastened on to a discussion of igloo building, but the children's minds were elsewhere. The teacher wondered what she did wrong. The following are excerpts from the discussion:

Unit Coordinator: ". . . And the key line (quoted above) was too subtle. Some of the children didn't seem to get its full import."

[17] *Ibid.*, pp. 16–18.
[18] *Ibid.*, p. 24.

Psychologist: "They got it all right, but they didn't get a chance to do anything with it."

Miss Amenta (Teacher): "The drama wasn't there. I felt like I was dehumanizing the children, asking them to be objective before they were ready. Some of the talkers wouldn't talk and that made the silent ones doubly uneasy. And that awful silence at the end! Where were their questions?"

Unit Coordinator: "I thought you were right in asking them to talk about Netsilik opinions rather than their own, that it would make it easier for them, but it didn't work out that way."

Psychologist: "That's where the lesson went astray. Celeste (the teacher) is right. We were asking for objectivity before they had a chance to exercise their involvement with some powerful subjective images. After all, as Jerry said, 'it's their mother' who was left out there to die. And Billy's 'You'd think they'd have some feelings.' He's right and what are those feelings? Let's begin with ours and end with theirs, rather than the other way around."

Master Teacher: "Wouldn't that be harder on them?"

Assistant Teacher: "I think it was harder on them this way. Like we dangled something juicy in front of them and then took it away."

Psychologist: "Right. We're interested in teaching them cognitive and emotional skills as well as the subject matter. What emotional skills would they have learned this morning if they followed our example? 'Here's a story about a useless old lady who's expected to commit suicide. Get it? Now let's see how they build an igloo.' What else could the children have learned from this, but how to deny or isolate feelings? Admittedly denial and isolation are emotional skills and sometimes very handy. But were they the ones we wanted them to use in this lesson?"

Psychometrist: "Yes, but do we want to get them bogged down in their own feelings so early in the course? Do we want to spend the time necessary to deal with such strong emotions before they have any empathy for the society they're studying? They don't yet appreciate the harshness of the environment nor the difficulties of surviving in it. I still think it's too soon to bring up the whole topic."

Psychologist: "If we want the children to empathize with the Netsilik winter environment, we had better figure out a way for them to experience temperatures of 40 and 50 degrees below zero. But if we want them to empathize with the people who live in that environment we're on the right track by confronting them with emotionally charged issues they can locate in their own lives. Hell, these children are not strangers to the problems a senile person can raise in a family. Some of them live in families who have used the same solution—abandonment. But let's slow down and do this right. We're treating it all like a hot potato to be dropped at all possible speed. In fact it's the best opportunity we've had yet to teach about 'man.' "

Miss Grossman (Second Teacher): "I agree with that. Until this morning these kids haven't really cared a darn about this course. Every day in the individual interviews I ask what problems the Netsilik have and it's always 'food, clothing, and shelter; food, clothing, and shelter.' We don't need Jerome Bruner to design a curriculum to teach children that Eskimos have problems with food, clothing, and shelter. But this morning I got: food, clothing, shelter and grandmothers! I agree with Celeste that the lesson was poor, but I'll settle for it for openers. Next I'd look to hear: 'food, clothing, shelter, grandmothers, and babies.' And then 'food, clothing, shelter, grandmothers, babies, and too few wives.' I mean if all ESI wants to do is provide better materials for teaching the same dry old stuff then why bother with experimental try-outs at all?"

Unit Coordinator: "It sounds like you'd be willing to try a lesson on infanticide tomorrow."

Miss Grossman: "I'll try it if we can answer Celeste's question: what did she do wrong this morning? I too felt the kids were potentially there and that we lost them."

Psychologist: "Miss Amenta did one thing wrong. She stuck to the lesson plan instead of following her own good professional ear. You say, Celeste, you felt you were dehumanizing them in asking them to be prematurely objective about the story. What would you have preferred to do?"

Miss Amenta: "Well first I'd have liked the story to have more dramatic appeal. It wasn't just that the reading level was a bit over their heads. Maybe if ESI would make a slide-tape with drawings, interesting voices, and music or sound effects. Something that would pull the children into the key line rather than just letting it flit across their attention. Then I'd want the children to do something with their own reactions before listing the Netsilik reactions. After this morning I'm not sure I'd trust the discussion medium, although I do think they'd have offered their own reactions if I'd asked for them. But if discussion didn't work then some other expressive medium— art or creative writing or playacting. Something that showed the kids I was interested in them first and the Netsilik second. And then I'd go to the Netsilik, and their harsh environment, and their problems, and so forth. Finally I'd like to end with some comparison exercise that required the children to be objective not only about the Netsilik but about themselves."

School Principal (a rare one): "Yes. Couldn't we put a feather in our collective caps if we could set these youngsters to rationally considering our society's problems with overpopulation, birth control, increasing life span and old age, before they have to vote on them."

Unit Coordinator: "Yes, in your school, in Newton. But what about the average teacher in the average community in Kansas? What's she going to do about the Birchers in the P.T.A.?"

Principal: "Not use the course. According to Bruner we're to see what's possible, not what's practical."

Miss Grossman: "If I'm going to do a lesson on infanticide tomorrow morning, could we get back to the point please? What do you think of Celeste's plan?"

Psychologist: "I think it's a sound one, provided the expressive exercise is designed to do more than let off emotional steam. We want that steam to power the children's mastery of the subject. But I think that's what she had in mind for the comparative exercise at the end."

Miss Grossman: "Well, it's too late to find an infanticide story, but there is something I'd like to try following Celeste's strategy—on one condition: no observers tomorrow, except the people in the room right now. Last week I myself was violently against exposing the children to any of this, and I don't want to try it with that kind of opposition looking over my shoulder." [19]

The next day the second teacher, Miss Grossman, reviewed with the children the Netsilik culture and environment, showed a short film of igloo life while the father is out hunting, and continued with a discussion of it with the children. Part of the discussion of female infanticide follows:

Teacher: "Now let's suppose that the hunting isn't so good and the mother has a small child like Alexei and another little baby is born."

Student: "Give the baby to another family that didn't have any children."

Teacher: "That's what the Netsilik try to do. In fact, Umayapek, the boy we saw last week, was adopted. His parents had no children and arranged to take the next son of another father and mother who already had a son."

Student: "What if it had been a girl?"

Teacher: "That depends. If the father is a good hunter, they might keep her for themselves."

Student: "What if there are no families with no children?"

Teacher: "Then there is a difficult decision: whether to keep the new baby, or to abandon it and hope that another family will take it for their own. That is their custom."

Student: "Do they just leave it there until another 'troop' comes?" (The children had just completed a unit on baboons.)

Student: "What happens if another 'troop' doesn't come?"

Student: "Do they put clothes on it first?"

Student: "They must leave it outside so it will cry so another family will hear and come to get it."

Teacher (timidly): "What would happen if no one came to get it?"

Student: "It would starve."

Student: "Freeze."

Student: "It would die."

Teacher (confidently): "Yes, how do you feel about that?"

Student: "Oh!"

Student: "It's mean."

Student: "They're cruel."

Student: "The baby has a right to live."

[19] *Ibid.,* pp. 34–37.

Student: "The grandmother 'could do no more.' But they're taking away the baby's future life."

Student: "If there is an older daughter, say fifteen, couldn't she help to take care of it?"

Student: "Don't they have any feelings?"

Teacher: "What feelings would you have?"

Student: "They said it wasn't wicked about the grandmother. But with the babies it's wicked."

Student: "It's worse than eating fish eyes."

Student: "How can they do it?"

Student: "But the baby doesn't know it."

Student: "They shouldn't get married if they're going to do that to the babies."

Student: "Does it hurt to freeze?"

Student: "They're stupid."

Student: "Why do they live there?"

Student: "They'll be sorry when they don't have good hunters to take care of them when they are old."

Teacher: "This has been a very good discussion. Now I'd like to tell you something. When I first heard about this custom that the Netsilik have, I almost had a sick feeling much like you had: 'It's mean, it's cruel, it's stupid.' Then I found out something else that made a difference. The Netsilik don't really like to abandon babies, but they believe a baby has no soul until it has a name. So what might they do to help their feelings out?"

Student: "Not name the baby if they're going to abandon it."

Teacher: "Right."

Student: "Then they're not murderers. But why do they have to live there in the first place?" [20]

The difference in the children's interest and discussion was obvious. And the difference in their behavior was also noticed by the dance teacher to whom the children went for their next class. This teacher had the day before complained about the preoccupation of the children with violence and death when they had come to her class. After this lesson she reported that they were different, and were interested in dancing.

This should provide an answer to critics who might object that allowing children to become involved in emotions and affective education, with the cruel realities of life, is undesirable and will lead to disturbance—preoccupation with death and violence. *It is only when children are prevented from expressing and facing such feelings that they become disturbed.* The fact that the usual curriculum prevents and avoids this

[20] *Ibid.,* pp. 40–41.

expression, and tries to hide the existence of feelings and emotions—especially negative ones—causes much of the unrest, disturbance and acting out of violence in classrooms.

Utilizing standard curriculum materials for the purpose of affective or humanistic education is difficult, and the teacher needs help, and special training, to do so.

Jones discusses a class in which the material on the Netsilik Eskimo culture had been used, as reported by Bruner. Jones had been involved in this situation and writes:

A good deal had transpired between the superficial and the profound in this class. In fact, the children had been growing increasingly restive and unreachable as they were shown the films of spring sealing, summer fishing at the stone weir, and fall caribou hunting. Moreover, they had begun to develop attitudes toward the Netsilik which were the opposite of those the course was designed to instill. The Netsilik were coming to be seen alternately as savages with no hearts (and therefore too disagreeable to comprehend) and just one more distant society of which it can be said that "they have their customs, and we have ours" (thus, too trivial to comprehend). In other words, instead of cultivating deepened awareness of the humanizing forces at work in all human societies, we were dangerously close to teaching generalized attitudes of prejudice and apathy. Mr. Martin (the teacher) sought out a consultant to talk over what might be done to remedy the situation.

Was this behavior typical of the children? "No, they were 'Newton children.'" What, then, did he sense the trouble to be? "The films!" . . . "The kids have had a daily diet of blood and cruelty, and the eating of fish eyes. I think they just want to holler 'Ouch.'" Why not let them? "I'm not sure I know how. . . . Besides, they're supposed to be thinking of Arctic ecology, and the advantages of social organization, division of labor, and so forth. . . ."

The children, as their teacher well knew, had every cause to be "restive." But why "unreachable?" What did Mr. Martin think? "I think they need to vent some steam before they can appreciate the points about social organization and division of labor." Why not let them, then? "How?"

We should first appreciate Mr. Martin's style of conducting a class. He is always very calmly on the move. Within any span of five minutes, every child has tangibly felt his presence—the brush of a trouser leg, the tap of a finger, a palm on shoulder, or, when necessary, the firm grip of his eyes. All very soothing to the children. It says to them: there is little danger in this class of anyone getting out of control, so you can think as you wish. In this atmosphere the first signs of boisterousness in response to the films had merely required "None of that!" and emotional control held sway. This was inhibitory control, however, and Mr. Martin was now concerned that it was being carried too far. How to help the children to replace their inhibitory emotional skills with regulative emotional skills?

The following plan was devised: a short lesson on language would first be given in which the children would distinguish "instruction" messages from "feeling" messages. The teacher would then confront the children with a mock dilemma: someone had put it to him the day before that the Netsilik were, in fact, not human beings at all, but some other species! How would the class instruct him to answer that person? Then, assuming the children to be on the side of Netsilik humanness, they would be given an opportunity to share the feelings they had until now inhibited in respect to some of the more repellent aspects of Netsilik behavior. The children would then be given an opportunity to use these feelings by trying to empathize with Alexei in what was known to be the most repellent scene in the Netsilik footage: the stoning of the seagull. Finally, they would be shown a film of Netsilik children at more familiar kinds of play, and asked to contrast it with the seagull sequence." [21]

With this preparation, the children were shown a film depicting the snaring of a seagull, a film which the research and evaluation staff felt would be too much for the children to handle. The reaction is described by Bruner:

It has to do with Alexei who, with his father's help, devises a snare and catches a gull. There is a scene in which he stones the gull to death. Our children watched, horror struck. One girl, Kathy, blurted out, "He's not even human, doing that to the seagull." The class was silent. Then another girl, Jennine, said quietly: "He's got to grow up to be a hunter. His mother was smiling when he was doing that." And then an extended discussion about how people have to do things to learn and even do things to learn how to feel appropriately. "What would you do if you had to live there? Would you be as smart about getting along as they are with what they've got?" said one boy, going back to the accusation that Alexei was inhuman to stone the bird.[22]

Clearly, it takes a skilled and well-prepared teacher to do this kind of teaching. The materials themselves are not sufficient.

We have taken the position here that the academic curriculum, particularly the social sciences, can and should be utilized for the purpose of education in the area of feelings and human relations, and that this, and not knowledge of subject matter per se, should be their primary objective. Though we have drawn upon the excellent illustrations of Jones to show how this can be done, Jones does not take the view that the primary objective is the education or development of the emotions. To him this is

---

[21] *Ibid.*, pp. 89–90, 90–91.
[22] Jerome S. Bruner. "The Growth of the Mind, *American Psychologist*, 1965, 20, 1007–1017. Quoted in Jones., p. 88.

psychotherapy, apparently even when we are dealing with the "normal" emotions of "normal" children. He says:

> Let us enter it as a fundamental rule, then, that cultivation of emotional issues in classrooms, whether by design or in response to the unpredictable, should be the means to the ends of instructing the children in the subject matter. This is not only for the reason that resolution of emotional issues, when integral to learning, tends to deepen learning; but also for the reason that in the setting of a school room emotional issues cannot be optimally resolved until they become relevant to educational objectives.[23]

This view, which confuses the facilitation of normal emotional development with psychotherapy, is what has prevented and still prevents teachers, educators, and psychologists from accepting the education of the emotions as a function of the school. It is a narrow, and incomplete, view of education and educational objectives.

In the second attempt, George Brown has presented an extensive program which he calls "confluent education," which he defines as "the integration or flowing together of the *affective* and *cognitive* elements in individual and group learning—sometimes called humanistic or psychological education." [24] The development of the program was supported by the Fund for the Advancement of Education of the Ford Foundation. Approaches to affective learning developed at Esalen which seemed to be appropriate for classroom use were adapted in workshops there, and then tried out in the classroom in an appropriate curriculum context.

Forty examples of affective techniques, which were presented to professionals at workshops at Esalen, are described briefly by Brown. "Ideally," he says, "a teacher or leader should have an extensive repertoire of techniques and approaches and should also be able to create new techniques the moment the need arises. Of course, the decision to present a particular technique is at times arbitrary and will depend on the emerging needs of the group or situation." [25]

An example of a technique is the trust circle:

> Under Gloria's guidance, the group next worked on the development of communications and trust. Some of the participants went around the circle talking to each individual, completing the sentence "I want to communicate with you by . . ." Later, others did the same with the sentence "I think I can/cannot trust you because . . ." After some trust had been established or identified among various members of the group, small groups of eight

---

[23] *Ibid.,* p. 160.
[24] George I. Brown, *Human Teaching for Human Learning: an Introduction to Confluent Education* (New York: Viking, 1971), p. 3.
[25] *Ibid.,* p. 28.

people formed trust circles. One of the group stood in the center and, letting himself go, fell and was caught and supported by those in the circle, who then passed the person around the circle. Through these techniques, the need for trust and the need for support was demonstrated to the group.[26]

These techniques are not related to academic or subject matter content, and can be used as direct instruction in affective education. In fact, they are so used in sensitivity or encounter groups with adults. But in the present context, they are to be introduced in the teaching of subject matter. They include a number of Gestalt techniques, some of which, adapted for classroom use, are included in a book by Janet Lederman, who was involved in the Ford-Esalen project.[27] Here, although used in the classroom, the techniques may have no relation to the subject matter being taught, but may be used in response to the emotional reactions of children. This is particularly the case at the kindergarten and first grade level, for here the children are less inhibited and respond to games and exercises more naturally.

The project developed a number of units and lesson plans involving secondary school social studies and English content. One of these was a unit in a course in American Government and World Geography. The presentation included the showing of the pictures in Edward Steichen's "The Family of Man", a lecture on theories of the nature of man, and a brief statement on the unique self and the self as an example of man. Then followed nine affective exercises toward self-discovery, and the writing of two essays, one entitled "Who Am I?" and the second "What Is Man?" followed by a list of some things common to the two essays. One of the exercises was the following:

Exercise. (Pass out scratch paper.) Tear these pieces of paper into eight parts. They don't have to be even parts, because you're going to throw them away in a while. Now, on each of those scraps of paper, write one of the words that came into your consciousness a few moments ago—words that describe your character. If I were doing this, I might say that I'm usually pretty honest, that I tend to use people to get what I want, that I'm pushy, that I'm . . . (Etc., whatever the teacher feels at that time. GET IN-VOLVED YOURSELF!) Remember, one word or short phrase on each slip of paper. You are the only one who is going to see these words, so you don't have to be afraid to be honest with yourself. Now read what you have written. Arrange them in order, placing the one you are happiest about or like the most on top, and the one you like least or are least happy about on the bottom. Make a stack of them and place the stack right in front of you.

[26] *Ibid.*, p. 41.
[27] Janet Lederman, *Anger and the Rocking Chair* (New York: McGraw-Hill, 1969).

Now for a while confine your eyes to the surface of your desk. Don't look at anyone or anything except the top of your desk and the pieces of paper. Take each piece of paper in order and really spend some time with that word. Stay with it for a few minutes and try on the word just as you try on clothes hanging in your closet. Our characters are like a wardrobe. We are sometimes one way, sometimes another. Today we are going through the wardrobe and examining our clothes and trying them on. Really see how they feel. Become the words you see. Accept them as *you* at one time or another, then do with the word and the piece of paper what you want to do. Put it back in your wardrobe, tear it up and throw it away, or whatever you wish. All right, you may begin. Take plenty of time with each word.[28]

In other units the exercises are woven into the more cognitive requirements. The relationship of the exercise to the subject matter content is not always clear nor direct, and there is a contrived element present: the units are contrived to allow the bringing in of the exercises, and the exercises sometimes appear to be introduced in a contrived manner. Thus some seem to be natural but others seem to be techniques. The affective elements do not appear always to flow from the materials, as seemed true for "Man: A Course of Study." Here the major, even sole, objective seems the selection of the content and materials for their utility in fostering the use of the techniques of affective education, rather than for any subject matter achievement. Thus this method approaches direct instruction, utilizing subject matter rather incidentally. This is particularly the case with the individual lessons as compared to the units.

Brown, in his evaluation, feels that all the techniques were "extremely successful both in getting across the subject content and in getting the students in touch with their feelings," [29] but he provides no data to support this evaluation. Teachers in the project report better learning of cognitive material; heightened motivation and response to learning situations; greater appreciation of self, nature, and others; greater pupil responsibility; and, at the secondary-school level, lessened desire for drug use by some students. The teachers were obviously pleased and happy, and offer testimonials. One writes: "This year is the first in which I have felt like a real educator and not just a purveyor of information and a 'people-pusher.' I feel that as a result of the Ford-Esalen project I have grown as a person and as a teacher. . . . the change in the students has also been fantastic. They have grown and matured faster this year than in any other I have experienced. They are more aware, more creative, and better students as a result of this project." [30]

[28] George I. Brown, *op. cit.*, p. 57.
[29] *Ibid.*, p. 96.
[30] *Ibid.*, p. 200.

But that all this was due to the techniques can be seriously questioned. The teachers were well liked, and in two cases were given elaborate surprise parties by the students. At one of the parties, one girl said to the wife of the teacher: "For me, it's not just the teacher-student bit. It's not all those field trips he took us on, but it's what he did for me as a person. I'm a better person because of him! I mean, I can tell him anything and *he listens and understands.* I'm a better person." [31] Clearly, this kind of reaction was not created by techniques! It is a response to the person of the teacher—his empathic understanding, respect and warmth, his genuineness. Techniques cannot be separated from the teacher's person, and fade into insignificance in contrast to him. The teachers were selected (in part, perhaps, self-selected) and were obviously good, dedicated and devoted teachers, enthusiastic about the project, and about participating in a novel experience. This whole aura partakes of the well-known Hawthorne effect. (see pp. 6–7)

While, in appropriate situations where they would naturally fit, some of the techniques could no doubt be used successfully by other teachers, most teachers could not successfully use many of them, because they would not be natural to the teacher. Techniques must cease to be techniques, and must be a part of the genuine teacher, before they can be effective in the everyday, continuing teaching situation. Techniques can be built into a role, making the teacher a showman, unable to function as a real person without them. Such teachers are sometimes considered to be successful—they hold the children's interest and entertain them, but in spite of their success, their techniques are also their crutch.

But when exercises and games are simple and natural, they can facilitate the expression of feelings. Our society encourages the repression rather than the expression of feelings, inhibition rather than spontaneity or genuineness. Thus people need to be given "permission" to be themselves, to be spontaneous, to express their feelings. Thus a simple exercise, such as "For the next ten minutes I want you to talk to each other and say nothing but positive things about each other" gives permission to express feelings which otherwise would not even be recognized, let alone expressed. Games may also make it possible for people to touch each other—a taboo in our society except under special conditions.

But if exercises and games are continued or over-emphasized, or treated as an end, people are not helped to be genuine and spontaneous in everyday life. It is the teacher who is or becomes a real person in all his relationships with students who has a real and lasting effect on the personal development of his students.

[31] *Ibid.,* p. 202. (*Status* added.)

A Curriculum of Affect

The third attempt (see p. 167) is a Curriculum of Affect. If the development of the emotions is a function of the schools, along with the development of the intellect, then feelings, emotions, and their place in interpersonal relations are subject matter themselves. People are now attempting to deal with them directly as subject matter.

This is by no means a new area of concern in education. For many years mental hygiene and human relations content has been provided in subject matter form, usually as units in another course, or sometimes as part of a secondary-school course in psychology, but these materials have not been widely accepted or used.

One reason for this is that this inclusion has not been effective. (Another reason is a general lack of interest and concern of educators with this area.) The lack of effectiveness stems from at least two sources. First, the materials have not been interesting or relevant, unrelated as they have been to the actual experiences—feelings and attitudes—of students. Subject-matter rather than person-oriented, they serve perhaps as just another instance of how educators (curriculum writers) render sterile subject matter which can and should be highly relevant and educational.

A second reason for unsuccessful mental hygiene instruction lies in the method and teachers. The method has been structured, didactic, and essentially the teaching of abstract subject matter. Teachers, not being psychologists, have not been familiar with the material, have not really understood it or been involved in it, and have been through this ignorance hesitant to get into the subject in any way relevant or meaningful to students.

Thus, we shall not review or consider these traditional attempts to introduce psychology and mental hygiene into education.

In an attempt to introduce relevance into affective education, Weinstein and Fantini have attempted to develop a curriculum based on the basic concerns of students.[32] The curriculum effort developed from the Elementary School Teaching Project of the Fund for the Advancement of Education of the Ford Foundation.

The assumption on which the development of relevant content was based was that *"Significant contact with pupils is most effectively established and maintained when the content and method of instruction have an affective basis.* That is, if educators are able to discover the feelings, fears, and wishes that move pupils emotionally, they can more effectively

[32] Gerald Weinstein & Mario D. Fantini (Eds.) *Toward Humanistic Education: a Curriculum of Affect* (New York: Praeger, 1970).

engage pupils from any background, whether by adapting traditional content and procedures or by developing new materials and techniques." [33]

Student concerns are more than a means of arousing interest in traditional content—they are content in themselves. The project attempted to identify the principal concerns of students, "to help teachers to recognize pupil concerns, use them in selecting and developing content, and devise techniques and procedures enabling students to deal with these concerns." [34] Materials and techniques were tried out in actual classrooms.

Concerns are more basic than interests or feelings, although they involve and include these. "Concerns are the most persistent, pervasive threads of underlying uneasiness the learners have about themselves and their relation to the world." [35] Three broad classes of concerns were identified: (1) concern about *self-image* (identity); (2) concern about *disconnectedness* (alienation), i.e., where one fits into the scheme of things; and (3) concern about *control* over one's life (power). The manifestation of these concerns will vary in different age, socioeconomic, geographic, cultural and racial or ethnic groups. Desirable outcomes are not changes in concerns, but in behavior representing an improvement in dealing with concerns.

Subject matter from the standard disciplines, including psychology, may be used to achieve the desired outcomes. In addition, classroom incidents, out-of-school experiences and the children themselves provide content.

Weinstein and Fantini provide units and materials for a study of the self-concept, designed to help children recognize that the self-concept develops out of experiences with others, leads to certain ways of seeing the world and to responses to what they, the children see that tend to reinforce the self-concept. The technique of "one-way glasses" was used to help children realize that much of our world is created through our perceptions, which then determine our responses as well as our views of ourselves.

Their use is illustrated in a class of 10- and 11-year olds in an ungraded University demonstration school. The children were very concerned about power and self-concept, which were tied together. They seldom listened to each other, and reactions to what others said were generally negative. The objective was to replace the disconnectedness in the classroom with connectedness, so that the children would have feelings of constructive power and positive self-concepts—the children would then listen to each others' viewpoints, acknowledge each others' strong points; withdrawn children would respond more. Teaching was organized around three ideas: (1) there are many ways of seeing the same situation;

[33] *Ibid.,* p. 10. (Italics in original.)
[34] *Ibid.,* p. 11.
[35] *Ibid.,* p. 22.

(2) perceptions and responses depend on the feelings and thoughts accompanying them; and (3) limited perception constricts the person's view of himself and of the world. No subject matter content was used. An example of the use of "one-way glasses" is the following:

> The teacher now held up two pairs of sunglasses, each with different color lenses. He explained that these were very special glasses, that each pair colored the wearer's view of the world with a particular feeling.
>
> TEACHER: The first pair of glasses are "suspicious" glasses. When a person wears them, he regards whatever he sees or hears with suspicion. [The teacher asked for a volunteer to put on the suspicious glasses and tell the class what he saw.]
>
> VOLUNTEER (looking at two children who were talking and laughing, as he put on the glasses): I wonder if they're talking about me. Are they laughing at me? [The teacher asked that questions be addressed to the volunteer.]
>
> STUDENT: Who's your best friend?
>
> VOLUNTEER: Why does he want to know that? Are they going to try to take my friends away?
>
> TEACHER (holding up second pair of glasses): I have a second pair of glasses, which are rose-colored. They make whoever wears them see and hear with this feeling: "No matter what anyone says to me, I know they really care for me."
>
> [Teacher asked for and secured the cooperation of another volunteer. Throughout the dialogue that followed the teacher sought to clarify the volunteer's responses by asking: "Are you acting suspicious or just curious?" "Do you really feel that way, or are you exaggerating your reactions?" "Do you really think they might be trying to do that to you?"]
>
> TEACHER: Let's get some reactions from our volunteer.
>
> STUDENT (to second volunteer): You're just a noisy little pipsqueak!
>
> VOLUNTEER 2: He always calls me a little pipsqueak, but that shows he really notices me and probably likes smaller people like me.
>
> STUDENT: How come you're always hanging around with Betty?
>
> VOLUNTEER: I bet she asked that because she really wants me to try and make more friends.[36]

In the last lesson, the class was asked to put away their put-down and suspicious glasses and wear another pair called "strong-point" glasses, which are very difficult to wear:

> TEACHER: Now we'll choose somebody to come to the front of the room and tell us how he sees himself through his strong-point glasses.
>
> At the teacher's request, members of the class dropped slips of paper

[36] *Ibid.,* pp. 79–80.

bearing their names into a hat, and one was drawn. The person chosen went to the front of the room.

TEACHER: How do you think this person feels?

STUDENTS: Embarrassed.

TEACHER: You can help him overcome his embarrassment by not making faces at him or making fun of him and by looking at him supportively.

The teacher warned the selected person that his strong-point glasses might occasionally slip, in which case he might don his "crack-a-joke-about-me" or put-down glasses. The group was asked to be on the lookout for such lapses. Now the teacher suggested that in the event the target person ran out of positive things to say about himself, he was to feel free to admit it and ask the class for help in finding additional strong points. The class was cautioned once again about the difficulty of its assignment. With this in mind, the teacher, too, was prepared to help students find strong points if necessary.

FIRST PERSON (a strong, quiet, interested, class leader): I'm good in science and in playing baseball and all kinds of sports and at home when it comes to helping around the house. I'm strong in the classroom in writing poetry and discovering and exploring new things. I like to do a lot of reading. I think I can produce a lot of ideas and create things. I think that's all, does anyone have anything else?

STUDENTS:—You're creative.

—You as a person are nice. You're not a boaster, putdown, or suspicious. You're a good worker and compatible—not always criticizing.

—You're good at organizing, like when you were class president.

—You have a good sense of humor. You can hold up against your three brothers. You're tactful.

—You don't always try to be on top.

The strong-points situation was repeated several times, giving as many students as possible a chance to tell about their own strong points. . . .

TEACHER: How do you feel about this whole idea? How do you feel when this is going on? Why are these the most difficult glasses to wear? We're often taught to look at the worst in ourselves and others; to be overly critical. When we wear one-way glasses or only a few pairs of glasses— that is, critical or put-down glasses—we see only a piece of the world. The more different kinds of glasses we are able to wear, the more we are able to see.[37]

There were seven lessons, each lasting one to two hours, over a period of three weeks. The teacher felt they were successful:

[37] *Ibid.*, pp. 91–92, 93.

As the series of lessons drew to a close, the original participants seemed more attentive to others and less destructive. Positive observations about others were expressed more freely as the students glimpsed more strong points in themselves and others. One student, for example, exclaimed admiringly to the rest of the class about a target person during the strong-points episode: "Gee, I just never thought of John that way!" [38]

Some students objected to the use of real glasses as props, and the authors suggest that perhaps use of the glasses should have been discontinued after one or two lessons. Some students felt they were better able to "dope out" other children: "Now I can see through a person better," one said. This evaluative, judgmental, or critical attitude would appear to be an undesirable outcome. Some children, perhaps some of the inhibited or withdrawn ones, felt that the lessons didn't help a lot. Often these children are the very ones who dislike and fail to be drawn into games and exercises which may seem artificial and unreal. Other students gave more positive reactions:

> "I've learned how to see people in different ways and to see how other people look at us."
> "The glasses have helped me and other people mostly in realizing that different people do not always think the same, and it has helped me look at things as if I were another person."
> "It helped me to view other people's strong points and also to realize my own." [39]

Weinstein and Fantini propose their approach as simply a suggestive beginning, open to criticism and change. Several comments might be made regarding it. Weinstein and Fantini attempt to put their contribution in the form of a model. It would appear to be premature to attempt this at this point, for the model appears simply the usual model for developing a curriculum, and might be seen as a device to appeal to educators obsessed with formal statements of curriculum. The model places emphasis on diagnosing student "concerns"—another term for what are commonly referred to as "needs". But while it is true that basic concerns may be expressed differently by different groups, they are also expressed differently by each individual in any group. More important, however, is the fact that all individuals, and all groups, share these basic common concerns, self-image, alienation, and control, and it is not necessary to go through the process of diagnosing before teaching—a point which Weinstein and Fantini incidentally recognize.

[38] *Ibid.,* p. 97.
[39] *Ibid.,* p. 99.

A strong impression given by Weinstein and Fantini is that the teacher is always in control. Teaching is a highly structured situation, following a detailed, in effect, lesson plan. The approach is highly cognitively oriented —in effect it is *the teaching of affect by cognitive methods.*

Finally, one is conscious of the technique orientation, as in the case of confluent education. It is almost as if Weinstein and Fantini are afraid to face a class of children without a well prepared program of techniques, and would be uncomfortable in a free, open, unstructured situation. As teachers take refuge in a lesson plan, they take refuge in techniques. This attitude is apparent when they write: "In the sense that they get children to talk about themselves, the people they live with, and the aspects of their lives which they feel are most significant, these [three diagnostic techniques] are learning techniques for both students and teachers." [40] But techniques are not necessary to get children to talk about themselves, as Herndon, Kohl, Kozol and others have clearly shown. It takes an understanding warm, real, sensitive human being who will listen.

Deliberate Psychological Education

We shall consider one other specific proposal in the area of affective education. This is what Mosher and Sprinthall call "deliberate psychological education." [41] These writers, together with their students and others, have attempted to formulate the beginnings of a curriculum in personal and human development, consisting of "a comprehensive set of educational experiences designed to affect personal, ethical, aesthetic and philisophical development in adolescents and young adults." [42] They base their work on Piaget, Erikson, and Kohlberg. The curriculum will be a series of courses focusing on the various stages of the life cycle. Adolescents would thus study child development. Students would participate in experiences in observing mother/child interactions and children in nursery school, and in "parenting" and teaching children. The adolescent period would be studied in part through a seminar and practicum in counseling. Teachers, counselors and parents study the problems adolescents bring to counselors, and the counseling process. "The course focuses heavily on the processes of listening to another individual, listening for feeling and for ideas and learning to respond both to another person's feelings and his

[40] *Ibid.,* p. 123.
[41] Ralph L. Mosher & Norman A Sprinthall, "Psychological Education in Secondary Schools: a Program to Promote Individual and Human Development," *American Psychologist,* 1970, 25, 911–924; Ralph L. Mosher, Norman A. Sprinthall, and others, "Psychological Education: a Means to Promote Personal Development During Adolescence," *The Counseling Psychologist,* 1971, 2 (No. 4), 3–82.
[42] Ralph L. Mosher, Norman A. Sprinthall, and others, *ibid.,* p. 9.

ideas. These skills are developed in role-play, simulated counseling and in actual counseling by the students of other high school or junior high school students." [43] The results of a study of a high school class which participated in a course in counseling indicated that the students learned to listen, and to withhold judgments and prescriptions about others' behavior. They increased significantly in empathy.

A comment of one student is significant in terms of the purpose of humanistic education proposed in this book:

> "I think it would be better if you could train everybody in the whole world to be a counselor than it would be to have enough counselors to go around and counsel everybody. If that makes sense. . . ." [44]

Affective or human relations education is in effect educating everyone to be a counselor, to offer the conditions for self-actualizing behavior to others.

This is one of the most comprehensive, and thus most promising approaches to psychological or affective education. Yet, while there is an attempt to place it on theoretical and research bases, these bases have not been adequately developed. Their rejection of humanistic psychology and existentialism may certainly be questioned. Their attempt to avoid the value question involved in goals and objectives is not only unsuccessful, but an impossible one.

SOME CRITICAL COMMENTS

While recognizing that the approaches described briefly in this chapter are tentative beginnings in a new field, it appears to be desirable to make a few comments which might be of help to those who wish to further advance the field of affective education.

The overemphasis upon techniques and structured, teacher-controlled procedures is inconsistent with the goals of affective education, which include spontaneity, student initiated activity, open and free discussion in a natural setting, and self-directed exploration and learning. Content and structure can be provided by materials such as films and reading, rather than by the teacher.

This overemphasis also requires that teachers, and student teachers, must be warned that the adoption of any or all of these and other techniques, games, exercises, etc., will not make a humanistic teacher or facilitate affective learning. It is possible that an approach such as that of

[43] *Ibid.,* p. 14.
[44] *Ibid.,* p. 32.

Weinstein and Fantini could become the basis for new methods courses in teacher education, but to go in this direction would be a mistake. Current methods courses do not prepare teachers for the teaching relationship, and new methods courses focusing upon new techniques will not do so either. Robert E. Samples, in his review of Borton's book, sounds a relevant warning when he says that "these instructional strategies may well have as many shortcomings as the mechanistic approaches to subject matter that the past ten years of curriculum revision have supposedly replaced. In addition, students are deeply sensitive to contrivances of any sort. . . . Whenever we get rational about needs and feelings, our efforts usually create relatively meaningless and contrived lessons." [45]

Perhaps the greatest difficulty or deficiency in current approaches to affective education is that they are not based on any systematic theory of human behavior, of human development and interpersonal relations. Bruner has emphasized that if subject matter is to be taught effectively, it must be organized in terms of basic principles or propositions. It would appear that before we can develop a curriculum of affect or of human development or of psychological education, we must have some knowledge, understanding, and agreement upon the psychology of emotional development. Mosher and Sprinthall recognize this when they say: "A major problem confronting psychological education is the lack of an adequate theory of personal or emotional development." [46] They attempt to build their approach to adolescents upon the work of Piaget, Erikson and Kohlberg. But when they teach counseling to high school students they do not indicate their definition of, or theoretical approach to, counseling.

This book is based upon a systematic theoretical approach to human behavior, which is outlined in Chapters 2 and 6. This theoretical system can be used as a basis for the direct teaching of human relations. If the basic conditions for facilitative interpersonal relationships are empathic understanding, respect or warmth, and genuineness, then the development of these conditions should be the objective of a curriculum in interpersonal relations. The direct teaching of these conditions should be a major part of the curriculum. There are many other aspects of personal development which are important and necessary for the development of these conditions—these include the concerns of Weinstein and Fantini—and these should be included in the curriculum. But they must be integrated into a systematic or theory based approach.

The teaching of counseling is an effective—perhaps the most effective —but not the only way of teaching the core conditions. Counseling or psychotherapy is, or should be, the purest form of a facilitative interper-

[45] Robert E. Samples, "Tools for Everyone," review of Terry Borton, *Reach, Touch and Teach, Saturday Review,* September 17, 1970, 82.
[46] Ralph L. Mosher, Norman A. Sprinthall, & others, *op. cit.,* p. 10.

sonal relationship, and thus training in counseling is a highly effective method of education in interpersonal relationships. This is, to some extent at least, implicit in the Mosher and Sprinthall approach. Carkhuff has pioneered efforts to teach these conditions to other groups, including parents.[47]

SUMMARY

In Chapter 1 we argued that the major function of the schools is to produce self-actualizing persons, persons who can understand themselves and others and can relate to others.

In this chapter we have reviewed several attempts to introduce affective or psychological education into the curriculum. One approach is to utilize existing subject matter as a basis for affective education. Since subject matter areas vary in their adaptability to this purpose, the social sciences are perhaps most adaptable.

The education of the emotions, and the learning of interpersonal relations through the standard curriculum may be considered an indirect approach. It can even be considered simply as a by-product, although when so considered—as it has been in the past—it is not likely to be effective. On the other hand, when the standard curriculum, especially in the social sciences, is directed specifically toward affective education it can and may be perhaps the most effective approach, since the history of the development of man and the human race provides inherently relevant content. Such content can be inherently relevant if it is used to show problems humans have faced in living together.

However, other approaches are also useful, including the direct approach to education in human relations or psychological development. Currently, such approaches are technique-oriented and lack systematic or theoretical foundations. It seems that we have lost our basic humanity, since we are unable to relate to students—or to each other—without the intervention or use of techniques. It is interesting in this connection that we are recognizing that the essence of the psychotherapeutic relationship is that it is a relationship devoid of, or without, techniques.

The implication is that teaching should also be a relationship devoid of techniques. Children have—inherently and until we deprive them of it— this ability to relate to others naturally, honestly, trustingly, understandingly. *We don't need techniques to relate to children*—in fact techniques interfere with establishing a relationship with children.

In this book we have proposed a theory of human behavior and inter-

---

[47] Robert R. Carkhuff, *Helping and Human Relations: a Primer for Lay and Professional Helpers,* Vols. I & II. (New York: Holt, Rinehart & Winston, 1969).

personal relationships as a basis for humanistic education. If this theory is useful in the teaching relationship—and it appears that it is, as it has been demonstrated to be, through research, in the psychotherapy relationship—it should also be relevant to all interpersonal relationships. It is therefore proposed that this theory become the basis for a curriculum in affective or emotional education.

One of the contributions of the Mosher and Sprinthall proposal for psychological education is that it is not limited to didactic instruction. Any approach must include an experiential aspect. One of the most useful experiential approaches to affective education is the group experience. In the next chapter we turn to this approach to affective education.

11 Groups In Humanistic Education

*Encounter and sensitivity groups "are the most
rapidly spreading social phenomenon in the country.
They are helping break through the alienation and
dehumanization of our culture."*

—Carl R. Rogers, PSYCHOLOGY TODAY, December, 1969

*"One of the most effective means yet discovered for
facilitating constructive learning, growth, and
change—in individuals or in the organizations they
compose—is the intensive group experience."*

—Carl R. Rogers, FREEDOM TO LEARN *

The group movement is one of the social movements of our current
society—Rogers calls it a "social invention." [1] Various names have been
used for different groups: T-groups (T for training), sensitivity groups, encounter groups. There are differences within groups going under each of
these terms, as well as between them, and groups going by different names

* (Columbus, Ohio: Merrill, 1969), p. 304.
[1] Carl R. Rogers, *Carl Rogers on Encounter Groups* (New York: Harper & Row,
1970), p. 1.

may be quite similar. These differences introduce confusion in the field, and it is necessary to find out just what kind of a group is being referred to in order to understand and evaluate it. In this chapter we will be concerned with what Rogers calls a "basic encounter group," defined as a group whose purpose is "to emphasize personal growth and the development and improvement of interpersonal communication and relationships through an experiential process." [2]

The group movement has developed outside the universities, and appears to represent a spontaneous social movement. Groups of course are not new—man has always lived in groups. Membership in a group, such as the family, is necessary for human survival. The individual becomes a person and develops a self only in a group. The inherent need in man to associate with others is expressed in the formation of clubs of all kinds, lodges, and fraternities. Adolescents and youth form peer groups, often taking the form of gangs. Sociologists have designated the small, informal, face to face groups, such as the family, neighborhood groups, and church groups, as primary groups.

The development of interest in groups coincides with changes in our society which are leading to the decrease of primary groups. The family has become smaller. Churches, lodges and other clubs and groups have become larger and more formal. Neighborhoods are disappearing. Youth leave home more frequently for college and work, and perhaps earlier than in the past. As our society has become more highly specialized and urbanized it has become more impersonal, with resulting feelings of loneliness and alienation in many people. Our culture is becoming dehumanized. It is interesting that it is mainly young people who recognize this and resist it most strongly. Older people are turning to encounter groups—if they can afford it, and many can.

The fact that so many people want and are willing and able to pay for group experiences, though, has led to the commercialization of groups. Some years ago a psychologist wrote a book on individual psychotherapy in which he suggested that psychotherapy was the purchase of friendship.[3] This phrase characterizes many encounter groups today. Though conducting groups has become a growth industry, there has among some people been a reaction against such a development, for in part this commercialization has drawn in unqualified or marginally qualified persons as group leaders, and has led to the development of sensational and potentially harmful gimmicks, techniques and procedures designed to attract customers.

[2] *Ibid.,* pp. 4–5.
[3] William Schofield, *Psychotherapy: the Purchase of Friendship* (Englewood Cliffs, N. J.: Prentice-Hall, 1964).

GROUPS IN THE SCHOOL

The reaction against groups, and the feeling by some, influenced by sensational publicity, that the movement is simply a fad, has led to some reluctance and even strong opposition to the use of groups in schools. It would be unfortunate if encounter groups were denied a place in education because of this.

Students, as well as adults are interested in and need groups. The usual clubs and other student activities are not sufficient. These are exclusive, in the sense that a certain interest, skill or ability is required for membership. They are relatively formal, with a limited purpose—they are what is called task-oriented groups. Academically oriented, they exclude less academically oriented students and as a result these students are more apt to belong to nonschool groups, such as gangs. The less socially oriented or less socially adept students are often not drawn to or accepted in student activities groups, and even less so in the informal, spontaneous student groups. Adolescent groups, particularly, even though their members may be sensitive to their own needs for acceptance and group membership, are often insensitive to others and cruel in their rejection.

Adolescents are often lacking or awkward in social skills. They are often self-conscious, and feel different from and inferior to others. They are often afraid to express their innermost feelings, except possibly to a very close friend. Many are not sure how much they are accepted by others, since most adolescents, especially boys, do not easily or openly express positive feelings toward others. Some feel alienated and many if not most pass through an identity crisis or stage. The concern about self-identity, referred to in the last chapter, is a common if not universal concern of adolescents. It is to this concern that many of the methods and techniques of affective education are directed.

The reserve, inhibition, self-consciousness, anxiety, and even fear which characterize adult interpersonal relations in our society was remarked upon in the last chapter also, and mentioned as a reason why so many of those in affective education (as well as encounter groups) resort to exercises and techniques. These same factors are present in adolescents. But those who are experienced in group counseling, and in encounter groups, with adolescents find that such gimmicks or techniques are not necessary if the leader is secure and at ease himself.

There are those who feel that verbal procedures, in individual counseling or in groups, are not appropriate with young children. However, this is clearly not borne out by experience with children: young children, compared to adolescents and adults, are characterized by openness, spontaneity, honesty and genuineness in their social relationships. Indeed, adults are sometimes embarrassed when children show these characteristics. Groups are much more easily developed with children than among adults, or adolescents. Rogers, who has worked with a wide variety of persons in groups, makes the following ranking, from greatest to least, of difficulty in initiating encounter groups: administrators, college faculty, high school faculty, elementary teachers, college students, high school students, elementary school students.[4] Thus, children are more ready for a personal group experience than most adults. Furthermore, if they are not to become like these adults, they should have the opportunity for a continuing group experience in school.

The teacher who faces a class of from 25 to 40 children in September does not face a group. And usually, the teacher leaving that same class in May or June does not leave a group. A class is usually an "aggregate," defined by Gorman as "a collection of human beings brought together to accomplish some task." He continues: "An *aggregate* differs from a group in that members of an *aggregate* maintain their individual defenses at all times, interact in a formal manner, refuse to deal with their feelings with each other, and remain fairly tentative, untrusting and suspicious of each other. The typical school classroom is a setting in which students do not know other students, and no one really knows the teacher as a person." [5]

A class may become a group. One of the requirements of a group is that there be interaction and communication among all its members. In the usual classroom communication is almost entirely from the teacher to the students, with some, but usually little, communication from the student to the teacher. Even in active, informal, and effective classrooms there is usually little if any communication among the students; this is true usually of so-called discussion groups in the classroom.

The fact that in a group there must be communication—or the opportunity for communication—among all possible pairs of students places a limit on the extent to which a classroom can become an effective group. This is the basis for small group work in many college classes. The larger the group, the less opportunity there is for each person to interact with each other person in the group. This becomes a limitation upon the group process and progress.

The classroom is thus too large for an effective group. Though the optimum number for a group is not known, it probably varies with the group's composition, duration, and purpose. Authorities suggest anywhere from 6 to 20 members. Experience suggests that for the basic encounter group concerned with personal development, ten is a good size.

[4] Carl R. Rogers, *Freedom to Learn* (Columbus, Ohio: Merrill, 1969), p. 338.
[5] Alfred H. Gorman, *Teachers and Learners: the Interactive Process* (Boston: Allyn & Bacon, 1969), p. 3n.

THE PURPOSE OF ENCOUNTER GROUPS
IN THE SCHOOL

The purpose of the encounter group, broadly, is to contribute to affective education and to its goal of developing self-actualizing persons. Its particular contribution is in providing experience in interpersonal relations, thus involving learning by doing, or through experience. The learning of interpersonal relations would appear to be one place where cognitive instruction and computer assisted learning would be inappropriate, or at least relatively ineffective. You can't teach human relations by machines. Actual experience in groups seems so clearly superior to any other method of learning that it is amazing that it hasn't been widely used long before this. There is no substitute for learning human relations through interacting with others. Sitting in a classroom while actually being alone, not really knowing the other students, while listening to the teacher talk about "mental hygiene" or "human relations" is not sufficient. Nor is being in a classroom and going through a series of games and exercises which, while involving some realistic interpersonal reactions are not actually "for real."

In the encounter group students can learn through experience:

to listen to others

to accept and respect others

to understand others

to identify and become aware of feelings

to express one's own feelings

to become aware of the feelings of others

to experience being listened to by others

to experience being accepted and respected by others

to experience being understood by others

to recognize the basic commonalities of human experience

to explore oneself

to develop greater awareness of oneself

to be oneself

to change oneself in the direction of being more the self one wants to be

In groups learning occurs without the input of external content, in contrast to the approaches to affective education described in the last chapter, where, through the use of techniques, content is used to teach human relations, or new content is created for this purpose. Groups provide learning in human relations without needing to provide content or techniques which put distance between the learner and what he learns. Group encounters also eliminate this distance.

The encounter group differs from T-groups in a significant respect, and when used in affective education should not be confused with them. The T- or training group is concerned with consciously teaching so-called "human relations skills" (often reduced to "techniques of handling others"), and are thus a mixture or alternation of spontaneous interaction and cognitive analysis of the interaction—the so-called dynamics operating in the group. The development of skills is primary; personal development in the broader sense is secondary or accidental.

In encounter groups there is no separate, cognitive analysis of "the process." The interaction is not stopped to study group dynamics, nor is it a training group in group dynamics. It is not necessary that cognitive analysis or awareness—"insight"—be present for learning to occur.

Encounter groups provide the most relevant and the most realistic education in human relations. It is learning through practice, or a practicum in interpersonal relations.

In addition to this direct contribution to the personal development of students in the school, encounter groups are extremely useful in areas where there are problems of interpersonal relationships. These include relations between administrators and teachers, teachers and parents, and administrators and parents. Certainly there is need for greater understanding among these groups, and the relationships among them influence the education of children.

But our concern here is with the students and their relationships with others. The teacher-student relationship could be improved if students and teachers could participate together in encounter groups. Students and administrators could also benefit. In the few instances where meetings between students and faculty and administrators do occur they are formal and stilted, or at times angry confrontations, with little if anything being accomplished. Teachers and administrators seem to resist open, free encounters with students; yet they complain about lack of understanding by students. Students and parents also should be brought together. The lack of understanding—the so-called generation gap—could be reduced by encounter groups. A few schools have used encounter groups to bring black and white students together with good results.

The only remedy for conflict and lack of understanding between groups is a group experience of the kind provided by an encounter group where understanding and acceptance are fostered.

THE ENCOUNTER GROUP PROCESS

In the encounter group where there is an atmosphere of safety, individuals are free to express their feelings toward themselves and each other. Mutual trust, liking, concern, and understanding develop. Each individual sees himself as he is and as he is capable of becoming. Not needing to be defensive, the individual is open to change in attitudes and behavior. He can learn from others who are concerned about him, including learning how he affects others. He becomes freer to become his potentials, to become a more self-actualizing person—more understanding, warm, and genuine.

Rogers has defined and described the stages in the process. The stages are not separate or discrete but constitute trends, sometimes overlapping and reversing, but roughly sequential. The following is an adaptation of Rogers.[6]

1. MILLING AROUND. When the group is initially given freedom, with little structure except that it is a place where individuals can relate to each other and get to know each other, there is a period of confusion, silence, frustration, small-talk, lack of continuity. There is often a demand for the leader to "do something." In one group conducted by the writer, after two hours of this one member addressed me and said: "Why haven't you done something; why don't you do something?" Before I could respond she said: "Well, I'm going to do something," and then she launched into a very personal expression of her problems.

2. RESISTANCE TO PERSONAL EXPRESSION OR EXPLORATION. Although one member may reveal something personal, there may be a hesitancy, reluctance or refusal of others to respond on a personal level. There may be an embarrassment in others, who may even cover over the personal statement. People don't disclose themselves in ordinary social situations, and it takes time for them to feel comfortable in doing so even when they have been, in effect, given permission to do so. A trust in the group must develop first.

3. DESCRIPTION OF PAST FEELING. Expressions of feelings begin with telling about past feelings. They are experienced as in the past, not in the present. They do not involve members of the group.

4. EXPRESSION OF NEGATIVE FEELINGS. The first current feelings to be expressed, about other members in the group, are at first negative. The feelings are often first directed at the leader or facilitator, as in the illustration above. Negative feelings are apt to be expressed first because of feelings of threat, anxiety, defensiveness, and because we are not used to expressing positive feelings, and also perhaps as a testing of the freedom and safety of the group.

5. EXPRESSION AND EXPLORATION OF PERSONALLY MEANINGFUL MATERIAL. The voicing of negative feelings is followed by someone revealing himself to the group. Rogers says that "the reason for this no doubt

[6] Carl R. Rogers, *Carl Rogers on Encounter Groups, op. cit.,* pp. 15–37.

is that the individual member has come to realize that this is in part *his* group. He can help to make of it what he wishes." This was beautifully illustrated by the woman in the writer's group referred to above, who took responsibility for her contribution to getting the group started. A climate of trust begins to develop. Members are willing to take the risk of disclosing themselves.

6. THE EXPRESSION OF IMMEDIATE INTERPERSONAL FEELINGS IN THE GROUP. Members became able to express their feelings and attitudes about each other, both positive and negative. The negative feelings are not critical, bitter attacks, but simple statements of feelings and reactions. The result is not conflict, but exploration in an atmosphere of trust.

7. THE DEVELOPMENT OF A HEALING CAPACITY IN THE GROUP. Members of the group begin to help each other. They begin to care for each other, to understand each other, to try to help, each in his own way.

8. SELF-ACCEPTANCE AND THE BEGINNING OF CHANGE. This is an awareness of what one is, an admission, even, of what one really is behind the facade. This recognition of what one is, is necessary before one can begin to change. One can then explore what one is. A growing sense of realness, genuineness, or authenticity, develops. Members feel they can be *themselves,* both their strong and weak selves.

9. THE CRACKING OF FACADES. The growing recognition of oneself leads to the throwing off of defenses, the taking off of masks and facades. Each group member, apparently realizing the possibility of a deep encounter when everyone is real and open and honest, demands or requires that other members be themselves.

10. THE INDIVIDUAL RECEIVES FEEDBACK. As the group members become open and honest with each other, the members learn how they seem to others, how they affect others. Again, this is positive and negative, but the negative takes place in a concerned and caring environment. Feedback can lead to greater self-understanding. Glasser reports on a group in which two class leaders were quite shocked to find that they were feared rather than respected, and that their behavior was considered irrelevant rather than funny. They recognized that their self-image differed considerably from the way they were perceived by their peers.[7] Feedback lets us see ourselves as others see us.

11. CONFRONTATION. When one member reacts to another very strongly, usually in a negative manner, confrontation seems to be a better term

[7] William Glasser, *Schools without Failure* (New York: Harper & Row, 1969), pp. 150–151.

to use than feedback. Sometimes people do feel strongly against others and these feelings have to come out. But it is only when people have come to know each other well that these feelings can be meaningfully expressed with the possibility of constructive results.

12. THE HELPING RELATIONSHIP OUTSIDE THE GROUP SESSIONS. Group members relate to each other outside the group in a more human way, and often are very helpful to another member of the group who is going through the painful process of self-awareness and change.

13. THE BASIC ENCOUNTER. Group members feel close to each other, are highly empathic with each other, feeling for each other. An extremely close personal relationship develops, a basic human encounter, an I-thou relationship.

14. THE EXPRESSION OF POSITIVE FEELINGS AND CLOSENESS. The group becomes warm, trusting, with a sense of human togetherness and closeness.

15. BEHAVIOR CHANGES IN THE GROUP. Group members change and become different right before one's eyes. They become more empathic and understanding, they become more accepting, respecting and warm, they become more honest, real, and genuine—they act like self-actualizing persons! Interpersonal relationships change, personal problems are resolved. A member in one of the writer's groups, who had presented himself as needing to be strong and independent, to have people lean on him (at the age of 6 he had taken his younger brother on a train halfway across the country) began openly to ask for and accept help from others. A man who could not bear to be touched by a woman was unaware later when a woman touched him, and when he touched her. There is considerable evidence that people are different following even a brief but intensive group experience. Too often, though, in the reality of the world outside the group, changes fade away. It is difficult to be really human in a world where there are so few really human beings— or where so few human beings express their humanness.

This description of the process of the encounter group is not derived from therapy groups with disturbed people. It is based on experiences with average, normal people, including adolescents. To be sure, the same process occurs in therapy groups. The only difference between encounter groups and therapy groups is the nature of the members—some have more problems or are more disturbed than others.

The development of a group to the point where its members can be open, honest, trusting and really themselves takes time, for there is no such thing as "instant" group, instant intimacy, or instant relationship. One of the problems in many groups is the desire of the inadequately trained facilitator to produce this, or to speed up the group process; to do this, exercises and gimmicks are often introduced, as indicated in the last chapter. It is a characteristic of our society that things must be done in a hurry, must be speeded up. But if a group is to be highly facilitative for its members it cannot be pushed, and the facilitator must be patient and allow the group to grow into relationships at its own pace. While a few couples may meet and marry after one date, most go through a process requiring time, called "courtship," in which a relationship leading to the intimacy of marriage develops. This is aptly expressed in a song title: "You Can't Hurry Love." Groups must also have time to develop.

FACILITATING A GROUP

The encounter group is not, or should not be, a place where the facilitator (or teacher) engages in a controlled, planned program of exercises, games, etc., of the kind characterized by the approaches of Brown, and of Weinstein and Fantini, to affective education. No content should be introduced by the facilitator; the content arises from the participants, and consists of their feelings and relationships with each other. The major function of the facilitator is to create, set up, or "permit" a situation where group members can express themselves, can start out on and continue along the pattern delineated in the last section. The facilitator is not a controller, with his hand on the throttle, pushing and pulling to speed up or slow down the process by manipulating the behavior of group members, as if he were trying to reach a preconceived destination on a time schedule. The encounter group is a real life situation and should be allowed to develop naturally. The purpose of the facilitator should be to help provide an atmosphere in which the members can interact more naturally, more realistically, more honestly, and more humanly than is possible in the so-called real, but actually artificial, social environment in which we live. How does the facilitator do this?

The facilitator is not a leader in the usual sense of the word. He is definitely not a teacher, in the usual sense of the word. But his role and function may be defined quite like that of a humanistic teacher who is attempting to make possible self-initiated learning, exploration, and the achievement of personal meaning. There is no specific goal for the group, or for individuals, as there is in lesson plans in teaching. The goal is simply to make possible personal interaction on a human level.

1. STRUCTURING. The amount of structuring necessary or desirable depends on the group and the situation. If the group has no idea of what

is expected of them, some structuring is necessary. If the group, or some of its members, have some misconceptions about the group and how they are to function, then structuring is necessary.

In general, structuring should be kept to a minimum. Because of the fact that in encounter groups people are expected to function differently than in "real life", some structuring seems to be necessary. Rogers, in starting the group depicted in the Academy Award winning film "Journey into Self," began as follows:

I'm glad we all had a chance to have dinner together because it gives a little chance to get acquainted, at least a few of us; but I feel as though really, we really are strangers to each other in spite of that—with lots of geographical distance and occupational distance, and everything. And, I feel like saying just one or two things to start with, from my point of view. One is that this is our group. We really can make of it anything we want to make of it, and, for myself, I don't have any prediction, except that by the time we end Sunday afternoon, we'll probably know each other a lot better than we do right now; but how we may want to go about it, or what we want to do, that's really up to us. And I think that it is an opportunity to *be* in the group as fully as we can; maybe in some respects to try ways of being or ways of relating to each other that we never quite have had nerve enough to try before, where in ordinary life situations it seems like it's too impossible. In a sense, it's an opportunity to try out new ways of behaving with other people; there's that in it too: things that we have sort of wished we might be or do with others and never have quite had the nerve,— maybe we will have the nerve here. I don't know, but at any rate from here on in, as far as I'm concerned, it's up to us. . . . Oh, yes, one thing I did want to say: I feel a lot of anticipation about this group; I really look forward to getting to know you. And at the same time, I'm apprehensive; and I don't think it has much to do with the lights and the cameras. I think I'm always a little apprehensive in not knowing what a given group is going to be like. I don't know who we are, how we're going to get along, whether anything is going to come of this. Ah, so I feel a very double feeling: I feel excited and full of anticipation; I feel a little on the scared side, too.[8]

Structuring is designed to give participants some idea of what to expect, and what is expected of them, thus reducing initial anxiety and threat. With students in a school setting, the structuring would be different, and perhaps briefer. It is perhaps necessary to indicate that the group is different from a class discussion, that there is no topic or problem, that the facilitator is not a teacher and will not "lead" the group. The purpose can be stated as a chance to get to know each other in a different situation and way than in the classroom or other social situations.

[8] Included in William Coulson, "Inside a Basic Encounter Group," *The Counselling Psychologist,* 1970, 2(2), 1–27.

2. LISTENING. The facilitator listens carefully to *everything* everyone says, focusing upon the feelings being expressed. This is an intense, personal listening, to whatever the member of the group is expressing.

3. ACCEPTANCE AND RESPECT. Each member is accepted and respected as he is, as a person. There is no pressure for change, no attempt to make the group "jell," "get down to business," begin expressing feelings, or to "speed up" the group process. There is no attempt to get each member involved, to force participation, to "psyche out" a silent member, or to delve beneath what persons say. Each person's contribution is taken at face value.

4. UNDERSTANDING. The facilitator attempts to understand what each member is thinking, feeling and trying to express. He attempts to place himself in the shoes of each person, so he can understand the personal meaning of what he is saying and feeling.

5. RESPONDING. The facilitator attempts to convey his understanding of what is said by his responses. It is not necessary, nor desirable, that the facilitator respond to every statement by a member of the group, for to do so would tend to lead to the development of a two-way inter-action. Group members respond to each other, and the facilitator must allow for this. But, as a trained and experienced person, the facilitator can often better understand what a member may be trying to say, and can often, in communicating his understanding, put it in a clearer form, reducing the incoherence or lengthy attempts at expression. By responding to feelings rather than intellectualizing, the facilitator can focus the group upon feelings. The facilitator can sharpen differences among participants by bringing them out clearly, thus helping participants see their differences more clearly and engage in a more meaningful inter-action.

The reader will recognize these methods of facilitating a group as being familiar. They are the basic conditions of a learning or facilitative inter-personal relationship we saw in Chapter 5. The encounter group is no exception when it comes to them. As a model for good, open, honest interpersonal relationships, these conditions must be present in the encounter group. While some groups might be able to function as an encounter group without the presence of a facilitator, since these characteristics are present, to a greater or lesser extent, in most individuals, their presence to a sufficient degree cannot be counted on. Groups without a facilitator would at best be less efficient—that is, move more slowly. The facilitator, as a trained person, an expert, and as a constant model provides a stability to the group as its members flounder and struggle in their relationships with each other. The facilitator is thus necessary. Attempts to encourage "leaderless" groups through providing audiotapes are questionable.

The presence of the conditions provided by, and fostered by, the facilitator leads to a nonthreatening, safe atmosphere in which people can become less defensive, less inhibited, less constricted, and more open, free, and honest. They can become more real, more human, and thus more the kind of person they are capable of being. And in doing and in being so, they make it more possible for others to be so. *They become facilitators for each other.*

For the person who has been used to directing, leading, guiding and controlling others, and who has been concerned about cognitive learning involving thinking and rational problem solving, facilitating an encounter group means a great change in approach. This is one reason why teachers have such difficulty, and why, as indicated in the last chapter, educators tend to highly structure and introduce techniques into affective education. This is also one reason why teachers need special preparation for facilitating groups—or for that matter, to engage in any aspect of affective education.

Part of the difficulty in maintaining a "hands off" approach is perhaps a lack of trust or confidence in the group to function without direction and guidance. Perhaps this is a common problem of teachers—as well as of parents and other adults—with children and adolescents.

SOME QUESTIONS AND PROBLEMS

Encounter groups pose some questions or problems which need to be considered. One of the most serious of these will be considered first.

Are Encounter Groups Dangerous?

It is not possible to consider all the questions related to potential harmful effects of encounter groups. While there are some instances of people being hurt psychologically, they are very few in number. With the lack of controls over who leads groups, who participates in groups, and what is done in groups, the incidence of harm is amazingly small, giving testimony to the toughness of human beings. If groups are composed of "normal" individuals there is little danger. More important, in the writer's opinion, is the role of the facilitator. If the facilitator functions as indicated above, and avoids stimulating or provoking feelings, putting pressure on group members, and introducing bizarre gimmicks and techniques, the danger is slight. Love—real love—is very unlikely to hurt anyone.

Are They Effective Only Through Provoking Aggression?

One of the widespread misconceptions of encounter groups is that to be successful or effective the members must be at each other's throats, and the sooner the better. This misconception, fostered by some leaders, who are, in the opinion of the writer, incompetent and dangerous, is so widespread that many persons who become members of groups believe that aggressive behavior is expected of them, and do their best to show it. Now it is true that while most persons (though not all) have suppressed or repressed aggressive feelings (aggression is not universal or innate, it will be remembered from Chapter 5), it is not desirable that such feelings be expressed immediately in the group and directed to its other members. There are good psychological reasons for this, which can't be gone into here. But one reason is that it can be harmful to the persons to whom aggression or anger are directed, who might not, for many reasons, be able to understand, empathize with, or help the aggressor, but only react in self-defense.

If aggression is not innate, an instinct, but a response to frustration and threat, then, in a group where threat is minimized, aggression should be reduced rather than stimulated. Aggressive feelings toward others outside the group may be present, of course. But why should members feel aggressive toward each other, unless aggression is deliberately stimulated and provoked? Some leaders do this, insisting that everyone, in effect, hates everyone else, including other members of the group, and that this must be expressed. Members are made to feel abnormal, uncooperative, resistant, unless they come up with their quota of anger and aggression. If they are provoked enough, they will. And they may suffer from guilt and remorse later, wondering where their anger came from, being convinced that it must have been in them all the time, when in fact it was provoked by the leader, and often by other members of the group.

This is a source of some of the damage an encounter group can cause, and leads to another problem which should be considered.

What Is the Responsibility of the Facilitator?

There are some who disclaim any responsibility of the facilitator for what happens (particularly of a negative nature) in the group. This is irresponsible behavior. The facilitator is in the group, and presumably as the most highly trained person is responsible, not only for his own behavior, but for the behavior of others *at least insofar as he provokes it.*

The facilitator is responsible for creating the atmosphere or the conditions under which the group functions. If he follows the procedures discussed above, there should be no problem regarding harmful aggressive behavior or vicious attacks by members of the group on each other. But if such attacks do occur, through misconceptions of a group member as to what is desirable or permissible, or because a group member is a seriously disturbed person, then it is the responsibility of the facilitator to protect the attacked group member from harm, both physical and psychological. In addition, no member of a group should be forced or coerced by the facilitator or any other group member, to do anything which he does not wish to do.

Should There Be Selection of Group Members?

Reference to who should participate in encounter groups, and to group members who are seriously disturbed, leads to questions about the selection of group members. In the writer's opinion, selection of members for a group is undesirable, except for individuals who are seriously disturbed emotionally. In general, any student who is permitted to attend school should be permitted to be in an encounter group.

Should All Students be Required To Participate in Encounter Groups?

The quick answer to this question might be "no," but there are some considerations which lead to "yes." There is no more danger in an encounter group conducted as recommended in this chapter than in the usual classroom. In fact, it could be contended with considerable justification that there is *less* likelihood of psychological harm. Second, if the encounter group is, as the writer believes, the most effective method of affective education and of learning in the area of interpersonal relations, it is more justifiable to require this of students than it is to require any other course or experience.

Is the Encounter Group Actually a Counseling Group?

The only difference between an encounter group and a counseling group is that in the latter case the members consist of persons who in their own eyes or the eyes of others, have "problems," at least to a greater extent or degree than other persons. The conditions of facilitative interpersonal relationships, which are the conditions of an encounter group, are also the conditions of counseling or psychotherapy, as has been pointed out in earlier chapters. The encounter group is therapeutic, while the counseling group is therapy. It is true that the facilitator (or counselor) in a counseling group should have greater training and experience than the facilitator of an encounter group.

The Facilitator as a Group Member

We have emphasized the lack of control or direction of the facilitator. The facilitator becomes, as much as it is possible, another member of the group—more experienced in human relations perhaps, but still a member. True, he cannot become just like any other member—because of his status the group will usually be unable to allow him to become exactly like themselves. And he does have certain responsibilities, as indicated earlier, which distinguish him from the other members of the group. But, if he remains outside the group, psychologically, he is not a facilitator, but a teacher, observer, or commentator. This leads to his being evaluative rather than being understanding, being detached rather than being involved, inhuman rather than human—an unnatural appurtenance to the group. No natural social group has such a person in it—or rather outside of it—observing and evaluating.

How, Then, Does the Facilitator Affect the Group?

Part of the answer to this question has already been implicit in the discussion so far. The facilitator is (usually and at the beginning) the most experienced, knowledgeable, empathic and genuine person in the group, and his responses are thus more effective and facilitative. In addition, as such a person (and having some prestige and recognition) he is or becomes a *model* for the group.

Students thus learn the conditions through modeling and through practicing them with each other. One of the most difficult things to be learned is the ability to listen to and hear what another person is saying without analyzing, judging or evaluating. The evaluative attitude is the prevalent one in our society, and is the major deterrent to real empathic understanding. We don't hear what another person is really saying or feeling, and understand how he sees things, because we listen from our own frame of reference—an external rather than internal one.

Rogers has suggested a way to facilitate listening and understanding which can be used in any group, whether encounter or discussion. This method can often get a group to the point of listening to each other quickly, and may be presented as a rule when a group is getting started—before a member of the group can respond to something another member has said, he must restate what the other person has said in a way that the other person agrees reflects what he was saying or feeling. This is, in effect, a technique, but it should not be used routinely or as a technique. It is not necessary in many groups. But in a group where it is apparent that members are not listening to each other, it can be helpful if the facilitator suggests that, for a brief period, this rule be followed, as a way to help the members to really listen to each other.

OTHER GROUPS IN THE SCHOOL

The small encounter group is perhaps the most effective method for learning interpersonal relationships. In many schools, however, it may not be possible, at present, to provide a small group experience for every student.

While, as has been noted earlier, the classroom size group is too large for the intense, intimate encounter process, it is possible to provide a learning experience in interpersonal relationships, and psychological education, in the large classroom group, using an unstructured approach rather than the planned lesson approach discussed in the last chapter.

Clark Moustakas at the Merrill Palmer School in Detroit began offering a two-semester Seminar in Interpersonal Relations for teachers, counselors and principals over twenty years ago. The purpose of the seminar was "to help the individual teacher express and explore the values, meanings, and dynamics of personal and professional experience, to achieve self-awareness, and to develop sensitive, understanding, responsive attitudes in relations with children and parents." [9] Teachers in the seminar worked with students in classroom groups on a regular basis of one or two periods a week, sometimes more. Although some teachers structured the meetings, and some introduced activities such as drawing or writing of student journals, the meetings usually consisted of free discussions, particularly in the upper grades.

John Seeley conducted a project a number of years ago in which teachers were trained in human relations over a period of a year. Part of the training consisted of conducting "Human Relations Classes" in schools.

[9] Clark E. Moustakas, "A Human Relations Seminar at the Merrill Palmer School," *Personnel and Guidance Journal*, 1959, 37, 342–349. Reprinted in C. H. Patterson (Ed.) *The Counselor in the School: Selected Readings* (New York: McGraw-Hill, 1967).

These were designed "to afford 'normal' children in everyday classrooms a regular exposure to . . . 'free' discussion . . . to aid the child to understand himself, his peers, and the rest of the world in which he lived, at least in its most immediate bearing on his self-definition and his most general and profound feelings." [10] The classes were based on "the belief that people (in this case children) really free (externally) to talk about anything will finally talk about everything, but also, in the curious circling way such communication has, will concentrate on those matters that have for them vital psychodynamic import." The sessions were conducted weekly in several classes from the fourth to the twelfth grades by a teacher (or a project staff member) from outside the school, unlike the Merrill Palmer seminar procedure, where the teachers worked with their own students.

The reactions of the students and teachers in these group meetings are interesting. Moustakas reports that the teachers had difficulty in convincing the students that what they talked about would be held in confidence. Seeley notes that the teachers in his project were surprised at the lack of problems of discipline or control, at the emotional involvement of the children, at their active participation, and at the content of their discussions. Some teachers were uncomfortable about the lack of logical problem-solving, the "waste of time" in coming to a point—taking hours for what a good teacher could tell them in ten minutes—the jumping about from topic to topic, and leaving things unfinished.

William Glasser emphasizes the use of groups to reduce failure in children in the school.[11] He recommends "classroom meetings," led by the teacher, beginning with the first grade. In the lower grades the meetings should last from 10 to 30 minutes, and from 30 to 45 minutes in the upper elementary grades (or through grade 8). He describes three types of meetings: (1) *educational-diagnostic* meetings, dealing with student understanding of the curriculum; (2) *open-ended meetings,* concerned with intellectually important subjects; and (3) *social-problem-solving meetings,* relating to the students' social behaviors which constitute problems in the school.

In all of the meetings the teacher leads a nonjudgmental discussion. It is the social-problem-solving type of meeting which is most closely related to the kind of groups discussed in this chapter. Here the students deal with any problem brought up by a student about himself or another student, by the teacher, or by an administrator. The discussion is directed toward solving the problem, not to judge or punish the student or students in-

---

[10] John R. Seeley, "The Forest Hill Village Human Relation Classes," *Personnel and Guidance Journal,* 1957, 37, 424–434.
[11] *Op. cit.,* Chapter 10.

volved. The class, though not the teacher, may make judgments which work toward positive solutions.

The class forms in a circle for these meetings, since they are not successful when the students are seated in the usual classroom arrangement. Glasser states that teachers often resist this requirement.

According to Glasser, in these meetings "each child learns that he is important to every other child, that what he says is heard by everyone, and that his ideas count . . . children learn that their peers care about them. They learn to solve the problems of their world." [12]

SUMMARY

People live in groups. Interpersonal relations thus are an important aspect of living. One of the functions of the school, particularly from the point of view of humanistic education, is to prepare people to live together.

Although principles of human relations can be taught didactically, the evidence is that such teaching is not very effective. There is no substitute for learning by experience here. The basic encounter group is probably the most effective vehicle for the teaching and learning of interpersonal relations. In this chapter the objectives of such groups are considered, the group process is described, the functioning of the facilitator or leader is investigated, and some questions and problems considered.

Every student in our schools should be a participant in small encounter groups throughout his entire school career. Such a continuing experience holds the greatest promise for changing our society from one which is characterized by lack of understanding and conflict to one which is characterized by understanding and cooperation.

If teachers are to engage in facilitating encounter groups, as well as to function as humanistic teachers, they must be prepared to do so in teacher education programs. We therefore turn, in the final chapter, to a consideration of the preparation of teachers for humanistic education.

[12] *Ibid.*

12 The Preparation Of Humanistic Teachers

I see the facilitation of learning as the aim of education. . . . We know . . . that the facilitation of such learning rests not upon the teaching skills of the leader, not upon his curricular planning, not upon his use of audio-visual aids, not upon the programmed learning he utilizes, not upon his lectures and presentations, not upon an abundance of books, though each of these might at one time or another be utilized as an important resource. No, the facilitation of significant learning rests upon certain attitudinal qualities which exist in the personal relationship between the facilitator and the learner.

—Carl R. Rogers, FREEDOM TO LEARN *

In Chapter 1 it was stated that preparation for teaching in the school of the future, the humanistic school, would consist of education in human relationships. It should be clear now why this is so. In Chapter 7 it was emphasized that it is not teaching methods which make a good teacher, but the person of the teacher. It is thus paradoxical, and difficult to understand, that the emphasis in teacher education has been on methods, as well as on subject matter.

* (Columbus, Ohio: Merrill, 1967), pp. 105–106.

Teacher education, along with education, has been the object of criticism. Coladarci states that "the contents and procedures of teacher education frequently have no demonstrable relevance to the actual teaching task." [1] Teachers have been highly critical of and dissatisfied with the preparation they have received. Silberman concludes: "That the preparation should be substantially different from what they now receive seems hardly open to debate; there is probably no aspect of contemporary education on which there is greater unanimity of opinion than that teacher education needs a vast overhaul. Virtually everyone is dissatisfied with the current state of teacher education: the students being educated, the teachers in the field, the principals, superintendents, and school board members who hire them, the liberal arts faculties, and the lay critics of education." [2]

Those who have been concerned about student achievement in subject matter areas have focused upon the inadequate preparation of teachers in subject matter content, as well as in the liberal arts in general. Changes have been made toward this end in many teacher education programs. Other than this, there has been very little change in the preparation of teachers for the last fifty years. Although knowledge of subject matter is clearly necessary, it is not sufficient to make a good teacher. More emphasis on methods courses does not seem to be the answer, since there are probably too many now, with much overlapping, and repetition. Yet these two alternatives appear to be the only solutions to the problem of teacher education which have been seriously considered. Neither Silberman nor the other critics of education propose any approach to the preparation of humanistic teachers.

It might appear that the answer would be more courses in psychology, an area in which teachers certainly have too little background. A course in general psychology and one in educational psychology and/or child development is all that most teachers have, and experience with teachers who have just completed their undergraduate education leads one to conclude that they might as well have had none, as far as what they remember or have learned. It seems apparent that something is wrong with the courses.

If one looks at what is taught in these undergraduate courses, one quickly realizes what is wrong. The standard courses have nothing to do with people, with real students in real classrooms. They focus upon research done in laboratories (often with rats) or in special experimental situations. The courses consist of review of research study after research

---

[1] Arthur P. Coladarci, in Foreword to Seymour B. Sarason, Kenneth S. Davidson & Burton Blatt, *The Preparation of Teachers: an Unstudied Problem in Education* (New York: Wiley, 1962).

[2] Charles E. Silberman, *Crisis in the Classroom* (New York: Random House, 1970), p. 413.

study which are irrelevant to teaching since no generalizations can be made to the real classroom situation. There is little attempt to teach principles, or a theory which can be applied in real life situations. To do this would be to depart from a rigorous approach to psychology as a science.

THE TEACHER AS A PSYCHOLOGIST

The teacher works with human beings. Since teaching is a psychological relationship, a helping relationship, it should be apparent that teaching is applied psychology, and that the basic science of education, and the basic preparation of teachers, is, or should be, psychology. There has been some recognition of this: the psychology of learning has received increasing attention in education. But not without difficulties, however. First, the psychology of learning currently available is, as suggested above, essentially irrelevant to classroom teaching. Bruner and Skinner have attempted to remedy this situation, by working on a psychology (or technology) of teaching or instruction.

But this is not sufficient, because of the second difficulty. The psychology which has been applied to education and teaching is too *narrow* a psychology, being essentially a cognitive psychology of learning and teaching. If teacher education is inadequate to prepare teachers to facilitate cognitive learning, it has been nonexistent for the preparation of teachers to facilitate affective learning.

The psychology appropriate to teaching must then be broader. It must encompass the total behavior of the teacher in interaction with the student. It must focus upon those characteristics and behaviors of teachers which are most important in the teaching-learning relationship, upon those conditions of learning which are more important than subject matter knowledge, methods, or techniques.

These characteristics, as has been emphasized in this book, are the personal characteristics of the teacher—empathic understanding, respect or warmth, and genuineness. It is the person of the teacher which is the most important factor in teaching and learning. It is therefore apparent that teacher education should focus upon the development of the person of the teacher. Teacher education must center upon the feelings, attitudes, and beliefs of the teacher, including attitudes toward himself, or the self-concept.

That good teachers differ from poor teachers in their attitudes and beliefs is shown in studies by Combs and his associates. It was found that good teachers, as compared to poor ones, perceived others as able rather than unable, as friendly rather than unfriendly, as worthy rather than unworthy, as internally rather than externally motivated or controlled, as dependable rather than undependable, and as helpful rather than hindering.[3] Good teachers also operated from an internal rather than from an external frame of reference; that is, they were sensitive to and concerned about how others saw and felt about things and reacted to people on this basis. In addition, good teachers were more concerned about people and their reactions than about things and events.[4]

These same studies also found that good teachers perceive themselves differently than poor teachers. Compared to poor teachers, good teachers see themselves as more adequate, trustworthy, worthy, wanted and identified with others. Their beliefs about themselves, their self-concepts, are different from, and more adequate than, those of poor teachers.

What does this imply for teacher education programs? It is not our purpose here to deal with the total teacher education program, but only with that part of it relevant to humanistic or affective education. We shall first propose a basis for the psychological preparation of teachers, and then consider some necessary aspects of a humanistic teacher education program.

HUMANISTIC PSYCHOLOGY

It would seem logical that humanistic teaching should be based upon a humanistic psychology.

Humanistic psychology has been developing rapidly in America since World War II. Many prominent psychologists have participated in its development, including Gordon Allport, Sidney Jourard, Abraham Maslow, Clark Moustakas, and Carl Rogers. Although their influence is being felt throughout the field of psychology, it has not reached down to the teaching of undergraduate or, indeed, graduate courses in psychology. Thus, neither psychology nor teacher education students are exposed to this system or point of view, though it is the most relevant and practical approach to understanding human behavior. When the writer has presented this approach to beginning graduate students in education they have responded by asking why they hadn't learned about this theory of human behavior as undergraduates.

The basic characteristic of this humanistic or perceptual psychology is that it assumes an internal frame of reference rather than the external frame of reference of so-called scientific psychology. It is interesting that,

[3] Arthur W. Combs, Donald L. Avila, and William W. Purkey, *Helping Relationships: Basic Concepts for the Helping Professions* (Boston: Allyn & Bacon, 1971), pp. 12–13.
[4] Arthur W. Combs, *The Professional Education of Teachers: a Perceptual View of Teacher Education* (Boston: Allyn & Bacon, 1965), p. 55.

as noted above, the best teachers were found to look at their students in this way, since they had not been taught this point of view. Combs writes: "Apparently, good teachers arrive at this frame of reference with respect to people as a consequence of their experience. If this is true, it is time we introduced it much more widely into our teacher-training programs." [5]

This systematic approach to human behavior provides the necessary theoretical base for a humanistic approach to education, which, as noted in the last chapter is lacking in the writings in humanistic and affective education.

In Chapter 5 we provided an introduction to this theory. The most complete and systematic presentation is found in the book by Combs and Snygg referred to in that chapter.[6] Every teacher education student should be familiar with this book.

A HUMANISTIC ATMOSPHERE

Teacher education is more than the teaching of subject matter, even the subject matter of a humanistic psychology. It must be concerned with the development of persons with humanistic beliefs about people and attitudes toward them. It must make it possible for the student to develop an adequate self-concept. In short, it must foster the development of self-actualizing teachers.

We have been concerned in this book with the conditions for facilitating the development of self-actualizing persons in our public schools. *These are the same conditions necessary for the development of self-actualizing teachers in teacher education programs. Thus, this book is not only a text for teachers, but for the teachers of teachers.* If we want teachers who are capable of fostering self-actualization in their students, they must be self-actualizing persons themselves, and they can become such persons only by experiencing the conditions which are necessary for the development of self-actualizing persons.

This, perhaps more than anything else, is the defect or lack in teacher preparation programs. We cannot *tell* teachers how to teach humanistically; we can teach them how only by teaching humanistically ourselves. Combs says this in referring to the saying among counselor educators that "students teach like they have been taught rather than the way we taught them to teach." [7] Teacher educators are models upon which teacher edu-

---

[5] Ibid., p. 59.
[6] Arthur W. Combs and Donald Snygg, *Individual Behavior: a Perceptual Approach to Behavior* Rev. Ed. (New York: Harper & Row, 1959).
[7] *Op. cit.*, p. 40.

cation students base their teaching. Unfortunately, too often they are not models of humanistic education.

SOME MORE SPECIFIC ASPECTS
OF TEACHER EDUCATION

Laboratory and Supervised Practice Experiences

A universal aspect of teacher education is practice teaching. Though it is necessary, practice teaching is far from adequate as it is presently conducted, as will be noted later. But in addition to necessary changes in practice teaching, teacher education students need some pre-practice teaching experiences, a graded sequence of experiences culminating in practice teaching. One of the reasons that practice teaching is not as effective as it could be is that students are not adequately prepared for it. Teacher education could benefit from examining the methods of preparing counselors or psychotherapists in graduate programs.

Laboratory experiences should begin with *observation*. Courses in child psychology, child development, and adolescent psychology should include experiences in observing children and adolescents—not only in classrooms, but in a variety of situations.

Now it is true that in many instances these courses do include some observation. Combs notes that:

> Most teacher-education programs require students to spend many hours observing the behavior of students or teachers. Many instructors put great faith in this technique despite the fact that student teachers often find it distasteful and a waste of time . . .
>
> Many of us have made such a fetish of objectivity in the making of observations that we have blinded students to the real meaning and values of observing. Because we want to develop in students "disciplined observation," to see what is *really* going on, we have insisted that they report exactly what occurred, precisely and in detail.[8]

The kind of report which results is illustrated by the following:

> "Jimmy picked up his pencil, examined the end of it. He saw that it needed sharpening so he got out of his seat and walked to the back of the room. He sharpened his pencil, looked out the window for a moment and returned to his seat. On the way back to his seat, he tapped his friend, Joe, on the head with the pencil as he passed him. He sat down and straightened

[8] *Ibid.,* pp. 64–65.

his paper. He looked at the board where the teacher had placed the problem. He read the problem to himself. He sucked on the end of his pencil. He twisted his feet around the bottom of his desk and then he started to write the answer. He worked very slowly and once in a while he would look up and around the room. Once he put his head down on his arm and wrote from that position . . ." [9]

Combs asks: "Is it any wonder that students often find this kind of reporting sheer drudgery?" But the major criticism is that this procedure directs the student's attention to the wrong things. It ignores feelings, attitudes, perceptions, goals and purposes—the meaning of behavior.

Observation should be directed toward these factors, towards trying to see things from the child's point of view. Combs has abandoned requiring "objective" observation and reports:

> I now ask them to do what I myself do when I watch a child behaving or a teacher teaching—to get the "feel" of what's going on, to see if they can get inside the skin of the person being observed, to understand how things look from his point of view. I ask them "What do you think he is trying to do?" "How do you suppose he feels?" "How would you have to feel to behave like that?" "How does he see the other kids?" "What does he feel about the subject?" and so on.[10]

The point of view of humanistic psychology must be applied to the teaching of courses in child behavior, especially to the observation of behavior.

A second phase of laboratory experiences should include some practice in taking the internal frame of reference in interaction with individuals. Such training can or should include several aspects:

The first stage of this phase can begin with learning to recognize the existence of various levels of the conditions of empathy, respect, and genuineness. Carkhuff's book provides materials for such training.[11] Collingwood reports a study of eight female junior high school teachers, whose teaching experience ranged from one to ten years. They received eight hours of training in a one week workshop, learning to discriminate and communicate the core conditions using taped stimulus expressions. Following this they spent five hours roleplaying with each other, and five hours discussing the application of the experience to teaching. They were tested before and after the workshop. A significant increase in facilitative func-

---

[9] *Ibid.*, p. 65.
[10] *Ibid.*, p. 66.
[11] Robert R. Carkhuff, *Helping and Human Relations. Vol. I: Selection and Training* (New York: Holt, Rinehart, & Winston, 1969).

tioning was found.[12] Collingwood suggests that the communication of the core conditions is a concrete, operational definition of being pupil-centered, a concept which is usually vague and relatively meaningless. This study by Collingwood supports the results of other studies which were referred to in Chapter 8.

The practice of the core conditions in roleplaying constitutes the second aspect of laboratory experience in developing the conditions. The third stage is actual supervised experience in talking with other people. The scales developed by Carkhuff can be applied to tape recordings of these interviews so that the level of the core conditions can be evaluated.

This kind of experience offers opportunity for the student to engage in self-exploration regarding his beliefs and attitudes, leading to a better understanding of himself and the possibility of change in himself and his self-concept.

A third phase of laboratory and supervised practice is the observation of the teaching situation. This phase should come relatively early in the student's education, so that he may re-evaluate his decision to go into teaching, but not before the student has had the opportunity to learn enough about teaching and human relationships to know what to look for. It could be concurrent with the laboratory experience in the core conditions. Sarason, Davidson and Blatt report on an interesting project of teaching students' observation of a teacher in which fifteen students beginning their junior year participated.[13] One of the things which they learned was that their perceptions, or their observations, were selective, being influenced by the student's own values. It is interesting that the teacher which the group observed (an unusually good teacher) had no discipline problems. The students began to realize that this was related to the nature of her relations with the students. It was obvious to them that she was warm, that she had consistent limits for student behavior, and that she was available to help when needed. One student seemed to sum it up when she said: "You get a lot of talk about how you have to respect your pupils and that there is something about each of them that you can develop. When you watch Miss _____ you *know* she respects each one. It's as if she really respects each one and is going to bring out the best in them." [14]

Students should have the opportunity to observe more than one teacher, and for periods of time adequate to get to feel and understand the relationships between the teacher and the students. Such observation should be

---

[12] Thomas R. Collingwood, "A Further Delineation of the Integrated Didactic-experiential Training Approach for Teachers," Discussion Papers, Arkansas Rehabilitation Research and Training Center, University of Arkansas. Vol. III, No. 8.

[13] Seymour B. Sarason, Kenneth S. Davidson, & Burton Blatt, *op. cit.*

[14] *Ibid.,* p. 86.

accompanied by a seminar in which students discuss their observations. Closed circuit TV would be useful to extend the range and variety of teachers and students observed.

A final method of laboratory instruction, which has been recently developed, must be mentioned. This is micro-teaching. This involves the teacher education student practicing a specific method or technique with a small group of four to six students. The brief "practice period"—five to ten minutes in length—is videotaped. The student and an instructor view the playback, analyzing and evaluating the student's performance. The student may then engage in another practice session, which is then evaluated. This can continue for as many sessions as is desired.

This method of instruction would appear to be promising. Certainly the viewing of a videotape of one's performance can be instructive to a teacher. But the way in which this is done in micro-teaching is not necessarily helpful, and indeed the evidence regarding its value is limited, and indicates that results are small and short-lived.

Although it would appear that breaking complex behaviors into simpler components for instruction would be useful, this is not necessarily the case. There are perhaps optimum amounts in which things can be best learned, and micro-techniques such as asking questions, reinforcing student responses, answering questions, or similar small tasks may not be optimum for learning. In addition, one faces the problem of putting these all together in a classroom period.

A further problem is one which plagues our whole teacher education program, one which we have raised before and will raise again in connection with practice teaching. It concerns the basis on which we break the teaching process down, or upon which we choose specific techniques for use in micro-teaching. Silberman puts it as follows:

> Neither the techniques the student teachers practice nor their supervisors' analysis of their videotaped performance are related to any concept of education or any theories of teaching or learning. Thus there is no structure to the micro-teaching sessions themselves, no attempt to develop an hierarchy of skills. On the contrary, the education students are merely taught to use various techniques that are not related to one another, still less to any conception of what teaching is about or any notion of which strategies are most appropriate for which teaching objectives, or which kinds of students or which subject matters.[15]

The problem of the effectiveness of generalization to the real classroom is also present. It is not true that four to six students are similar to a group of thirty students, or that teaching in a specific way for five or ten minutes

[15] *Op. cit.,* p. 458.

is similar in any real or fundamental respects to teaching for forty or fifty minutes. Moreover, the so-called "students" in the micro-teaching situation may bear no resemblance to students in the real classroom. In a research study, a student of mine utilized some micro-teaching classes. The "students" who constituted the micro-teaching group were paid college students, who could care less about the whole thing. One sat with his hat on throughout the session, paying not the least bit of attention to the student teacher.

Micro-teaching, in my opinion, is of little value in teacher education. Even if it were changed to eliminate the criticisms considered above, it would appear that there are better, more realistic and more relevant ways to use the teacher education student's time. In the discussion of modeling in the last chapter, it was noted that this means of teaching and learning was efficient, as well as effective, because it involved the learning of wholes, or of patterns and sequences as wholes, rather than of parts which then must be assembled into wholes.

PRACTICE TEACHING

Practice teaching, which is one of the most important experiences in teacher education, is one of its major problems. Though there is widespread dissatisfaction with the way it is conducted, nothing is being done to change it, and changes in the rest of teacher education are useless if practice teaching is not changed. In fact, if the rest of teacher education becomes humanistic in its orientation, and practice teaching continues as it now is, it can be a traumatic and damaging experience for the student. This experience is similar to the supervised practicum in counseling or psychotherapy and should receive as much attention and support.

The classroom teacher (supervising or critic teacher) with whom the student does his practice teaching is an important influence on the teacher education student, often becoming a model for the student. Yet such teachers are not carefully selected, and are often chosen on the recommendation of a principal or superintendent, whose essential concept of a good teacher may be one who maintains discipline and control. Thus, as Silberman notes, "practice teaching may do more harm than good, confirming students in bad teaching habits rather than training them in good ones." [16]

Not only are supervising or critic teachers not adequately selected, but they do little if any real supervising. They have had no training in supervision, and get little if any help from the college or university supervisor of

---

[16] *Ibid.,* p. 451.

student teaching. The teacher education student also gets little if any supervision or help from the college or university coordinator, who is responsible for too many students to be able to give each individual help.

Supervising or critic teachers vary tremendously in how much actual teaching they permit the student teacher to engage in. Too many give the student little opportunity to teach, but much opportunity to become a teacher aide—handing out materials and supplies, writing material on the blackboard, maintaining bulletin boards—and constructing innumerable lesson plans which he is never given the opportunity to use. Thus he never gets any real experience in teaching, and if he does, he

> never experiences the 'real thing'—never gets the feel of what teaching is actually like. Because the regular classroom teacher remains responsible for everything that goes on in his room, the student teacher cannot feel the full impact of that responsibility. Neither can he experience the full responsibility of being a teacher. He is, after all, a visitor in someone else's classroom, and visitors are not welcome to rearrange their host's furniture, alter his schedule, revise his curriculum, or change the atmosphere he has labored to create. Nor is the student teacher likely to be able to make those kinds of changes if he wanted to.[17]

Not only do student teachers get little if any feedback from the supervising teacher or their college or university supervisor,[18] but they are not given adequate instruction prior to entering practice teaching on what is expected of them in their assignment, or informed just what the criteria are on which they will be judged and evaluated. This is in part because the teacher education program and its instructors have no consistent theory of instruction or, more basically, theory of human behavior, in or out of the classroom. Silberman's indictment may be too harsh but it is not without substance. Referring to college and university supervisors of practice teaching he writes:

> Lacking any conception of teaching, and without having thought about the ends or means of education, supervisors of student teaching tend to focus on the minutiae of classroom life, e.g., the fact that a child in the third row was chewing gum, rather than on the degree to which the student teacher was able to achieve his teaching objective, or relate to students, or evoke their interests, or what have you. Without any conception of teaching, moreover, the supervisors frequently disagree among themselves as to what constitutes good or bad teaching. Indeed, individual supervisors are frequently

---

17 *Ibid.*, p. 460.
18 See Sarason, Davidson, and Blatt, *op. cit.*, pp. 102–106, 110–114, for reactions of student teachers to their practice teaching.

unable to agree even with themselves, applying different criteria to different student teachers, or to the same student on different days.[19]

It is apparent that supervisors cannot tell students what the criteria are by which they are being evaluated if they are not clear what those criteria are themselves, or disagree on them. The need for a systematic theory becomes apparent again. If students know what they are supposed to do, they might be successful in doing it. They can then be aware of whether or not they are successful, or the degree or extent to which they are successful. They can, in effect, evaluate themselves, give themselves feedback, and change their behaviors.

If instructors and supervisors can agree upon a humanistic approach to education, then there are instruments which can be used in evaluating student teachers. These are the measures described and provided in Chapter 8.

It is possible that the concept of practice teaching as being a one-time experience is inadequate. Combs suggests a graded series of experiences in the classroom. The beginning student would function as a teacher-helper or aide a half day a week, and would progress to the place where he would be in full charge of a classroom for at least a four-month period.[20]

There is much that can be done to improve practice teaching and its supervision. Again, the model is to be found in the teaching of counseling or psychotherapy. The student must be given the opportunity to engage in practice teaching where he has responsibility for the teaching situation; one cannot learn to be responsible unless he has the opportunity. He must be adequately prepared, so that he knows what he should do and what he is expected to do by his supervisors. This involves more than a series of how-to-do-it rules; it must consist of a theory and a system of principles to be applied to specific situations. Given these things, the student is able to evaluate himself—with the aid of audiotapes, or videotapes, and instruments to obtain feedback from his students. The supervisor then can become a facilitator for the student's development, not simply an evaluator assigning a grade to the student.

ENCOUNTER GROUPS AND GROUP TRAINING IN TEACHER EDUCATION

If the essence of successful professional work with people is the effective use of the self as an instrument, then teacher education should focus on the

[19] *Op. cit.,* pp. 453–454.
[20] *Op. cit.,* p. 125.

development of the teacher as a person, and as a person who can offer the necessary conditions of learning and self-actualization to others. The discussion of teacher education so far has related to this concept of teacher education. People feel or see themselves as adequate or able, worthy, wanted, acceptable, etc., when they are treated that way. Thus, the general atmosphere of the teacher education program contributes to the development of an adequate and helping self. Individual counseling can and does help, though to make it available to, or to require it of, all students would be prohibitive. It should certainly be available for those who need and want it. But perhaps the most direct and most effective method for developing teachers who can facilitate the personal development of their students is the experience provided by the basic encounter group.

In Chapter 11 we emphasized the basic encounter group as a method of humanistic education in the schools. If such an approach is helpful to students below the college level, it should be helpful to college students, and particularly to teacher education students. It is a most effective way to help students to greater experiences of self-fulfillment, "to perceive themselves in more positive ways, to confront themselves and the world with openness and acceptance, and to develop a deep sense of identification with the human condition"—or in short, to become what Combs calls "adequate personalities." [21]

Borton suggests that "it is helpful for teachers to have had some experience in exploring their own feelings before working with students on a feeling level," and that this can be obtained through a group experience. He warns that teachers should be careful about the qualifications of the leader.[22] For teachers in the field, group experiences should be provided by qualified leaders in workshops or in-service training programs. But teacher education students should be provided with this experience, under competent leadership, as part of their preparation.

Several of the humanistic critics of education recommend a group experience for teachers in training. Rogers sees it as being as important as the classroom situation for the education of teachers and administrators.[23] Dennison supports the idea of group therapy for teacher education students.[24] Knoblock and Goldstein suggest that a group experience is not only useful for the personal development of the teacher education student, but as preparation for classroom management. They write:

[21] *Op. cit.,* p. 73.
[22] Terry Borton, *Reach, Touch, and Teach* (New York: McGraw-Hill, 1970), p. 199.
[23] Carl R. Rogers, *Freedom to Learn* (Columbus, Ohio: Merrill, 1969), p. 141.
[24] George Dennison, *The Lives of Children* (New York: Vintage Books, 1969), p. 257.

It is our rather strong belief that guided experience in understanding one's own group behavior and the management of groups is a necessary prerequisite to effective functioning with groups. While there are texts written on dynamics of classroom groups, without a personal frame of reference for group participation the application of sound techniques remains elusive.[25]

Silberman, while warning against the potential dangers of sensitivity training, sees a place for a group experience for teachers.[26] Silberman apparently fails to recognize the difference between the active probing and cracking of defenses used by some extremists in the field and the encounter group experience described by Rogers and referred to in the last chapter.[27]

In addition to a group experience, teachers should also have some preparation in conducting groups. Experience in an encounter group, as Knoblock and Goldstein suggest, is helpful, even necessary, but not sufficient. Some understanding of the nature of groups and the group process, beyond that presented in Chapter 11, is necessary.

Goodman contends that "the only profitable training for teachers is a group therapy and, perhaps, a course in child development." [28] He also writes: "I see little merit, for teaching this age [the first five grades], in the usual teacher-training. . . . Since at this age one teaches the child, not the subject, the relevant art is psychotherapy, and the most useful course for a normal school is probably group therapy.[29]

If teachers are to be involved in conducting the kinds of groups discussed in the last chapter, whether classroom size groups of the kind suggested by Glasser, Moustakas, and Seeley or the smaller basic encounter groups, they need preparation. Such preparation is possible at the undergraduate level.

THE CONTINUOUS INTEGRATIVE SEMINAR

Encounter groups are concerned with personal development and interpersonal relations. Students should also have the opportunity to participate in seminars in which they can, with the instructor, and with each other,

[25] Peter Knoblock and Arnold P. Goldstein, *The Lonely Teacher* (Boston: Allyn & Bacon, 1971), p. 40.

[26] *Op. cit.,* p. 502.

[27] Carl R. Rogers, *Carl Rogers on Encounter Groups* (New York: Harper & Row, 1970).

[28] Paul Goodman, "No Processing Whatever," in Beatrice Gross & Ronald Gross, (Eds.) *Radical School Reform* (New York: Simon & Schuster, 1969), p. 100.

[29] Paul Goodman, quoted in George Dennison, *op. cit.,* p. 266.

consider, evaluate, and integrate their total experience in teacher education, including content, laboratory, and other experiences, and their personal development in terms of ideas, beliefs and attitudes. This seminar
should be a continuing one from the beginning of their college education
to its end, including the practice teaching experience. It need not consist
of the same group of students, or the same instructor. It should be small
enough for discussion, say 15 to 20 students.

Combs proposes a continuous seminar of from 15 to 30 students, re-
maining constant, and meeting 2 hours per week throughout the student's
education.[30] However, as students left the group for whatever reason,
including differing rates of progress through the program, they would be
replaced by beginning students, so there would be students at differing
levels.

Glasser also recommends a continuing four-year seminar for teacher
education students, which would include observation of teachers at every
level. Practicing teachers would be invited in for discussions. With a full
year of practice teaching, Glasser feels that few other education courses
would be necessary in teacher education.[31]

The seminar provides an opportunity for students to think and talk
about their observations, laboratory experiences, practicum, and their
reading. The seminar described by Sarason, Davidson, and Blatt illustrates
the value of such a seminar in conjunction with observation of classroom
teaching.[32] One of the purposes of this seminar was to start the students
thinking about the way children are usually taught in the schools and the
way *they* were learning in the seminar and observation. These writers suggest a series of seminars, the first beginning as soon as students have decided on a teaching career. This seminar would not be professional in
nature, but focused on an understanding of the observational process, and
will develop an attitude of critical inquiry toward self, others, and problems. Child psychology courses would also have an observational seminar.
A third kind of seminar would concern itself with what is covered in conventional methods courses.[33] Former students who have become teachers,
or practicing teachers could be involved in these seminars.

SUMMARY

In this chapter we have been concerned with the preparation of humanistic teachers. Such teachers will of course need some preparation in

---

[30] *Op. cit.,* pp. 119–121.
[31] William Glasser, *Schools Without Failure* (New York: Harper & Row, 1969),
p. 10.
[32] *Op. cit.*
[33] *Ibid.,* pp. 107–108.

subject matter areas, but the emphasis in their preparation should be in human relations.

A major defect in the psychological preparation of teachers is that they are not provided with a systematic theoretical approach to human behavior. Such a theory, which is highly practical, is to be found in humanistic psychology, especially in the perceptual approach to behavior of Combs and Snygg. This should be the focus of the psychological preparation of teachers.

The importance of a humanistic atmosphere in teacher education is emphasized. It is essential that the methods of teacher education should exemplify the nature of what is being taught.

In addition to the didactic aspect of teacher education, an experiential aspect is necessary. This should include a graded series of laboratory experiences, beginning with observation. Practice teaching is also part of the experiential curriculum, but it must be modified and expanded if it is to be maximally effective. More adequate supervision is necessary.

A further aspect of the experiential curriculum is a group experience, which should exist in addition to a continuing seminar, to integrate the total educational experience of the student. Finally, the teacher education student must be prepared for leading groups of the kind described in the last chapter. While the experience of being in an encounter group is necessary, some didactic or course work in group methods and procedures is also required.

Davis says that "it may be that humanistic education can only exist in a humanistic society." [34] But it might also be contended that we can only achieve a humanistic society by developing a humanistic educational system. We must start somewhere, and society is too large and pervasive a place. Essentially, we can only work with individuals in developing humanistic—or self-actualizing—persons. It would appear that the most effective place to start is with the education of teachers. This, of course, assumes that the educators of teachers are themselves humanistic, which is perhaps unrealistic. But we must assume that somewhere there are humanistic persons to start with, and hopefully we are more likely to find them among educators than in most other groups. Perhaps this book can help to facilitate the development of humanistic educators—including administrators—as well as humanistic teachers.

[34] David C. Davis, *Model for Humanistic Education: the Danish Folk Highschool* (Columbus, Ohio: Merrill, 1971), p. 105.

Index
Of
Names

Index
Of
Subjects

A

Acceptance, 48, 56
Affect in learning, 94
Affective education, 14, 49, 93, 159–189
Agape, 72
Aggression
  as reaction to threat, 65
  in encounter groups, 204
Aggressive instinct, 64
Anger, 104–105
Authenticity, 72, 98–106
Authoritarianism, 102–103
Autocratic classroom, 102–103
Aversive control, 4, 8–9

B

Barret-Lennard Relationship Inventory, 112–113, 131–134
"Beating the system," 89–90
Business and education, 10–11

C

Center for the Study of Democratic Institutions, 11
Challenge versus threat, 55, 69, 86, 145, 157
Class discussions, 83
Classroom
  as a factory, 10–11
  as a group, 194, 207–209
Class scheduling, open versus closed, 78–80
Committee for Economic Development, 60
Competition versus cooperation, 85–87
Compulsory attendance, elimination of, 11, 13, 46
Computer-assisted instruction, 3–10, 62, 150, 151, 152–153
Computers, anthropormorphized, 9
Concerns, 182
Conditions for self-actualization, 70–74, 98–112
  and behaviorism, 154–155
  conditionality of, 155

DATE DUE